CHRIST
FORMED IN YOU

To Brian,
   May the Holy Spirit use this
book to make you more like our
Lord Jesus Christ.
      Grace & Peace,
         Brian G Hedges
         2 Cor 3:18

CHRIST
FORMED IN YOU

The Power of the Gospel for Personal Change

BRIAN G. HEDGES

Shepherd Press
Wapwallopen, Pennsylvania

Christ Formed in You
©2010 by Brian G. Hedges

Trade paperback ISBN: 978-0-9824387-7-0
ePub ISBN: 978-0-9824387-8-7
Mobi ISBN: 978-0-9824387-9-4

Published by Shepherd Press
P.O. Box 24
Wapwallopen, Pennsylvania 18660

Italics or bold text within Scripture quotations indicate emphasis added by author. The abbreviation "cf." is sometimes used in scripture references; it comes from the word "confer" and means to "compare" or "consult" with the immediately preceding reference.

Page design and typesetting by Lakeside Design Plus
Cover design by Tobias' Outerwear for Books

First Printing, 2010
Printed in the United States of America

VP   21   20   19   18   17   16   15   14   13   12   11   10
14   13   12   11   10   9   8   7   6   5   4   3   2   1

Library of Congress Control Number: 2010936342

eBook Coupons
For an eBook of *Christ Formed in You* go to http://www.shepherdpress.com/ebooks
Mobi file for Kindle: **CFKE01**

ePub Edition: **CFEP01**

To my parents,
Ronnie and Gloria Hedges

Contents

Foreword

Do not try the following when you are discouraged by the lack of spiritual progress among those in your ministry setting. In other words, if you have been experiencing disappointment with the spiritual condition of those in your discipleship group, Bible class, or church, wait awhile before you attempt the experiment I suggest. For if you aren't discouraged before you try this little quiz, you almost certainly will be afterward.

Distribute pens and paper to all who are present. Then ask, "How many times do you think you have heard the gospel?" Some listeners, especially those who have been Christians for many years or who have attended Bible-preaching churches since childhood, may roll their eyes and say, "Thousands of times." Others will nod, affirming their repeated exposure to the gospel.

"Good!" you reply. "And since most of you profess to be Christians, you certainly had to not only hear the gospel, but understand it well enough to believe it and be saved, right?"

Again, you'll see relaxed, confident affirmations all around.

"Great! Since you're all so familiar with the gospel, I'm sure you won't have any problems with this simple exercise. Please take a sheet of paper and write down the gospel. In a paragraph or so, write the message people must hear, understand, and believe in order to be right with God and go to heaven."

Watch people freeze.

"Please, go ahead now and write a paragraph declaring the gospel which you say you have heard perhaps thousands of times and which you understood and believed when you were saved."

Now, in an increasingly uncomfortable silence, people will begin shifting in their seats, shuffling their feet, and staring at the sheet of paper. Many will not know what to write. The only thing more discouraging than these empty sheets will be some of the things people actually do write.

What will likely become depressingly apparent in this pop quiz is that an alarming number of those in your group are unclear on the most basic and important message of the Bible. Despite the fact that by their own admission they have read or heard countless presentations of the gospel and claim to have experienced new life in Christ through its power, they are unable to convey even the ABCs of the message of salvation.

What are the implications of this inability to articulate the gospel? For some, it surely reveals the reality that they aren't Christians at all. If you maintain—as I hope you do—that no one is saved apart from believing the gospel of Jesus Christ, it is rather hard to argue that a person has savingly believed the gospel if they cannot convey—in their own words and at their own level of understanding—the message they claim to have believed.

For those who are genuine Christians, but for whatever reason are unable to articulate the gospel, there's another implication: Their efforts at personal evangelism are likely to be seldom and shallow. If someone cannot communicate the gospel in the loving environment of a gathering of Christians, how can they possibly do so with unbelievers out in the world? No amount of pulpit encouragement or shame about evangelism will motivate them to speak words under pressure that they cannot express in the best of circumstances.

Still another implication for true Christians who are unclear on the gospel—and the one most relevant to this book—is that a weak grasp of the gospel is a hindrance to holiness. Or to put it positively, those who know the gospel best are those most likely to become closest to Christ and most like Christ. Brian Hedges understands that the pursuit of "the holiness without which no one will see the Lord" (Heb. 12:14) requires a clear understanding of the gospel. For it is in the gospel that we see Christ in His glory most clearly. And the better we understand and feast our souls on the gospel of Christ, the more intimate with and like Jesus we become. This, writes the author of the book in your hands, is the message of 2 Corinthians 3:18, "And we all, with unveiled face, beholding the glory of the Lord, are being transformed into the same image from one degree of glory to another." Or as Hedges puts it, "God changes us by giving us a vision of his glory revealed in the Lord Jesus Christ."

Turn the page now, and in the lines that follow, may you more clearly see "the light of the knowledge of the glory of God in the face of Jesus Christ" (2 Cor. 4:6).

—Donald S. Whitney

Associate Professor of Biblical Spirituality
& Senior Associate Dean
The Southern Baptist Theological Seminary, Louisville, KY

Acknowledgments

Writing and shaping a book, like the process of transformation itself, is a community project. The community surrounding the publication of *Christ Formed in You* is precious to me. It is a joy to acknowledge my gratitude.

Much of the book's content originated in a series of sermons preached at Fulkerson Park Baptist Church in Niles, Michigan, where I have happily served as Pastor for Preaching since 2003. I'm thankful for the privilege of pursuing Christ together with this special group of people.

Several people read either parts or the whole of my original manuscript and offered both encouragement and constructive criticism. Special thanks to Andy Hedges, Jeremiah Bass, Charles Clarke, and especially Paula Hendricks, for giving valuable time towards making this a better book. Thanks also to Mike Neises for his helpful advice in the early stages of this book.

My good friend Del Fehsenfeld III has his fingerprints all over this book. The seminal ideas were sharpened through our discussions about spiritual formation over Mexican food during the first year of my pastorate at Fulkerson Park. We have continued to swap books, insights, and ideas over the years—many of which have found their way into my thinking and this book. I'm grateful for both Del's enthusiasm for this project and his regular encouragement. But I value even more the joy of sharing life and shepherding people together, along with the other elders with whom we serve.

I am very grateful to Shepherd Press, and especially Rick Irvin, for taking an interest in this book. I have always wanted to write, but didn't expect the opportunity to publish a book during this stage of life. But Shepherd Press announced their interest in new authors at a conference I was attending in 2008, so I stopped by their table and pitched my idea for this book. They were interested and so began our relationship. It has been a pleasure.

I can't imagine working with a better editor than Kevin Meath. He spent many hours on this book, suggesting revisions, restructuring, and rewrites along the way. Throughout the process of editing, Kevin has been sensitive to my goals as an author and has shown deference to my style of working and writing. His sharp editorial skills have increased the book's clarity, verve, and practical usefulness. Kevin, I thank the Lord for you.

I also wish to convey my appreciation to Dr. Donald S. Whitney, Associate Professor of Biblical Spirituality at The Southern Baptist Theological Seminary in Louisville, Kentucky, for graciously agreeing to read and supply the foreword to *Christ Formed in You.* Don not only wrote the foreword, but encouraged me in my desire to write when we first met several years ago (and also infected me with a love for fountain pens!). I am thankful for both his personal encouragement and his ministry to the church through his teaching and writing.

The biggest cheerleader for this book has been my best friend, sweetheart, and life partner, Holly. No one has encouraged me more in pursuing the dream to write. She has listened as I've read aloud countless paragraphs and given me high fives, hugs, and kisses in many milestone moments. Along with our wonderful kids, Stephen, Matthew and Susannah, she cheerfully sacrificed time during our vacation in 2008 as I hammered out much of the first draft. Her support throughout has been a great blessing, but living life together as we seek to become more like the Lord Jesus is a greater blessing still. Holly, you're the love of my life. Thanks for traveling this journey with me.

Finally, I never would have written anything had it not been for the encouragement of my fourth grade teacher who first taught me how to organize my thoughts and put them down on paper, while encouraging me in the then daunting task of writing nine book reports. This teacher is particularly special to me, because she is my mom. Even more important than my intellectual shaping, however, is the spiritual shaping I received through both of my parents. Their confidence in God's sovereign goodness, love for Scripture and historical Christian literature, and humble trust in the gospel have left an indelible mark on me. Before Christ was formed in me, he was formed in them. They were the instruments God used to bring me to faith in Christ. And so, I gratefully dedicate this book to my parents, Ronnie and Gloria Hedges.

Introduction

Have you ever been in a situation where you knew your destination but couldn't find your way? It happens to me with almost predictable regularity. In fact, I've been lost in nearly every big city I've ever visited. Just ask my wife. In these moments of dislocation and disorientation, we need two things for our journey to be a success: a map and someone to show the way. When you come right down to it, we usually need a third thing as well. Especially men. When our journey has been reduced to an ineffective mix of hunches and guesswork, we need to admit that we're lost and need help!

Following Jesus is also a journey. Our destination is clear: conformity to the image of Christ. To be holy. Most Christians realize this and desire it. But we often feel disoriented in the midst of our journey. Though we know where we should be going, it can seem like we've lost our way.

A primary reason for this disorientation is simply that becoming more like Jesus—a process theologians often call "sanctification"—takes a lifetime, and life gets complicated. As the years unfold it can become unclear how sanctification really works, and how it fits with other elements of Christian life and thought. For anyone who takes faith seriously, honest, important questions will eventually arise.

- How do my current struggles with sin affect my standing with God?

- What practical steps must I take to deal with sin and nurture spiritual growth?

- What should I expect as I pursue change?

- How do I measure progress?

- And how do other aspects of my life—my longings for happiness, my personal disciplines and habits, my sufferings and trials, and my relationships with other people—fit into all this?

Dangers, Toils, and Snares

This journey towards holiness is further complicated by what the well-known hymn, "Amazing Grace," describes as "many dangers, toils, and snares." It is both terribly sad and undeniably true that a fair number of these perils have emerged from within Christianity itself.

Distortions of Emphasis

Many Christian traditions, all of them undoubtedly well-intentioned, emphasize certain aspects of biblical teaching to the neglect of others, leaving unsuspecting Christians with distorted ideas or false expectations about spirituality.

- Some put so much emphasis on having correct doctrine that the heart and affections get left behind in an overly intellectual approach to discipleship.

- Others so heavily emphasize inward piety and the importance of spiritual experience that they effectively replace joyful faith in Christ with an unhealthy and myopic introspection.

- Some neglect the work of the Holy Spirit altogether, leaving Christians with the impression that being holy is wholly dependent on moral effort and self-discipline.

- Still others put so much focus on the Spirit that believers wrongly view the Christian life as nothing more than a passive acquiescence to the Spirit's work.

Misrepresentations of the Gospel

Even worse are teachings that eclipse the transforming power of the gospel altogether. These appear in two basic forms.

On one side of the spectrum are views that distort God's grace in ways that give license to ongoing patterns of sin. This is the error that Dietrich Bonhoeffer called "cheap grace ... the grace which amounts to the justification of sin without the justification of the repentant sinner who departs from sin and from whom sin departs."

> Cheap grace is the grace we bestow on ourselves. Cheap grace is the preaching of forgiveness without requiring repentance, baptism without church discipline, Communion without confession, absolution without personal confession. Cheap grace is grace without discipleship, grace without the cross, grace without Jesus Christ, living and incarnate.[1]

But on the other side of the spectrum, and even more contrary to the gospel and more detrimental to spiritual health than "cheap grace," are approaches to holiness that stress moral effort while neglecting the rich resources of God's grace in the gospel. This legalistic approach to holiness rips the heart out of Christianity, leaving people with nothing but the dead form of performance-based religion.

In his essay, "The Centrality of the Gospel," Tim Keller captures the gospel-centered balance we need:

> The key for thinking out the implications of the gospel is to consider the gospel a "third" way between two mistaken opposites ... Tertullian said, "Just as Christ was crucified between two thieves, so this doctrine of justification is ever crucified between two opposite errors." Tertullian meant that there were two basic false ways of thinking, each of which "steals" the power and the distinctiveness of the gospel from us by pulling us "off the gospel line" to one side or the other. These two errors are very powerful, because they represent the natural tendency of the human heart and mind ... These "thieves" can be called *moralism* or *legalism* on the one hand, and *hedonism* or *relativism* on the other hand. Another way to put it is: The gospel opposes both *religion* and *irreligion*. On the one hand, "moralism/religion" stresses truth without grace, for it says that we must obey the truth in order to be saved. On the other hand, "relativists/irreligion" stresses grace without truth, for

they say that we are all accepted by God (if there is a God) and we have to decide what is true for us. But "truth" without grace is not really truth, and "grace" without truth is not really grace. Jesus was "full of grace *and* truth." Any religion or philosophy of life that de-emphasizes or loses one or the other of these truths, falls into legalism or into license, and either way the joy and power and "release" of the gospel is stolen by one thief or the other.[2]

These "two thieves" of legalism and license have plagued the church throughout its history, doing great damage and hindering many in their journey. It is directly between these extremes, therefore, that we must live, safe in the truth of the all-sufficient cross of Christ. This is how we reliably make progress toward the destination of Christlikeness.

To aid us on our way we need a good, accurate map. A map that not only tells where we are in the journey, but one that marks the path clearly and warns us of the dangers, toils, and snares—from our own hearts, from the temptations of this fallen world, and from well-meaning but misguided Christian teachers—that we will encounter along the way.

Piecing Together a Puzzle

My personal journey towards Christlikeness has certainly not been a straight line from conversion to transformation. I've often felt disappointed with my lack of progress and confused by the conflicting perspectives on how to change. But I've also experienced surges of growth as the Lord has opened to my mind the glories of Christ's work in the gospel and the ways of his Spirit in the heart. Nor is my journey complete. I continue to fight sin and learn of my daily need for repentant faith in the crucified and risen Christ. My spiritual growth has been like putting together a jigsaw puzzle—slowly the borders have been formed and key pieces have fit into place, and the big picture has gradually taken shape.

The goal of this book is to explain where the process of transformation fits and how it happens in the Christian life. I hope to bring together various aspects of spiritual formation in a way that is unusual for most books. Many authors do a wonderful job of focusing on one or two of the following areas.

- The content of the gospel—unfolding what God has done for us in the cross and the resurrection of Christ.

- The application of the gospel—discussing the implications of the cross for daily life.

- The priority of holiness and the necessity of mortifying sin— explaining what holiness is and how putting sin to death is an essential and ongoing responsibility in any Christian's life.

- The motivating power in Christian spirituality—describing the inner dynamics of grace and joy in helping us glorify God through the pursuit of holiness.

- The nature and means of spiritual transformation—explaining how people grow spiritually through the use of various methods (such as meditation and prayer).

- The role of suffering in spiritual growth—encouraging us to embrace trials as one of God's means of changing us.

- The importance of community in our discipleship—reminding us that we need others to help us in our journey to Christlikeness.

I have been greatly helped by many of these books, authored by contemporary theologians and pastors such as J. I. Packer, John Stott, John Piper, Sinclair Ferguson, D. A. Carson, Don Whitney, Paul Tripp, Jerry Bridges, Richard Lovelace, and Tim Keller; as well as classic books on spirituality from previous generations written by great stalwarts of the faith such as Saint Augustine, John Calvin, John Bunyan, Jonathan Edwards, John Owen, Charles Spurgeon, Martyn Lloyd-Jones, and C. S. Lewis. As I've read these and other authors over the past fifteen years, different pieces of the puzzle have slowly come together, giving shape to a larger vision of what the gospel is about and how it connects to the various dimensions of my spiritual life. My purpose in this book is to bring these pieces together, presenting a single, unified, gospel-centered vision of how to understand and live the Christian life.

The Power of the Gospel for Personal Change

Because you have picked up this book, you must feel the need for change in your own life. When you examine your attitudes, relationships, thought-patterns, and personal habits, it doesn't take long to realize how far you still have to grow, does it? If you are like me, such self-assessment can quickly become discouraging! We know we need to change, but how do we pursue it?

My central claim in *Christ Formed in You* is that it is God's purpose to change us by progressively making us more like Jesus, and that this happens only as we understand and apply the gospel to our lives. In the pages that follow we will explore the transforming power of the gospel from several angles.

> **Part One** focuses on the *foundations* for personal change. We will look at God's ultimate goal in transforming us (Chapter 1); the key to transformation, which is the gospel itself (Chapter 2); and the application of the gospel to our lives in three specific ways (Chapters 3, 4, and 5).
>
> **Part Two** then takes up the *pattern* of personal change. We will explore the captivating beauty of gospel holiness (Chapter 6); with its demands that we both kill sin (Chapter 7); and grow in grace by the power of the Spirit (Chapter 8); and the quest for joy that motivates us in this pursuit and strengthens us in the battle for holiness (Chapter 9).
>
> **Part Three** of the book focuses on the *means* of personal change, the tools God uses to transform us. These final three chapters, while building on the foundation of the gospel discussed earlier in the book, are the most practical. We will learn how God uses spiritual disciplines (Chapter 10); suffering (Chapter 11); and personal relationships in the body of Christ (Chapter 12) to conform us to the image of Christ.

In each of these chapters, my aim has been to "connect the dots" between the gospel, the goal of Christlikeness, and the specific aspect of spirituality under discussion. As Keller writes, I want us to see that "we never get 'beyond the gospel' in our Christian life to something more 'advanced.'"

The gospel is not the first "step" in a "stairway" of truths, rather, it is more like the "hub" in a "wheel" of truth. The gospel is not just the A-B-C's but the A to Z of Christianity. The gospel is not just the minimum required doctrine necessary to enter the kingdom, but the way we make all progress in the kingdom. We are not justified by the gospel and then sanctified by obedience, but the gospel is the way we grow (Gal.3:1–3) and are renewed (Col.1:6). It is the solution to each problem, the key to each closed door, the power through every barrier (Rom.1:16–17).[3]

This explains what I mean by the subtitle of this book: *The Power of the Gospel for Personal Change*. The seventeenth-century English Congregationalist pastor and theologian, John Owen, put it well in a sentence that summarizes the entire thrust of my book. He said, "Holiness is nothing but the implanting, writing, and realizing of the gospel in our souls." [4] His treatises on the glory of Christ, the work of the Holy Spirit, communion with God, the nature of indwelling sin, temptation, and the mortification of sin provided a road map for pursuing gospel-driven holiness.

While I would never venture to compare either the depth of my knowledge or the historical significance of my ministry to Owen's, I have benefited greatly from his writings (along with those of Tim Keller and others) and hope that this book might serve in a similar way as a map for twenty-first-century believers who long to experience the life-changing power of the gospel in their own journey toward holiness.

PART ONE

THE FOUNDATIONS FOR PERSONAL CHANGE

Anyone who knows me well knows that a handyman I am not. When it comes to home repairs, I attempt only the simplest of tasks. Attempting to do more would be willfully setting myself up for the temptation to sin through frustration and anger! My father-in-law, thankfully, excels where I do not, and every time he comes for a visit from Georgia, Holly and I provide him a long list of house projects to do. And, being the smart, amiable man that he is, he never fails to get the jobs done, effortlessly maintaining a winning attitude all the way. As he usually quips with a smile, "It's one of the many services we offer."

But you don't have to be another Bob Vila to know that foundations, blueprints, and taking the right steps in the right order are important when building things. And this also holds true in our spiritual lives, which is why part one of this book is about the foundations for personal change.

The first chapter focuses on the goal of transformation. Allow me to mix in a couple more metaphors. When piecing together a puzzle, it helps to look at the picture on the box. Before setting out on a journey, it is generally best to know your final destination. The purpose of chapter 1 is to provide that picture, to define that destination, as it relates to spiritual transformation.

The intention of chapter 2 is somewhat different. Since the claim of this book (for more, I refer you to the Introduction) is that the gospel is the key to transformation, I have devoted chapter 2 to explaining what the gospel is.

This is followed by three chapters about the application of the gospel to our lives. Fair warning: this is where the heavy lifting in this book comes in. We'll be dealing with some big theological concepts, like justification, regeneration, and sanctification. I suppose it would be tempting for the theologically trained people to skip these chapters (because you already know this stuff) and for the non-theologically trained people to skip these chapters (because this stuff is too deep and you're more interested in the practical parts of the book).

But I hope you won't skip them. For one thing, some of the most practical things I have to say in this book are carefully woven into these chapters. For another, I've tried to write these chapters in a way that both captures the beauty of what God has done for us in a fresh way and connects the dots between theology and the rest of life.

So, whatever your level of interest in theology may or may not be, I hope that you will prayerfully dive in to these chapters and discover new depths of joy in what God has accomplished through Christ and the Spirit to deliver you from both the guilt and grip of sin.

Restoring God's Broken Image

The Goal

The glory of God is man fully alive, and the life of man is the vision of God.

—Irenaeus

By the time David Garrett was eight years old, he was studying violin with the world's finest teachers, practicing seven hours a day, and making solo appearances with legendary orchestras, including the London Philharmonic. As an adolescent, he studied at the Juilliard School in New York City.

In 2003, for the price of one million dollars, Garrett purchased a Guadagnini, a rare 236-year-old violin made by a student of Stradivarius. But on December 27, 2007, after a brilliant performance at the Barbican in London, David Garrett tripped, fell down a flight of stairs, and landed on the valuable instrument. Though still in its case, the violin was smashed, sustaining damage to the body, neck, and sound post. Restoration was predicted to take eight months and cost more than $120,000. Experts doubted the finely crafted instrument would ever sound the same.

Garrett's unfortunate accident and crushed violin recall a darker tragedy—the Fall of Man and the devastation that followed. We live in the rubble of the world's resulting brokenness. Pain, sickness, suffering, sin, crime, violence, war, alienation from God, shattered relationships, disease, natural disaster, and death are on every side, the ruins of our broken world. Can it all be made right? Is restoration possible?

Scripture teaches that restoration is not only possible, but is a certain reality, secured by God himself through the redeeming death and resurrection of his Son and realized in our lives by the power of his Spirit. The gospel is about nothing less than the redemption of fallen human beings and the perfect, complete restoration of our broken world. As Christ himself says in the closing pages of Scripture, "Behold, I am making all things new" (Rev. 21:5).

Restoration through the gospel is the hope of all Christians. But the practicality of the good news for personal transformation *here* and *now* sometimes escapes us. Someday, everything that is wrong with the world will be made right forever. God will wipe away every tear from our eyes; mourning, crying, pain, and death will be no more (Rev. 21:4). But is genuine change in *my* life possible *now*? And if so, how does it happen?

I believe transformation is possible. The goal of this book is to explain how. More than that, I hope to bring together various aspects of the Christian life in a way that is somewhat unusual in Christian books. As I mentioned in the introduction, many books do a wonderful job of clearly presenting the *content* of the gospel so that we might clearly understand what Christ did for us, or helping us grasp the *practical significance* of the gospel for daily life, or offering us *fresh motivation* for the Christian life in God's purpose to glorify himself and satisfy our souls, or teaching us to embrace the various *means of grace*—such as spiritual disciplines, suffering, and community—by which God matures us in the faith. This book attempts to bring all these approaches together, presenting a single, unified vision for how to change.

To best understand and fully experience the transforming power of the gospel, we must begin with the end in mind. What is God's ultimate goal in saving and changing us? To answer this we need to grasp why God created us in the first place, what has been lost by human sin, and what God through Christ and the Spirit has done and is doing about it. In other words, we need to frame our concerns about personal change in the larger story of God's saving work, the story of creation, fall, redemption, and restoration.

Creation: Images of His Glory

Why did God create us? For what purpose? The *Westminster Shorter Catechism* answers, "Man's chief end is to glorify God and enjoy him forever."[1] Speaking originally of the scattered exiles of Israel whom God promised to redeem, Isaiah 43:6–7 agrees:

> I will say to the north, Give up,
> and to the south, Do not withhold;
> bring my sons from afar
> and my daughters from the end of the earth,
> everyone who is called by my name,
> whom I created for my glory,
> whom I formed and made.

In the first chapter of Genesis we don't read that man was created for God's *glory*, but in God's *image*. What's the difference? Not much. As Sinclair Ferguson has noted, "In Scripture, image and glory are interrelated ideas. As the image of God, man was created to reflect, express, and participate in the glory of God, in miniature, creaturely form."[2] The *Heidelberg Catechism* agrees, "God created man good, and after his own image, in true righteousness and holiness, that he might rightly know God his Creator, heartily love him and live with him in eternal happiness to glorify and praise him."[3]

God created human beings in his image so that they would glorify him by rightly representing him. In other words, the more we resemble God, the better we honor him. With this in mind, look at Genesis 1:26–27.

Then God said, "Let us make man in our image, after our likeness. And let them have dominion over the fish of the sea and over the birds of the heavens and over the livestock and over all the earth and over every creeping thing that creeps on the earth." So God created man in his own image, in the image of God he created him; male and female he created them.

Human beings were God's crowning achievement in creation. We alone are made in God's image, after his likeness. Our creation alone was prefaced with the transcript of God's consultation within himself: "Let us make man in our image." For the creation of everything else Scripture simply records God's words, "Let there be . . . and it was so." But man and woman were different. We were designed and commissioned by God with a special assignment in creation: to display God. As the early church father Irenaeus said, "The glory of God is man fully alive, and the life of man is the vision of God."[4]

Let's unpack what it means to be created in the image of God by briefly looking at three interrelated aspects of it.

To Reflect

To be created in the image of God means we are designed to display God's nature, character, and glory. As a mirror is made for reflection, so God created us to be mirrors of his character, instruments for reflecting his glory.[5]

Created in God's image, we are invested with special dignity and entrusted with particular duties. Our distinct worth as human beings springs from being God's image-bearers, the unique reflectors of his character on earth. The rest of creation *declares* God's glory, speaking of it vividly in a great variety of ways (Ps. 19:1). But we *reflect* it, actually making it, in small part, visible and tangible.

One of the supreme ways we reflect God's glory is by relating to other human beings in God-honoring ways. We ascribe glory to God's name by reflecting his character to others. As Anthony Hoekema writes, "We should not think of the image of God only as a noun but also as a verb: we are to *image* God by the way we live, and the heart of the image of God is love for God and for others."[6]

To Relate

To be God's image-bearers means we are created for relationships. This is implied in Genesis 1:26–27: "Then God said, 'Let us make man in our image, after our likeness.' So God created man in his own image, in the image of God he created him; male and female he created them."

Why does the text connect being created in God's image with being created male and female? Not because God himself is both masculine and feminine—he is unequivocally masculine. It is because God himself is a community—a trinity of persons, existing in eternal self-giving love. In creating man and woman together, he created a community. God created man to image his glory, but his glory could not be adequately displayed by an individual living in isolation from others. God himself says in Genesis 2:18, "It is not good that man should be alone." As John Ortberg writes,

> Community is rooted in the being of God . . . The Trinity exists as a kind of eternal dance of joyful love among Father, Son, and Spirit . . . God created human beings because he was so in love with community that he wanted a world full of people to share it with. He wanted to invite them all to the dance. And life within the Trinity was to be the pattern for our lives.[7]

At the core of our nature as God's image-bearers, we are *relational* beings. This involves a threefold relationship: "between man and God, between man and his fellowmen, and between man and nature."[8]

To Reign

As God's image-bearers, we are also to exercise dominion over the earth (Gen. 1:26, 28). God created human beings to serve as his vice-regents, reigning as his representatives and stewards over the created world. God placed the first man in the Garden of Eden "to work it and keep it" (Gen. 2:15). As God's delegated representatives on earth, human beings are intended to reign over the world—tending and maintaining it—not in exploitation, but in wise, responsible stewardship. Exercising this stewardship, human beings can reflect to the world the radiance of God's infinite worth and glory.

The Fall: Shattered Mirrors

The tragic reality, however, is that the mirror itself has been shattered. We rebelled against God and now live under his judgment and wrath (Gen. 3:16–19; Rom. 1:18). The image of God is therefore distorted. In Calvin's words, God's image is deformed, vitiated, mutilated, maimed, disease-ridden, and disfigured.[9]

This is true for all of us. "All have sinned and fall short of the glory of God" (Rom. 3:23). We have failed to glorify God by not loving his person, obeying his laws, and delighting in his glory. Rather than exclusively worshiping our glorious Creator, we have served and worshiped created things (Rom. 1:21–23). We are "alienated from the life of God" and "dead in trespasses and sins" (Eph. 4:18; 2:1). The image of God within us has become so marred and distorted that each of us, without exception, fails to display his character in fullness.

The Gravity of Sin

But we don't realize the gravity of this evil. Our souls are so calloused by sin that we do not sense its infinite offensiveness to God. J. I. Packer observes that the biblical words for "sin" portray it:

> in a variety of different ways: as rebellion against our rightful owner and ruler; as transgression of the bounds he set; as missing the mark he told us to aim at; as breaking the law he enacted; as defiling (dirtying, polluting) ourselves in his sight, so making ourselves unfit for his company; as embracing folly by shutting our ears to his wisdom; and as incurring guilt before his judgment seat.[10]

These pictures reveal several distinct aspects of our sin, but the common denominator they share is their *Godwardness*. All sin—even so-called little sins—are evil because they are ultimately committed against our infinitely holy God. When we sin against God we spurn his honor, preferring other things to his glory. Even when we sin against other human beings, we simultaneously assault God's glory by hurting those who bear his image. James condemns us for using our tongues to curse others because they are "people who are made in the likeness of God" (James 3:9).

David committed adultery with Bathsheba, murdered her husband, and covered his sin so the public would not know. Yes, these were grievous and horrible sins against people, but David's confession to God reveals his deeper understanding. They were not just sins against people. They were sins against God: violations of his law, infractions of his will, assaults on those who bore his image, and therefore, on God himself. That is why David confessed, "Against you, you only, have I sinned and done what is evil in your sight" (Ps. 51:4).

Every sin against a human being is also a sin against God. Egotism, lust, bitterness, gossip, slander, racial prejudice, violence, the devaluing of human life—these are sins against God's image-bearers, and therefore sins against God himself.

The Consequences of Sin

The consequences of sin are devastating; damaging each of the three relationships for which we were created—that is, relationships humans have with God, one another, and nature.

We see these consequences in Genesis 3, following the sin of the first man and woman. Before sin, they had enjoyed unbroken friendship with God. But after their sinful rebellion, they hid from him in shame and fear, trying without success to cover their shame with fig leaves. Before sin, they had also enjoyed the only perfect marriage that ever existed (Gen. 2:21–25). But following that fatal taste of the forbidden fruit, their relationship was characterized by shame, blame-shifting, and conflict. Before sin, they lived in paradise—a perfect environment. But ever since, humans have lived in conflict with a world under God's curse (Gen. 3:7–19).

- Sin alienates us from God, leaving us spiritually dead, enslaved to our passions, and subject to God's just wrath (Eph. 2:1–3; 4:18–19).
- Sin also brings conflict into human relationships: between husbands and wives; parents and children; and people of different races, languages, and nations.
- Sin is also what put us in conflict with the created order. Originally a welcoming environment, the earth is now hostile to human life

in significant ways. Natural disasters, environmental devastation, and the harshness of the elements are just some of the consequences of our rebellion against God.

Glorious Ruins

So, do human beings still bear God's image, given the extent of sin's devastation? The answer is Yes . . . sort of. Genesis 5:1–3 and 9:6—both written of the post-fall world—echo Genesis 1:26–28 by indicating that we do continue to bear God's image. But as Calvin said, "even though we grant that God's image was not totally annihilated and destroyed in him, yet it was so corrupted that whatever remains is frightful deformity."[11] A trace of his image is still present, but not enough for people to rightly perceive his glory and give him the honor he deserves. Alistair Begg provides a helpful illustration:

> One of the charming aspects of touring in Scotland is the discovery, often in remote regions, of ancient castles. While some of them are occupied, many of them are now in ruins. But they continue to attract our attention and cause us to pause in wonder because, although they have fallen into disrepair, there is still a grandeur to them. Ruins they may be, but they are still possessed of enough of their former dignity to be justifiably regarded as "glorious ruins." So it is with man. As offensive as it may seem to be, the Bible says that we are ruins! On account of sin, God's image in us has been obscured, but not obliterated.[12]

We humans are amazing in our ability to imitate the Creator in countless ways: composing symphonies; painting beautiful landscapes; building cathedrals, skyscrapers, and bridges; and sending explorers into space. But as magnificent as these accomplishments are, they fall far short of God's intention, when done without regard for his honor and glory. We are glorious ruins! Tiny flashes of light flicker in our achievements. But these are merely distorted glimmers of glory in the broken shards of our fallen, fragmented world.

Redemption: The Gracious Rescue

The good news is that God is reforging the shards! When he is finished, no trace of the breakage will remain. For God has formed a rescue plan. Not willing to abandon his creation to evil, God has purposed to redeem and restore the world by setting a new people apart for himself.

Although hints of this plan are given even before the expulsion of Adam and Eve from the Garden (Gen. 3:15), God's redemptive mission truly began to take shape when he called Abraham.[13] God promised to give Abraham two things: A son (and descendants) through whom the world would be blessed (Gen. 12:1–3), and a special land that would belong to his heirs forever (Gen. 17:7–8).[14] The promised son was Isaac. The descendants were the children of Israel. The land would be Canaan. God later rescued this people from slavery in Egypt and consecrated them as a special nation (Ex. 1–15) over which he himself would reign as sovereign king (Ex. 19:3–6; Num. 23:21; Deut. 33:2–5).

Once Canaan was settled, God promised David, the greatest of Israel's earthly kings, a son who would be forever enthroned over his people (2 Sam. 7). The entire story of the Old Testament is the outworking of these two covenant promises to Abraham and David. It is the story of God's glory gradually returning to earth through this people, chosen and redeemed to bear his image.

Israel, however, failed to reflect the glory of the Lord as they should. Israel's history in Scripture is marked by repeated cycles of rebellion against God, exile from God, and deliverance by God. In spite of God's grace and longsuffering, the hearts of the people continually turned to idols instead of their Covenant Lord. God repeatedly sent prophets to denounce their rebellion and idolatry, warning of the impending judgment that would surely fall upon them. They usually refused to listen. But a kernel of hope was buried in the prophets' oracles of doom. God promised that he would not utterly forsake his people. He would preserve a remnant of people, to whom he would faithfully fulfill his promises (Isa. 6:9–13; 10:20–22). He would send a suffering servant to lead the people in a second exodus. And he would create a new world (Isa. 40–66).

This rescue plan comes to fruition in Jesus, the son of David, the son of Abraham (Matt. 1:1). Born in fulfillment of God's promises (Matt.

1:18–25), Jesus is the ultimate descendant of Abraham, the heir to David's throne, and the remnant of Israel (Gal. 3:16; Rom. 1:3). Jesus is the suffering servant who, through death and resurrection, ransoms God's people, inaugurates his saving reign, and ushers in the new creation (Mark 1:15; 10:45; 2 Cor. 5:17).[15] As the great theologian Herman Bavinck summarized, "The essence of the Christian religion consists in this, that the creation of the Father, devastated by sin, is restored in the death of the Son of God, and re-created by the Holy Spirit into a kingdom of God."[16]

This has been only the briefest overview of the ways in which God's promises are fulfilled in Christ. But there is one more dimension of God's work in Christ that we must understand.

Restoration: New Man, New Creation

In contrast to Adam, the first man, Jesus came as the second Adam, the true image-bearer of God. Paul, looking forward to the final resurrection, says:

> Thus it is written, "The first man Adam became a living being"; the last Adam became a life-giving spirit. But it is not the spiritual that is first but the natural, and then the spiritual. The first man was from the earth, a man of dust; the second man is from heaven. As was the man of dust, so also are those who are of the dust, and as is the man of heaven, so also are those who are of heaven. Just as we have borne the image of the man of dust, we shall also bear the image of the man of heaven.
> —1 Corinthians 15:45–49

Similarly, 2 Corinthians 4:4 calls Christ, "the image of God" and Colossians 1:15 says that he is "the image of the invisible God, the firstborn of all creation." Along with Hebrews 1:3, which describes the Son as the "radiance of the glory of God and the exact imprint of his nature," these passages refer to the divinity of our Lord as the eternal and preexistent Son of God. In the words of Herman Ridderbos, "When in this context he is called . . . the Image of God, this is to say nothing less than that in him the glory of God, indeed God himself, becomes manifest."[17] But, as Ridderbos also observes, these passages "are in all sorts of ways directly reminiscent of the creation story."[18] Jesus is not only fully God, he is fully man. He comes as the second Adam, the Last Man, the true image-bearer of God, the one who never sinned, never failed God, never fell short.

In the unique union of deity and humanity in the person of Jesus Christ, we therefore see not only the Word of God made flesh (John 1:14), but the perfect picture of what it means to be human.[19] Jesus bears the image of God as Adam should have. The divine visage which is marred, distorted, and perverted in all other human beings, shines untarnished in him. As Hoekema writes, "Christ is called the image of God par excellence . . . In Christ we see the image of God in perfection. As a skillful teacher uses visual aids to help his or her pupils understand what is being taught, so God the Father has given us in Jesus Christ a visual example of what the image of God is."[20]

Jesus Christ perfectly reflects the glory of the Father, not only because he is himself divine, but because he perfectly images God's character in his flawless humanity. In him we see what God intended all human beings to be in their relationships to God, to one another, and to creation. Consumed with a passion for his Father's glory, Jesus lived in unbroken fellowship with God. He devoted himself to loving others, his love culminating in his death as our substitute on the cross. And he commanded the winds and waves—indeed all the elements of creation—as their true Lord and rightful King.

Jesus is the true *Imago Dei*, the true image of God. But he also remakes human beings in his image through his work. His life on this earth was the perfect embodiment of all that is righteous, good, beautiful, and true. In his spotless obedience and sacrificial death, he took our place—living the life we should have lived and dying the death we should have died. And in his resurrection and exaltation, he now reigns as the second and last Adam, the True Man, the "firstborn among many brothers" (Rom. 8:29). The clear purpose of God's saving work in Jesus is to conform us to the image of his Son. Jesus is the new man, ushering in a new creation, in us (2 Cor. 5:21).

This is the unfolding of God's eternal purpose. God has predestined those chosen in Christ to be conformed to the glorious image of Christ (Eph. 1:4–5; Rom. 8:29). This divine goal will not be fully realized until the Lord Jesus returns from heaven to "transform our lowly body to be like his glorious body" (Phil. 3:21; cf. 1 John 3:2). But the restoration has already begun in the redemptive work of Christ, applied in our lives by the power of God's Spirit.

Beholding and Becoming

The question this book aims to answer is *how* do we become like Jesus? *How does the restoration of the image of God within our hearts take place?* In the following chapters we will explore how Scripture gloriously answers this question. For now, let's consider a passage that compellingly describes the transforming power of gazing at God's glory revealed in Jesus.

> But when one turns to the Lord, the veil is removed. Now the Lord is the Spirit, and where the Spirit of the Lord is, there is freedom. And we all, with unveiled face, beholding the glory of the Lord, are being transformed into the same image from one degree of glory to another. For this comes from the Lord who is the Spirit.... And even if our gospel is veiled, it is veiled only to those who are perishing. In their case the god of this world has blinded the minds of the unbelievers, to keep them from seeing the light of the gospel of the glory of Christ, who is the image of God. For what we proclaim is not ourselves, but Jesus Christ as Lord, with ourselves as your servants for Jesus' sake. For God, who said, "Let light shine out of darkness," has shone in our hearts to give the light of the knowledge of the glory of God in the face of Jesus Christ.
>
> —2 Corinthians 3:16–18; 4:3–6

God changes us by giving us a vision of his glory revealed in the Lord Jesus Christ. The sensory language in this passage is remarkable. Paul speaks of the gospel being veiled or unveiled[21] (3:16, 18; 4:3), of beholding glory (3:18), of blindness and sight (4:4), of darkness and light (4:4, 6). Can you imagine what it would be like suddenly to be given sight after a lifetime of blindness? This is what happens when a person is born of the Spirit. As we so often sing, "I once was lost, but now I'm found; 'twas blind, but now I see."[22] Though we were dead to God, blind to his beauty and glory, now we are God-conscious, God-aware.

This new vision of God is focused on God's glory. Paul describes "beholding the glory of the Lord" in 3:18, the "light of the gospel of the glory of Christ" in 4:4, and the "light of the knowledge of the glory of God" in 4:6. What is the glory of God? It is the beauty and radiance of his worth. Only when we see *this* about God, his beauty and worth, displayed in and through Jesus Christ and his glorious work (3:18; 4:4–6), are we really changed.[23] *Beholding the glory of Christ is the means of becoming like Christ in his glory.*[24]

Though God's image within us is disfigured and distorted by evil and sin, the good news is that God is bringing redemption and restoration, freeing us from sin's penalty and power, and recreating us in the image of his Son. The vision of God's glory in Christ in the gospel has transforming power. As we see him, we become like him.

Life in the New Creation

Paul describes the change believers have experienced as a new creation. In Ephesians 2:10, he says that we are the workmanship— the masterpieces!—of God "created in Christ Jesus for good works."[25] Similarly, Paul reminds his readers that when they "learned Christ," they were taught to "put on the new self, created after the likeness of God in true righteousness and holiness" (Eph. 4:20–24).[26] A parallel passage in Colossians 3 says the new man, "is being renewed in knowledge after the image of its creator" (v.10). And 2 Corinthians 5:17 exults that, "if anyone is in Christ, he is a new creation. The old has passed away; behold, the new has come" (cf. Gal. 6:15). For all who are joined to Christ by faith, this inaugural and decisive renovation of the heart has already taken place. They have put off the old man and put on the new man; they have put on Christ (Gal. 3:27; Rom. 13:14). New creation has begun![27]

Perhaps you remember the lyrics from the children's song, "Bullfrogs and Butterflies." Both were born again. The curse of sin has been canceled and its bondage has been broken. As a tadpole is transformed into a frog, and as a caterpillar leaves its earthbound cocoon a beautiful, airborne butterfly, so we experience a dramatic metamorphosis through the power of Christ and his Spirit. We are transformed. As fallen inhabitants of the old creation, our native environment is sin.

But as recipients of God's new creation in Christ, holiness is no longer alien to us. We are born again for God!

The Imitation of Christ

Today, we live in the interval between the inauguration of the new creation and its consummation and completion when Jesus comes again. In this gap between what has already begun and what is yet to come, we taste the joy of living under God's gracious reign as citizens of the new creation . . . even as we groan with the tension of living as residents in the world as it now is. We are *truly* new, but not *completely* new. The renovation has begun, but it is not finished. This is why Paul groaned as in the anguish of childbirth until Christ was formed in his fellow believers (Gal. 4:19).

Our transformation into the image of the Lord is *progressive*—it happens in stages (2 Cor. 3:18). And though spiritual change is a divine work of God's Spirit in our hearts and lives, it demands our *participation.* We must refuse to be shaped by this present age and instead be transformed by the renewal of our minds as we put sin to death and live in righteousness (Rom. 12:2; Eph. 4:25–32; Col. 3:5–14). This dynamic process lies at the heart of the Christian call to holiness.

The essence of this holiness is *likeness* to Jesus Christ—what some theologians call "Christiformity."[28] When we become like Jesus, our lives reflect God's glory and we live in right relationship to God, other people, and the world. This is the goal God destined us for, the vocation he has called us to. This is why we are redeemed.

This also explains why Scripture calls us to imitate Christ. In 1 Corinthians 11:1, Paul says, "Be imitators of me, as I am of Christ." In Ephesians 5:1–2, he writes, "Therefore be imitators of God, as beloved children. And walk in love, as Christ loved us and gave himself up for us, a fragrant offering and sacrifice to God." And in Philippians 2:5–11, he urges us to have the mind of Christ, expressed in humility and selfless service to others. The apostle John also exhorts us to follow Christ's example, walking as he walked, practicing righteousness as he is righteous, purifying ourselves as he is pure, and loving others as he loved (1 John 2:6, 29; 3:3, 7, 16–18; 4:16–17).

Charles Wesley captured the heart of Christlikeness in these prayerful words:

> *O for a heart to praise my God,*
> *A heart from sin set free,*
> *A heart that always feels Thy blood*
> *So freely shed for me.*
>
> *A heart resigned, submissive, meek,*
> *My great Redeemer's throne,*
> *Where only Christ is heard to speak,*
> *Where Jesus reigns alone.*
>
> *A humble, lowly, contrite, heart,*
> *Believing, true and clean,*
> *Which neither life nor death can part*
> *From Christ who dwells within.*
>
> *A heart in every thought renewed*
> *And full of love divine,*
> *Perfect and right and pure and good,*
> *A copy, Lord, of Thine.*[29]

This is a book about spiritual formation, the "grace-driven developmental process in which the soul grows in conformity to the image of Christ."[30] The acid test of all spiritual formation is this: *Are you becoming more like Jesus?* Are the contours of your character being shaped by his image, formed in his likeness? Do you increasingly hate sin and love righteousness, as he already does perfectly? Are you growing in humility and self-giving, which he has practiced flawlessly? Are you making progress in loving and serving others, as he has always done in perfection?

Ongoing transformation is possible for you. You can become more and more like Jesus Christ. But there is only one way: through your increasing understanding and application of the gospel.

The Spell Is Broken

In C. S. Lewis's *The Lion, the Witch and the Wardrobe,* four children learn that the land of Narnia is under the spell of the White Witch. In Narnia, it is "always winter and never Christmas."[30] The people and beasts of Narnia are enslaved to the White Witch; if they make her angry, she turns them to statues of stone. The crisis comes when the White Witch has claimed the life of one of the children, a boy named Edmund, who has betrayed Narnia. But Aslan, the great lion who created Narnia, takes Edmund's place and is killed by the White Witch. The next morning, a wonderful thing happens. Aslan comes back to life! After his resurrection, he storms the castle of the White Witch, which is filled with stone statues. When Aslan breathes on the statue of a lion, this is what happens:

> For a second after Aslan had breathed upon him the stone lion looked just the same. Then a tiny streak of gold began to run along his white marble back—then it spread—then the colour seemed to lick all over him as the flame licks all over a bit of paper—then, while his hind-quarters were still obviously stone the lion shook his mane and all the heavy, stony folds rippled into living hair. Then he opened a great red mouth, warm and living, and gave a prodigious yawn. And now his hind legs had come to life. He lifted one of them and scratched himself. Then, having caught sight of Aslan, he went bounding after him and frisking around him whimpering with delight and jumping up to lick his face.[31]

Aslan is alive. The spell is broken. Winter is over. The statues are coming to life!

Lewis's imaginative tale beautifully illustrates the True Story of what God has done through the work of Christ, and is doing by the power of the Spirit to renew and restore the world. Though we betrayed God through our rebellion and sin, Jesus became our representative and died as our substitute. But he has risen! The spell of evil is broken. The dead are coming to life. The winter is over and spring is on the way!

"Behold, I am making all things new."[32]

The Key to Transformation

The Gospel

The gospel is not just the minimum required doctrine necessary to enter the kingdom, but the way we make all progress in the kingdom. We are not justified by the gospel and then sanctified by obedience, but the gospel is the way we grow and are renewed. It is the solution to each problem, the key to each closed door, the power through every barrier.

—Tim Keller

Some of my favorite stories are about characters who find themselves transported into an extraordinary world through some apparently commonplace object. Lucy walks through an old wardrobe into Narnia. Milo enters The Lands Beyond through a tollbooth. Alice pushes her way through a mirror into Looking Glass Room. Neo leaves the Matrix by taking the red pill. In each adventure, something ordinary becomes a portal into a new world.

As we saw in chapter 1, the gospel is the most astonishing and life-transforming portal of all. The good news of what God has accomplished in his crucified and risen Son is much more than mere words. Paul says it is "the power of God for salvation to everyone who believes" (Rom. 1:16). The gospel is a portal into the new world. When we gaze on the glory of Christ in the gospel, we are changed—transformed into his image by the Spirit.

> And we all, with unveiled face, beholding the glory of the Lord, are being transformed into the same image from one degree of glory to another. For this comes from the Lord who is the Spirit.
>
> —2 Corinthians 3:18

Here, the word "beholding"[1] means "to reflect as in a mirror." That which we gaze upon is "the glory of the Lord." As we gaze, we are transformed into his image. And the medium by which this transformation takes place—the mirror in which his glorious image is viewed—is the gospel.

> And even if our gospel is veiled, it is veiled only to those who are perishing. In their case the god of this world has blinded the minds of the unbelievers, to keep them from seeing the light of the gospel of the glory of Christ, who is the image of God. For what we proclaim is not ourselves, but Jesus Christ as Lord, with ourselves as your servants for Jesus' sake. For God, who said, "Let light shine out of darkness," has shone in our hearts to give the light of the knowledge of the glory of God in the face of Jesus Christ.
>
> —2 Corinthians 4:3–6

While much could be said about this passage, the main point is that God's glory, revealed in Jesus, is seen in the message of the gospel. The gospel is the mirror which reflects God's glory. The gospel is our portal to personal transformation. As Tim Keller writes,

> The gospel is not just the minimum required doctrine necessary to enter the kingdom, but the way we make all progress in the kingdom. We are not justified by the gospel and then sanctified by obedience, but the gospel is the way we grow (Gal.3:1–3) and are renewed (Col.1:6). It

is the solution to each problem, the key to each closed door, the power through every barrier (Rom.1:16–17).[2]

In the following chapters we'll look at some specific ways God uses the gospel to change us. But first we need to push deeper into what the gospel actually is. Gospel means "good news." Central to the life-transforming good news of the gospel are the crucifixion, burial, and resurrection of Jesus. When Paul reminds the Corinthian believers of the essential contours of his message, he focuses on these events (1 Cor. 15:1–5).[3] In this chapter, therefore, we will focus on the cross and resurrection of Christ as well, along with the subsequent exaltation of Christ and his gift of the Spirit to the church, all of which are foundational to our understanding of how the gospel transforms our lives.

The Achievements of the Cross

The cross is central in the apostolic proclamation of the gospel. Paul said to the Corinthians, "I decided to know nothing among you except Jesus Christ and him crucified." To the Galatians, he wrote: "But far be it from me to boast except in the cross of our Lord Jesus Christ, by which the world has been crucified to me, and I to the world" (1 Cor. 2:2; Gal. 6:14).

When we meditate on the cross, our thoughts are often taken up with the details of Jesus' physical suffering. This is not inappropriate, but neither is it Paul's principal focus. When he rehearses the essential components of his message in 1 Corinthians 15, Paul highlights not the *manner* of Christ's death with a gory description of its violence and shame, but the *meaning*—its theological significance. "[He] died for our sins" (v. 3).

Substitution

Jesus did not die for his own sins, for he had none. He had committed no crime, "For Christ also suffered once for sins, the righteous for the unrighteous, that he might bring us to God, being put to death in the flesh but made alive in the spirit" (1 Peter 3:18). The cross was more than just the execution of a Jewish prophet. It was a *substitution*. Jesus died in our place. As J. Oswald Sanders says:

By substitution we do not mean the saving of a life by *mere assistance*, as in the throwing of a rope to a drowning man; or by the *mere risking* of one life to save another; it is the saving of one life by the *loss* of another. As substitute, Christ took on Himself the sinner's guilt and bore its penalty in the sinner's place.[4]

> *Bearing shame and scoffing rude*
> *In my place condemned he stood*
> *Sealed my pardon with his blood*
> *Hallelujah! What a Savior!*[5]

"In my place condemned he stood." This is substitution. This is the meaning of the cross.

But merely stating the doctrine doesn't cause the glory of substitution to rest with weight on our souls. We are numb to spiritual realities, our hearts dull and unfeeling as stones. We need more details—not of the torturous agonies of crucifixion, but of the abiding significance of what the cross achieved, and of its cost for our Lord. A closer look at some of Scripture's varied and descriptive language about the cross—specifically propitiation, redemption, rescue, reconciliation, and triumph—can help us.

Propitiation

A divine transaction between the Father and the Son took place on the cross. The Father laid the sins of unrighteous people on his Son and punished those sins with all the fury of his omnipotent wrath, compressed into six hours. When Jesus died, he completely appeased that wrath. This is what Scripture and theologians call *propitiation*. John Stott explains:

> At the cross in holy love God through Christ paid the full penalty of our disobedience himself. He bore the judgment we deserve in order to bring us the forgiveness we do not deserve. On the cross divine mercy and justice were equally expressed and eternally reconciled. God's holy love was "satisfied" . . . Divine love triumphed over divine wrath by divine self-sacrifice.[6]

Scripture teaches that on the cross God displayed Christ as an atoning sacrifice to declare his righteousness. As a merciful and faithful high priest, Jesus made propitiation for the sins of the people. Jesus is our advocate with the Father; he is the propitiation for the sins of the whole world (Rom. 3:25; Heb. 2:17; 1 John 2:1–2; cf. 4:10). The beauty of propitiation is that our just and holy God is more satisfied with the obedience and death of Christ than he is grieved and angered by our God-belittling sins.[7]

This is not to suggest that Jesus arm-twisted the Father into granting us forgiveness. The sacrifice belonged to both Father and Son. Because of his great love for the world, God gave his one and only Son for us (John 3:16).

Redemption

To describe what Christ has achieved for us, Scripture also uses the language of ransom and redemption. These ideas come from the first-century marketplace where slaves were bought and sold. They also recall the Exodus story, when God redeemed the nation of Israel from captivity in Egypt. For the writers of the New Testament, our Egypt is the bondage of sin and the curse of the law. Christ, in taking our place, has paid our ransom and set us free (Gal. 3:10–13).

The price for our ransom was the death of Christ. "In him we have redemption through his blood, the forgiveness of our trespasses, according to the riches of his grace" (Eph. 1:7). Peter says we were ransomed by the precious blood of Christ (1 Peter 1:18–19), and Jesus himself said to his disciples, "The Son of Man came not to be served but to serve, and to give his life as a ransom for many" (Mark 10:45; cf. Matt. 20:28, Rom. 3:24; Col. 1:13–14). And the four living creatures worshiping the enthroned Lamb exclaim:

> Worthy are you to take the scroll
> and to open its seals,
> for you were slain,
> and by your blood you ransomed people for God
> from every tribe and language and people and nation,
> and you have made them a kingdom and priests to our God,
> and they shall reign on the earth.
>
> —Revelation 5:9–10

Rescue

Closely related to redemption is the concept of rescue or deliverance. In Galatians 1, Paul teaches that Jesus Christ, raised from the dead by God the Father (v. 1), "gave himself for our sins to deliver us from the present evil age" (v. 4). What does this mean? In what sense are we rescued from "this present evil age"?

Richard Gaffin writes, "The expression 'the present evil age' reflects Paul's use of the distinction between 'this' or 'the present age' and 'the age to come.'"[8] The present age is marked by evil, corruption, and death: the consequences of human rebellion against the Creator. In contrast, the age to come is defined by righteousness, wholeness, and life.

> The purpose of Christ's death, according to Galatians 1:4 . . . is nothing less than the deliverance of the church from the present world order, marked by sin and its consequences, and with that deliverance, by implication, to bring believers into the coming world order, the new and final creation, marked by eschatological life in all its fullness.[9]

Paul sounds a similar note in Colossians 1:13, rejoicing that the Father "has delivered us from the domain of darkness and transferred us to the kingdom of his beloved Son." In the death of Christ, God's glorious future invaded and plundered the present evil age. A beachhead is established for the kingdom of God in the lives of the redeemed. We have been rescued from the sin and darkness of the fallen present world!

Reconciliation

Scripture also uses relational language to describe the effects of Christ's work on the cross. Sin created a breach between us and God. The once peaceful relationship is now marked by hostility and hatred. The cross brings reconciliation and restores us to God.

In Romans 5, Paul says that Christ died for us when we were ungodly sinners, and his enemies (v. 6, 8, 10). We were alienated from God by our sins, sworn enemies to the just and righteous God of glory. But in his amazing love, God sent Jesus to take our place, resulting in a restored relationship characterized by peace, harmony, and mutual love (cf. Eph. 2:11–22; 2 Cor. 5:18–21; Col. 1:19–23). Where once there was enmity, now there is grace and friendship.

Triumph

Finally, Scripture describes the work of Christ as the triumph over evil: his victory over Satan, sin, and death. John writes, "the reason the Son of God appeared was to destroy the works of the devil" (1 John 3:8). Paul says in Colossians that in the cross, Jesus "disarmed the rulers and authorities and put them to open shame, by triumphing over them in him." And in Hebrews we read that Christ became incarnate, "that through death he might destroy the one who has the power of death, that is, the devil, and deliver all those who through fear of death were subject to lifelong slavery" (Col. 2:15; Heb. 2:14–15).

In the death and resurrection of Christ, the decisive victory over sin, Satan, and death was won. Of course this raises a question: if this is so, why is there still so much evil and suffering in the world? Let me answer with a story.

There was an elderly widow who attended a little church I once pastored in Texas. Her name was Merleen, and though very kind, she was one of the toughest ladies I've ever met. She had grown up on a farm and could grow—or kill—anything! Merleen's utter fearlessness of rattlesnakes captured my interest. She had killed dozens of snakes, more than twenty in just one year! Merleen once found a rattlesnake on her farm, but didn't have a hoe nearby to kill it. She wasn't about to let it get away, so she dropped a boulder on the snake—not killing it, but pinning it to the ground. The decisive victory against the rattler was won then and there. Then she left to fetch her hoe and returned to take the snake's head off once and for all.

In the death of Christ, the decisive defeat of sin, Satan, death, and hell was won. Jesus crushed the serpent's head. Satan was disarmed and defeated, though not completely destroyed. He is like that rattlesnake pinned to the ground: still dangerous, still able to bite, but with far less authority. As Merleen returned to finish off the snake, so Jesus will return to establish his kingdom and defeat evil once and for all.

To summarize, Christ died *for* our sins and *in* our place. In his substitutionary work on the cross, Jesus saved us from the consequences of our sins.

- Through propitiation, he became our curse and bore the wrath we deserved.
- In redeeming us, he paid the ransom that set us free from slavery.
- He also rescued us from the darkness of this present evil age.
- Through reconciliation, he removed the hostility separating us from God.
- And he triumphed over our enemies: sin, Satan, and death.

These glorious achievements of the cross show why it lies at the heart of the gospel.

The Power of Christ's Resurrection

Jesus, of course, did not remain on the cross or stay in the grave. The Christian message would not be good news if there were nothing to report beyond Good Friday. But there *is* a report. "He was raised on the third day, in accordance with the Scriptures" (1 Cor. 15:4). The news is good because Jesus is alive!

What did Paul mean when he claimed that Christ was raised? Did he simply mean the spirit of Jesus had gone to heaven after he died? That Jesus had passed into life-after-death? Did he mean that he and others had seen visions of Jesus or had been visited by the Spirit of Christ or had a sense of his abiding presence with them? If asked, as one hymn does, "You ask me how I know he lives?" would Paul have answered, "He lives within my heart"? What does resurrection mean?

The Resurrection Is Physical

First, Paul meant that the physical body of Jesus of Nazareth—the same body that was killed through crucifixion, wrapped in linens, and laid in Joseph of Arimathea's tomb—was raised out of death into glorious, *physical* life. In 1 Corinthians 15:5–8, Paul named some of the many eyewitnesses of the risen Christ (including himself) as proof. When he wrote these words, many of those witnesses were still alive.

In one appearance, Jesus ate fish with his disciples, proving the tangibility and physicality of his resurrection body. As Luke says, Jesus "presented himself alive after his suffering by many proofs, appearing to [the apostles] during forty days and speaking about the kingdom of God" (Luke 24:33–43; Acts 1:3).

The resurrection means that the body of Jesus emerged from death in glorious triumph!

The Resurrection Is Eschatological

The resurrection of Christ is not only physical; it is eschatological. This means it belongs to, and effectively inaugurates, the age to come. This is why Paul draws the connection between the resurrection of Christ in the past and the resurrection of believers in the future.

> But in fact Christ has been raised from the dead, the firstfruits of those who have fallen asleep. For as by a man came death, by a man has come also the resurrection of the dead. For as in Adam all die, so also in Christ shall all be made alive. But each in his own order: Christ the firstfruits, then at his coming those who belong to Christ. Then comes the end, when he delivers the kingdom to God the Father after destroying every rule and every authority and power. For he must reign until he has put all his enemies under his feet. The last enemy to be destroyed is death.
> —1 Corinthians 15:20–26

Notice that Paul calls the resurrection of Christ "the firstfruits of those who have fallen asleep." This agricultural term derives its significance from the Old Testament, where worshipers brought their "firstfruits" sacrifices each year at the beginning of the spring harvest (Ex. 23:19; Lev. 23:10–11). The firstfruits offering was not only the first and best offering, it represented the entire harvest.[10] As Richard Gaffin states,

> His resurrection is not an isolated event in the past. Rather, in its undeniably full-bodied, past historicity, it belongs, in a manner of speaking, to the future. It can be said to be from the future and to have entered

the past and to be controlling the present from that future. In Christ's resurrection . . . the age-to-come has begun, the new creation has actually dawned, eschatology has been inaugurated.[11]

As C. S. Lewis observes,

The New Testament writers speak as if Christ's achievement in rising from the dead was the first event of its kind in the whole history of the universe. He is the "first fruits," the "pioneer of life." He has forced open a door that has been locked since the death of the first man. He has met, fought, and beaten the King of Death. Everything is different because He has done so. This is the beginning of the New Creation: a new chapter in cosmic history has been opened.[12]

The Great Eucatastrophe

J. R. R. Tolkien has been called *the* author of the twentieth century, and for good reason. His crowning achievement was *The Lord of the Rings*, a masterfully crafted and beautifully written story about the triumph of good over evil in a world full of heroic warriors, strange creatures, and frightening monsters. Most people, through the books, the films, or both, know the story of Frodo, Sam, and their quest to destroy the Ring of Power in the fires of Mount Doom.

What you may not know is that Tolkien was a professing Christian, and crafted his story within the framework of a robust Christian worldview—not with one-to-one parallelism, but through subtle Christian themes deftly woven into the whole literary tapestry of his work.

Tolkien once wrote an essay called "On Fairy-Stories." His essay explored one of the crucial plot-points in good fairy tales, which Tolkien coined the "eucatastrophe." The eucatastrophe was, "the good catastrophe, the sudden joyous 'turn' . . . a sudden and miraculous grace," which "does not deny the existence . . . of sorrow and failure," but "denies . . . the universal final defeat" and gives "a fleeting glimpse of Joy."[13]

The eucatastrophe in *The Lord of the Rings* comes in the third book, *The Return of the King*. When Frodo reaches Mount Doom, he is overcome by the seductive power of the Ring and refuses to cast it into the fire. Instead, he slips the Ring on his finger. All seems lost and Sam is near despair. But then Gollum, a pitiful creature enslaved by the Ring's power, emerges from the darkness, bites the Ring from Frodo's finger and falls into the cracks of doom, to perish in the fire. Gollum unwittingly fulfills a higher purpose, and the Ring is destroyed.

Exhausted and near death, Frodo and Sam are rescued. When they finally awaken two weeks later, they discover that the good wizard Gandalf (who had perished earlier in Tolkien's tale) is alive again. Sam, bewildered and overjoyed, says, "Gandalf! I thought you were dead! But then I thought I was dead myself. Is everything sad going to become untrue? What's happened to the world?"[14] That is eucatastrophe—the happy turn of events, the undoing of the tragedy, the *good news*.

Tolkien himself said, "The Birth of Christ is the eucatastrophe of Man's history. The Resurrection is the eucatastrophe of the story of the Incarnation."[15] Jesus' physical resurrection from the dead was the ultimate undoing of the tragedy of sin. In raising Jesus from death, the Father publicly vindicated his Son's work on the cross. God's future kingdom invaded the present age with triumphant power. Is it any wonder that the resurrection was the consistent theme of the apostles' preaching in the book of Acts?[16]

The Triumph of Christ's Exaltation

Our presentations of the gospel rightly emphasize the cross and resurrection of Christ. But sometimes we fail to notice what follows: his exaltation to God's right hand. Scripture frequently highlights this crucial gospel event, however, and so should we.

In Ephesians 1, for example, Paul prays that his readers would know "the immeasurable greatness of [God's] power toward us who believe." Then he illustrates that power in the resurrection of Christ from the dead and his coronation and enthronement at God's right hand. Christ rules far above all earthly powers and is given the supreme name in heaven and earth. God has "put all things under his feet," making him both Lord of the cosmos and head of the church (vv. 19–23).

All Things Under His Feet

Paul borrows the phrase "put all things under his feet" from Psalm 8, and the phrase is loaded with meaning. "[It captures] the idea of a victory over one's enemies. It is used of the winner of a duel who places his foot on the neck of his enemy who has been thrown to the ground, like Joshua who had his generals place their feet on the necks of the five defeated Amorite kings (Josh. 10:24; cf. 2 Sam. 22:39)."[17] Indeed, God invested Christ with all authority, placing all things, including his enemies, under his sovereign lordship (1 Cor. 15:27–28; Phil. 3:21; 1 Peter 3:22).

But what is most profound about Paul's allusion to Psalm 8 is that this psalm is about God's original purpose and intention for *human beings and their relationship to the created world*. As we saw in chapter 1, human beings were designed to reign over the created world as God's representatives on earth. Because of sin, they do not. Birds destroy crops. Insects spread disease. Wild animals maim and kill human beings. The environment is often more hostile than hospitable to human beings.

In taking this language from Psalm 8, however, Paul is saying that God has put all things under the feet of the risen and exalted Christ (cf. Heb. 2:5–9). In the person of Jesus, who is fully God *and fully man*, man has resumed his lordship over creation. Everything that Christ has done, is doing, and will do serves to recapture and complete God's original plan for the perfection of creation!

Human Nature Exalted in Christ

God's work in making Christ supreme has extraordinary implications—and not just theoretical or theological implications, but extremely personal implications for every Christian. For in Jesus Christ, *human nature itself has been resurrected, enthroned, and exalted.* As Martyn Lloyd-Jones said, "Human nature has been raised to [the] surpassing height of glory."[18] This is what the early church father Irenaeus called the "recapitulation" of humanity in Christ. Drawing on the Scriptural teaching that Christ has come as the Second Adam, and thus new "head" of the human race, he said, "God recapitulated in himself the ancient formation of man, that he might kill sin, deprive death of its power, and vivify man."[19]

C. S. Lewis captures the wonder of this truth, using the image of a diver.

> The story of the Incarnation is the story of a descent and a resurrection. When I say "resurrection" here, I am not referring simply to the first few hours or the first few weeks of the Resurrection. I am talking of this whole, huge pattern of descent, down, down, and then up again. What we ordinarily call the Resurrection being just, so to speak, the point at which it turns. Think what that descent is. The coming down, not only into humanity, but into those nine months which precede human birth . . . and going lower still into being a corpse, a thing which, if this ascending movement had not begun, would have gone back into the inorganic, as all corpses do . . . one has the picture of a diver, stripping off garment after garment, making himself naked, then flashing for a moment in the air, and then down through the green, and warm, and sunlit water into the pitch black, cold, freezing water, down into the mud and slime, then up again, his lungs almost bursting, back again to the green and warm and sunlit water, and then at last out into the sunshine, holding in his hand the dripping thing he went down to get. This thing is human nature; but, associated with it, all nature, the new universe.[20]

In Jesus, we see something of the pattern of what we will be. He is the firstborn of the new creation, the firstfruits of the resurrection in the age to come. His exaltation to a place of authority is something we will share. We are beneficiaries of the restoration of humanity that Christ accomplished through his resurrection. When Scripture tells us that we can anticipate being made like him, this is essentially what it means.[21]

The Gift of the Spirit

In his resurrection and exaltation Christ did far more than return to us our humanity. Even as the Son of Man departed from the earth, he sent us his Spirit. "This Jesus God raised up, and of that we all are witnesses. Being therefore exalted at the right hand of God, and having received from the Father the promise of the Holy Spirit, he has poured out this that you yourselves are seeing and hearing" (Acts 2:32–33). This was a pivotal event, unprecedented in the history of God's saving deeds. As Peter points out, it was also the fulfillment of Joel's prophecy that God would pour his Spirit out in the "last days" (Joel 2:28–32; Acts 2:17–21).

True, the Spirit of God was active before the coming of Christ. Scripture speaks of the Spirit's involvement in both creation and redemption (Gen. 1:2; Isa. 63:7–14). From Peter and Paul, we know that the Spirit was also the agent of God's self-revelation through Scripture (2 Peter 1:21; 2 Tim. 3:14–17). But it is especially in the life and ministry of Jesus that we make our acquaintance with the Holy Spirit. "In the coming of Jesus, the Day of the Spirit had finally dawned."[22]

The Spirit of the Son

The Holy Spirit was intimately connected with Jesus throughout his entire life. Prior to Jesus' virginal conception an angel said to Mary, "the Holy Spirit will come upon you, and the power of the Most High will overshadow you" (Luke 1:35; cf. Matt. 1:18, 20). When Jesus was baptized by John the Baptist in the Jordan River, the Father anointed him with the Spirit (Matt. 3:16; Mark 1:10; Luke 3:22). Then Jesus was immediately driven into the wilderness by the Spirit for a season of testing (Matt. 4:1; Mark 1:12; Luke 4:1). Luke says that Jesus was "full of the Spirit" when this happened; he afterward returned to Galilee in "the power of the Spirit" (Luke 4:14).

In Jesus' first sermon, he claimed to fulfill Isaiah's prophecy of a Spirit-anointed ministry of redemption and restoration to Israel (Luke 4:16–21). Peter's summary of Christ's ministry describes "how God anointed Jesus of Nazareth with the Holy Spirit and with power. He went about doing good and healing all who were oppressed by the devil, for God was with him" (Acts 10:38). When skeptical religious leaders accused him of casting out demons by satanic power, Jesus said, "if it is by the Spirit of God that I cast out demons, then the kingdom of God has come upon you" (Matt. 12:28).

In his death, Jesus offered himself as an atoning sacrifice through the Holy Spirit (Heb. 9:14). Paul tells us that Jesus was "declared to be the Son of God in power according to the Spirit of holiness by his resurrection from the dead" (Rom. 1:4). After Jesus' resurrection he breathed on his disciples, saying "receive the Holy Spirit" (John 20:22). Then followed Jesus' ascension and Pentecost, when the Spirit was poured out on the church, *as the Spirit of Christ.*

The New Age of the Spirit

The exaltation of Christ inaugurated the new age of the Spirit. Jesus, the quintessential Spirit-filled one, the Last Adam, has lived and died in our place. He is now exalted in glorified humanity. In this exalted position, the Spirit so identifies with the risen Lord Jesus that Paul speaks of Christ as "life-giving Spirit" (1 Cor. 15:45) and the "Lord of the Spirit"[23] (2 Cor. 3:18).

As Sinclair Ferguson writes:

> From womb to tomb to throne, the Spirit was the constant companion of the Son. As a result, when he comes to Christians to indwell them, he comes as the Spirit of Christ in such a way that to possess him is to possess Christ himself, just as to lack him is to lack Christ.[24]

This is important for us to grasp because the Spirit, as given by our exalted Lord, is the agent who personally effects our transformation.

When we embrace Christ as revealed in the gospel, he gives us his Spirit. The Holy Spirit remakes us after Christ's likeness, changing us by the sight of his glory into his very image (2 Cor. 3:18). We are dependent on the Spirit for every inch of progress in our pursuit of holiness and transformation. As Calvin wrote,

> It is the Spirit that inflames our hearts with the fire of ardent love for God and for our neighbor. Every day he mortifies and every day consumes more and more of the vices of our evil desire or greed, so that, if there are some good deeds in us, these are the fruits and the virtues of his grace; and without the Spirit there is in us nothing but darkness of understanding and perversity of heart.[25]

This is the life-giving ministry of the Spirit in the new covenant (2 Cor. 3:4–4:6). Writing with rich biblical insight of how "the Spirit's task is to restore glory to a fallen creation," Ferguson continues:

As Calvin well says, this world was made a theatre for God's glory. Throughout it he displays visibly the perfections of his invisible nature. Particularly in man and woman, his image, that glory was to be reflected. But they refused to "glorify God" (Rom. 1:21); they defiled the reflector (Rom. 1:28) and fell short of his glory (Rom. 3:23).

But now, in Christ who is "the radiance of God's glory" (Heb. 1:3), that glory is restored. Having become flesh for us, he has now been exalted in our flesh yet in glory. The eschatological goal of creation has been consummated in him as its firstfruits. Now he sends his Spirit, the intimate companion of his entire incarnation, to recover glory in us. So it is that "we, who with unveiled faces reflect the Lord's glory, are being transformed into his likeness with ever-increasing glory, which comes from the Lord, who is the Spirit [or, the Lord of the Spirit]" (2 Cor. 3:18 NIV).

The purpose for which the Spirit is given is, therefore, nothing less than the reproduction of the image of God, that is transformation into the likeness of Christ who is himself the image of God. To receive the Spirit is to be inaugurated into the effects of this ongoing ministry.[26]

Turning and Trusting

So how do we respond to the gospel, this good news of Jesus Christ, crucified, risen, and exalted? The answer is best expressed by two words: turning and trusting. Or, in biblical language, repentance and faith (Acts 20:21; Heb. 6:1).

Repentance: Turning from Sin

To repent is to change one's mind and alter directions: to turn around, to do an about-face. Perhaps the best illustration comes from baseball. A Major League baseball pitcher like Yohan Santana throws a 94 mph fastball, or a 76 mph changeup (which looks like a fastball, but drops in speed by 18 mph), or an 87 mph slider, straight through the center of the plate. Then, with a loud "crack" the ball meets the bat of a hard-hitting batter like Ryan Howard (58 home runs in 2006!). Do you know what the ball does? It changes directions. It repents! And when rebellious human beings encounter the life-transforming power of God through the good news of Christ crucified, risen, and exalted, they change directions.

Repentance always involves both turning *from* and turning *to*. Scripture speaks of turning from idols, turning from Satan, turning from sins, and turning from darkness (Acts 14:15; 1 Thess. 1:9; Acts 26:18; 2 Chron. 6:26). But repentance also means turning to light and to God himself (Acts 26:18; Hos. 14:2; Joel 2:19; Amos 4:8; Acts 14:15; 15:19; 2 Cor. 3:16).

Repentance, furthermore, is not a one-time event, but a life-long process. As Martin Luther said in his *Ninety-five Theses*, "When our Lord and Master, Jesus Christ, said 'Repent,' He called for the entire life of believers to be one of penitence."[27]

Faith: Trusting in Christ

The flip side of repentance is faith. Faith involves trusting in Jesus Christ and relying on what he has accomplished for us. As the *Westminster Confession of Faith* states, "the principal acts of saving faith are accepting, receiving, and resting upon Christ alone for justification, sanctification, and eternal life."[28]

Repentance and faith involve not only turning from sin and trusting in Jesus to save us from our *unrighteousness*, but also turning from our "goodness" and trusting Jesus to save us from our *self-righteousness* (see Phil. 3:7–9).

Finally, we should always remember that faith and repentance belong together. Genuine faith is always a repentant faith. And true repentance is always a believing repentance. As Richard Lovelace writes, "Faith and repentance are not separable qualities. To have faith is to receive God's Word as truth and rest upon it in dependent trust; to repent is to have a new mind toward God, oneself, Christ, and the world, committing one's heart to new obedience to God."[29]

Isaac Watts beautifully expressed the heart of repentant faith in the lyrics of this hymn:

> *No more, my God, I boast no more*
> *Of all the duties I have done;*
> *I quit the hopes I held before,*
> *To trust the merits of Thy Son*

Now, for the loss I bear His name,
What was my gain I count my loss;
My former pride I call my shame,
And nail my glory to His cross.

Yes, and I must and will esteem
All things but loss for Jesus' sake;
O may my soul be found in Him,
And of His righteousness partake!

The best obedience of my hands
Dares not appear before Thy throne;
But faith can answer Thy demands,
By pleading what my Lord has done.[30]

Where does this chapter find you? Have you entered through the gospel portal into the new life of the Spirit? Have you turned from sin and trusted in the all-sufficient work of the crucified, risen, and exalted Christ? He both commands and invites you to do so now (1 John 3:23; Matt. 11:28–30). This is the first crucial step toward genuine transformation.

The Curse Is Canceled

Justification

To see the law by Christ fulfilled and hear His pardoning voice,
Changes a slave into a child, and duty into choice.

—William Cowper

On a summer day in 1505, a short, stocky university student traveled a lonely road near the Saxon village of Stotternheim. The calm, overcast sky had turned menacing. As a bolt of lightning struck nearby, the twenty-one-year-old lad fell to the ground, terrified. Because his father was a miner he cried out fervently to St. Anne, the patron saint of miners, promising to become a monk if only his life were spared. He survived, and fifteen days later Martin Luther entered a strict Augustinian monastery.

For a year and a half, life in the cloister was peaceful for Luther. But a second storm broke on him when he performed his first mass in 1507. In Luther's own words, he was "stupefied and terror stricken" at the thought of addressing the living, eternal, and true God.[1] The experience plunged him into an austere asceticism as he sought peace for his tortured conscience. In 1510, he made a pilgrimage to Rome to climb on his knees the twenty-eight stairs of the *Scala Sancta*. That painful ascension was a metaphor for Luther's life: he was destroying himself in his attempt to climb his way to heaven. "If ever a monk got to heaven by his monkery, it was I," he said. "All my brothers in the monastery who knew me will bear me out. If I had kept on any longer, I should have killed myself with vigils, prayers, reading, and other work."[2]

But Luther found no relief in his efforts. Despite the thoroughness of his piety—sometimes confessing his sins for six straight hours—he could find no assurance of pardon. God terrified him. "I was . . . driven to the very abyss of despair so that I wished I had never been created," Luther later wrote. "Love God? I hated him!"[3]

In 1513, Luther was assigned a professorship in the University of Wittenberg, where it was necessary for him to study the Scriptures in preparation for his lectures. Two years later, while studying Romans, the breakthrough came. "I greatly longed to understand Paul's Epistle to the Romans and nothing stood in my way but that one expression, 'the justice of God,' because I took it to mean that justice whereby God is just and deals justly in punishing the unjust." He wrote:

> My situation was that, although an impeccable monk, I stood before God as a sinner troubled in conscience, and I had no confidence that my merit would assuage him. Therefore I did not love a just and angry God, but rather hated him and murmured against him. Yet I clung to the dear Paul and had a great yearning to know what he meant.
>
> Night and day I pondered until I saw the connection between the justice of God and the statement that "the just shall live by his faith." Then I grasped that the justice of God is that righteousness by which through grace and sheer mercy God justifies us through faith. Thereupon I felt myself to be reborn and to have gone through the doors of paradise. The whole of Scripture took on a new meaning, and whereas before "the justice of God" had filled me with hate, now it became to me inexpressibly sweet in greater love. The passage of Paul became to me a gate to heaven.[4]

Seized by the good news of justification by faith in Christ alone, the burden of guilt rolled from Martin Luther's shoulders. To his own surprise, Luther's discovery and preaching of God's grace in Christ eventually launched the Protestant Reformation. As his biographer writes, "He was like a man climbing in the darkness a winding staircase in the steeple of an ancient cathedral. In the blackness he reached out to steady himself, and his hand laid hold of a rope. He was startled to hear the clanging of a bell."[5]

Like Luther, sometimes we approach the need for personal change as if each step of obedience were one more stair to climb in the attempt to gain peace with God. We pursue holiness *for* grace, not *from* grace. But this reverses the order of the gospel. You will never get traction in your transformation until your feet are firmly planted in the freedom of God's justifying grace in Christ. The purpose of this chapter is to unpack the doctrine of justification by faith and show how embracing the truth of justification counters a performance-based, legalistic approach to the pursuit of transformation.

Your Day in Court

Imagine you are sitting in a jail cell. You are the defendant in a criminal trial and your court date is approaching. If convicted, your options are limited: you will either spend the rest of your life in prison or be executed. The judge hearing your case is known for rendering impartial justice, and when you reflect on this it terrifies you. For you are guilty as charged.

Enough imagining. This is not some hypothetical situation. Adjust the details a little, and this is reality. You *are* guilty, God *is* the Judge, and it's just a matter of time until your court date arrives.

This is the scenario Scripture envisions when it speaks of final judgment. Jesus spoke plainly and with full authority when he said, "I tell you, on the day of judgment people will give account for every careless word they speak" (Matt. 12:36). And Paul wrote:

> We know that the judgment of God rightly falls on those who practice such things. Do you suppose, O man—you who judge those who practice such things and yet do them yourself—that you will escape the judgment

of God? Or do you presume on the riches of his kindness and forbearance and patience, not knowing that God's kindness is meant to lead you to repentance? But because of your hard and impenitent heart you are storing up wrath for yourself on the day of wrath when God's righteous judgment will be revealed.

—Romans 2:2–5

We are all guilty and accountable to God for our sin. "For all have sinned and fall short of the glory of God" (Rom. 3:23). Sin renders us guilty—deserving God's righteous judgment. This is the bad news.

The good news, however, is that God, in his mercy, has made a way to pardon our sins, remove our guilt, and accept us as righteous. God, the perfect and holy judge, can look down from his judgment seat on guilty sinners like you and me, and with complete integrity and without any violation to truth or holiness, declare us "not guilty." How is this possible? Only through justification.

Justification isn't the easiest truth to grasp. But we must understand this unique aspect of God's grace if we are to pursue personal transformation with God-honoring motives, driven by joy and gratitude rather than guilt and fear.

Justification and the Law of God

Before we can really understand justification, we must be clear about the purpose of God's law. The ultimate purpose of God's law is *not* to give us a staircase to climb to heaven. Scripture is clear that the law itself can never make us righteous or earn favor with God. The law, rather, exposes our sin and shows us our need for grace.

Human beings seem hard-wired to trust in their own performance as the basis of their acceptance with God. We may do this by trying to keep the Ten Commandments or live by the Sermon on the Mount. But while it is true that God's law reflects his divine character and sets the bar by which we are judged, Scripture teaches that it is impossible to achieve a right standing with God through obedience (Gal. 3:21). This simply isn't the purpose of God's law. The attempt to gain God's acceptance through law-keeping or performance is *legalism*.

But the law was given to show us that we *cannot* satisfy God by what we do. In effect, the law gives us something tangible to bang our stubborn heads against until we throw up our hands and say, "I can't do this. I can't satisfy God's requirements of me. This is impossible! I need someone else to do it. I despair of my own strength. Help me."

The law, therefore, is like an X-Ray machine: useful for diagnosis, but not for cure; able to reveal a fracture, but not to reset a bone. The law shows us that we fall short, but cannot change our status in any way. It makes us conscious of sin, but has no power to rescue from sin's curse and control.[6] This is the significance of Paul's statement in Romans 3:

> We know that whatever the law says it speaks to those who are under the law, so that every mouth may be stopped, and the whole world may be held accountable to God. For by works of the law no human being will be justified in his sight, since through the law comes knowledge of sin.
>
> —Romans 3:19–20

With this understanding of the law in place, we are ready to take a closer look at justification. As we unpack the meaning of this vital biblical concept, we will see that it is legal in nature, declarative in function, and determines your status before God.

Justification Is Legal in Nature

As I have already suggested, justification—like its opposite, condemnation—is a word borrowed from the courtroom. In this particular courtroom, God is the Judge (Gen. 18:25), the law in question is *his* divine law, and sinful men—you and I—are the defendants. The divine judge requires nothing less than perfect obedience to his law (Gal. 3:10). Of course, this perfect obedience is precisely what all of us lack (Rom. 3:23). We, therefore, stand accused of violating God's law.

Justification Is Declarative in Function

More specifically, justification is a verdict, a declaration of a person's status in the view of the court.[7] The opposite of justification is condemnation (Deut. 25:1; Rom. 8:33–34). To condemn is to give the verdict of "guilty." To justify is to give the verdict of "not guilty." So, when a person receives a verdict from the court, he is declared either justified (righteous and innocent) or condemned (unrighteous and guilty).

It is important to understand that justification does not *make* someone righteous, any more than condemnation *makes* someone sinful. This is what we mean by justification being *declarative*. It declares, renders a verdict, and makes official a person's position in relationship to the law. Justification simply declares one's status as righteous, just as condemnation declares one's status as guilty.

We can see this in passages which speak of men justifying God. "When all the people heard this, and the tax collectors too, they justified God, having been baptized with the baptism of John" (Luke 7:29). It is obvious here that to justify God is not to make *him* righteous. God is righteous whether people acknowledge it or not. Righteousness is one of God's unchangeable characteristics. "Shall not the Judge of all the earth do what is just?" (Gen. 18:25). "What shall we say then? Is there injustice on God's part? By no means!" (Rom. 9:14). To justify God is simply to declare that he is just.

This declarative function of justification is also evident in Proverbs 17:15, which says, "He who justifies the wicked and he who condemns the righteous are both alike an abomination to the Lord." To justify the wicked is not to make a wicked man good, but to declare him righteous when in fact he is not. To condemn the righteous is not to change a righteous person into a wicked one, but to give the verdict of guilty to an innocent person. In each case—justifying and condemning—the function is declarative, not transformative.[8] The same is true when Scripture speaks of God justifying sinners.

Justification Concerns Our Status before God

So justification is *legal* in nature, and involves a *declaration* regarding our standing in view of the court of divine justice. This means, then, that justification concerns our *status before God*. Justification is the event that ushers you into a peaceful relationship with the Divine Lawgiver and Judge. As Paul says, "Therefore, since we have been justified by faith, we have peace with God through our Lord Jesus Christ" (Rom. 5:1).

Scripture teaches that all human beings will stand before God in judgment (Matt. 12:36; Rom. 2:1–16; 14:10; 1 Cor. 4:5; 2 Cor. 5:10). Scripture also teaches that all human beings are sinners—no one is righteous (Eccl. 7:20; Rom. 3:23). Therefore, the greatest question concerning each and every person is, "How can I, a sinner deserving condemnation, become right with a holy God?" How can I be acquitted on Judgment Day? When my day in court arrives, how can I be justified—declared righteous and not condemned—in the eyes of this God who sees all, never lies, and never makes a mistake?

Only one way. Through justification.[9]

Justification and the Gospel

We know that God judges the wicked. Yet Scripture is equally clear that, because of the gospel, God acquits the guilty. He justifies sinners!

"Now to the one who works, his wages are not counted as a gift but as his due. And to the one who does not work but trusts him who justifies the ungodly, his faith is counted as righteousness" (Rom. 4:4–5). Did you catch Paul's remarkable statement in this passage? God justifies *not the godly, but the ungodly*! God justifies sinners. He declares them righteous and treats them as if they had not sinned. This is what Martin Luther meant when he said that Christians are *"simul justus et peccator,"* righteous and sinful at the same time.

For every believer in Jesus, this is wonderful news! It means that though you are much more evil than you could ever imagine, you are also far more accepted than you ever dared to dream.[10] You are both ungodly *and* righteous! How can this be? How can a sinner be counted as righteous before a holy God?

A Tale of Two Men

The answer is found in Romans 5, where Paul explains that the destiny of every individual in the entire human race is wrapped up in the history of two men. The first man is Adam, the father of the human race, whose disobedience led to the condemnation and death of all. The second man is Jesus, whose obedience leads to justification and life for all who believe.

Therefore, just as sin came into the world through one man, and death through sin, and so death spread to all men because all sinned . . . But the free gift is not like the trespass. For if many died through one man's trespass, much more have the grace of God and the free gift by the grace of that one man Jesus Christ abounded for many. And the free gift is not like the result of that one man's sin. For the judgment following one trespass brought condemnation, but the free gift following many trespasses brought justification. If, because of one man's trespass, death reigned through that one man, much more will those who receive the abundance of grace and the free gift of righteousness reign in life through the one man Jesus Christ. Therefore, as one trespass led to condemnation for all men, so one act of righteousness leads to justification and life for all men. For as by the one man's disobedience the many were made sinners, so by the one man's obedience the many will be made righteous.

—Romans 5:12, 15–19

Notice the parallels and contrasts between Adam and Christ (see diagram 3.1). Each man serves as a representative for others. The performance of each one is described as it relates to God's law: Adam in his trespass and disobedience, and Christ in his righteousness and obedience. The actions of each lead to certain judicial verdicts: condemnation or justification. The verdicts of each lead to certain destinies: death or life.

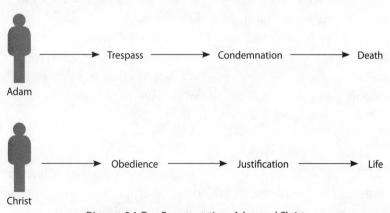

Diagram 3.1: Two Representatives: Adam and Christ

A sinner can only be counted as righteous before God when he or she is *found in Christ, rather than in Adam.* Adam sinned against God, was condemned, and died. Jesus obeyed God, paid the penalty for sin in his atoning death, and was justified in his resurrection to life.

Scripture says that Christ himself was "justified in the Spirit" (1 Tim. 3:16, KJV, HCSB),[11] and was "raised for our justification" (Rom. 4:25). If you are in Christ, then what is true of him is true of you. His verdict is your verdict. His obedience is your obedience. His righteousness is your righteousness. His justification is your justification. And his life is your life. "He is the source of your life in Christ Jesus, whom God made our wisdom and our righteousness and sanctification and redemption" (1 Cor. 1:30).

In Christ Alone

When we look closely at what Christ did for us on the cross we realize that he represented us in two ways. First, he represented us by taking the punishment of our sins—past, present, and future—"For our sake he made him to be sin who knew no sin" (2 Cor. 5:21a); "For Christ also suffered once for sins, the righteous for the unrighteous" (1 Peter 3:18a). And second, he represented us in his perfect obedience and righteousness; "By the one man's obedience the many will be made righteous" (Rom. 5:19b).

This double representation clarifies how we can be justified before God. We all begin with a two-fold need. We need to have our violations of God's law, our sins, paid for in full. And we need a perfect record of obedient righteousness by which to enter God's eternal kingdom and presence. Jesus has secured both of these benefits for us. He paid the penalty for our sins, and he lived a perfectly righteous life on our behalf.

On the cross, God treated Jesus as if he had lived my sinful life, so that he could then treat me as if I had lived the perfect, obedient life of Jesus. The only way I can be accepted as righteous by God is through the doing and dying of Jesus on my behalf. He died the death I should have died and lived the life I should have lived. God counted Jesus as a sinner so he could count me as righteous. The Father accepts me, not because of anything I have done or can do, not even because of anything he has done *in* me, but solely because of what Jesus Christ has done *for* me. His flawless record is counted as mine. As Paul says,

"For our sake he made him to be sin who knew no sin, so that in him we might become the righteousness of God" (2 Cor. 5:21).

So we have learned that justification means being declared righteous in the sight of God, our judge. And we have learned that this can happen only because Christ has become our representative, dying for our sins and obeying God on our behalf. So, how do we benefit from this grace?

By Faith Alone

We receive justification from God by faith alone. "For we hold that one is justified by faith apart from works of the law" (Rom. 3:28). "Therefore, since we have been justified by faith, we have peace with God through our Lord Jesus Christ" (Rom. 5:1). This joyful declaration is the summary of Paul's argument in Romans 3 and 4. One of the key paragraphs reads:

> But now the righteousness of God has been manifested apart from the law, although the Law and the Prophets bear witness to it—the righteousness of God through faith in Jesus Christ for all who believe. For there is no distinction: for all have sinned and fall short of the glory of God, and are justified by his grace as a gift, through the redemption that is in Christ Jesus, whom God put forward as a propitiation by his blood, to be received by faith. This was to show God's righteousness, because in his divine forbearance he had passed over former sins. It was to show his righteousness at the present time, so that he might be just and the justifier of the one who has faith in Jesus.
>
> —Romans 3:21–26

Having established that all men are sinners, Paul points to the cross as the solution to the mess sin created. God displayed his crucified Son before the world as an exhibition of his righteousness. His wrath against sin was poured out on Jesus and satisfied (as we discussed in chapter 2, this is the meaning of *propitiation*).

Earlier in this chapter, I said that God could look down from his judgment seat upon guilty sinners like you or me and, in complete integrity and without any violation to truth or holiness, declare us not guilty. Now we see how this is possible—God justifies us on the basis of Christ's life and death for us *through faith alone.*

Through the work of Christ, God's glory has been vindicated. His honor has been upheld. His righteousness has been displayed. The debt of sin has been paid. This is the meaning of the cross. And all this is received by faith. Paul describes "the righteousness of God through *faith* in Jesus Christ for all who *believe,*" and says that God has put Christ forward "as a propitiation by his blood, to be received *by faith.*" This was to declare God's righteousness "so that he might be just and the justifier of the one who has *faith* in Jesus."

Faith is believing in and relying upon God. It is "not a work, but a relinquishment of all work, an unqualified trust in God who gives life to the dead (Rom. 4:17), who raised Christ from the dead (4:24), who in Christ gave 'a righteousness from God.'"[12]

Justification is by grace alone, through faith alone, in Christ alone. God accepts us as righteous not because of anything we do, and not even because of anything he has done *in us,* but solely because of what Jesus Christ has done *for us.*

How Justification Changes Our Approach to Transformation

Now it's time to connect the dots. What does justification have to do with spiritual transformation? As I mentioned at the beginning of this chapter, a firm grasp on the truth of justification is essential to pursuing holiness with the right motivation. The doctrine of justification changes our understanding of three things: the *basis of our acceptance* with God, the *motivation for change,* and the *nature of our obedience.*

The Basis of Acceptance: Christ's Performance, Not Ours

All too often, religious people view their acts of piety or moral efforts as a means of gaining acceptance with God. Check yourself now. Even if you've been a Christian for a long time, don't you sometimes feel like God is more pleased with you on days when you've been faithful in daily devotions than those rushed days when you neglected time in the Word and prayer? Do you tend to view your relationship with God as a long list of "do's and don'ts"? Is your obedience to God motivated by love and characterized by joy—or guilt and fear? Is it easy for you to admit your failures and take ownership of your sins? Or does the possibility of being exposed feel threatening to your sense of well-being?

Like Luther, our relationship with God can easily become based on our own performance, rather than the performance of Christ. Even good spiritual disciplines, such as Bible-reading, prayer, and worship, become in our minds, like rungs on the ladder to heaven. We may not express it this way. In fact, we might even deny it. But functionally, and practically, we live as if approval from God depended upon our obedience, instead of Christ's obedience for us.

As Richard Lovelace wisely writes:

> Only a fraction of the present body of professing Christians are solidly appropriating the justifying work of Christ in their lives. Many have so slight an apprehension of God's holiness and of the extent and guilt of their sin that consciously they see little need for justification, although below the surface their lives are deeply guilt-ridden and insecure. Many others have a theoretical commitment to this doctrine, but in their day-to-day existence they rely on their sanctification for justification . . . drawing their assurance of acceptance with God from their sincerity, their past experience of conversion, their recent religious performance or the relative infrequency of their conscious, willful disobedience. Few enough know to start each day with a thoroughgoing stand upon Luther's platform: *you are accepted*, looking outward in faith and claiming the wholly alien righteousness of Christ as the only ground for acceptance, relaxing in that quality of trust which will produce increasing sanctification as faith is active in love and gratitude.[13]

Not only do I agree with Lovelace's assessment, but I think this uncovers one of the fundamental mistakes we make in our thinking about spiritual formation. Sometimes believers fall into a performance trap. We think that our obedience—our degree of cooperation with God's ongoing work of transformation—is the *basis*, rather than the *result*, of our acceptance with God.

The Motivation for Change: Grace, Not Law

This affects, secondly, our motivation for pursuing change. As believers we want to be holy, but sometimes we pursue holiness as if it were *for* grace—a condition for being welcomed by God, rather than *from* grace—an overflow of our love for the Father who freely welcomes us through Christ and his cross.

This is not only a misunderstanding, but a hindrance to our growth in Christ. To trust in our holiness as the ground of our acceptance with God is *legalism*. Legalism takes the law, rather than grace, as its starting point. Legalism is law-based and performance-oriented. Grasping the significance of justification protects us from this error.

This is not to say that the law is bad. Paul defended the essential goodness and holiness of the law (Rom. 7:7–12). But though the law is good, it is not able to save. As Luther himself later wrote:

> The law is divine and holy. Let the law have his glory, but yet no law, be it never so divine and holy, ought to teach me that I am justified, and shall live through it. I grant it may teach me that I ought to love God and my neighbour; also to live in chastity, soberness, patience, etc., but it ought not to show me, how I should be delivered from sin, the devil, death, and hell. Here I must take counsel of the Gospel. I must hearken to the Gospel, which teacheth me, not what I ought to do, (for that is the proper office of the law,) but what Jesus Christ the Son of God hath done for me: to wit, that He suffered and died to deliver me from sin and death. The gospel willeth me to receive this, and to believe it. And this is the truth of the Gospel. It is also the principal article of all Christian doctrine, wherein the knowledge of all godliness consisteth. Most necessary it is, therefore, that we should know this article well, teach it unto others, and beat it into their heads continually.[14]

All knowledge of godliness consists in this—knowing and embracing the truth of the gospel, that I am accepted by God not because of what I do, but because of what Christ has done for me. Until the sin-removing, curse-canceling power of Christ's death is understood and embraced, we will make no true progress in actually conquering sin and growing in grace. John Owen said, "There is no death of sin without the death of Christ."[15] The penalty of sin must be removed before the power of sin can be broken. But Scripture tells us that the penalty—the curse of the law—*is* removed! "Christ redeemed us from the curse of the law by becoming a curse for us—for it is written, 'Cursed is everyone who is hanged on a tree'" (Gal. 3:13).

Isn't this the greatest news in the world? The verdict of God's final judgment on the believer is given the moment he or she trusts in Christ—*Not Guilty!* "There is therefore *now* no condemnation for those who are in Christ Jesus" (Rom. 8:1). "Who shall bring any charge against God's elect? It is God who justifies. Who is to condemn? Christ Jesus is the one who died—more than that, who was raised—who is at the right hand of God, who indeed is interceding for us" (Rom. 8:33–34). Justice is satisfied in the death of Christ for sinners! We rejoice in this confidence: "If we confess our sins, he is faithful and *just* to forgive us our sins and to cleanse us from all unrighteousness" (1 John 1:9). Notice it is not only the faithfulness of God that assures us of pardon, but his *justice!* The debt of our sin was paid on the cross, and that payment is sufficient. God requires no further payment from us. *That* is divine justice.

> *If Thou hast my discharge procured,*
> *And freely in my room endured*
> *The whole of wrath divine:*
> *Payment God cannot twice demand,*
> *First at my bleeding Surety's hand,*
> *And then again at mine.*[16]

Therefore, we do not pursue personal transformation *for* grace, which would be legalism, but *from* grace. We live holy lives not in order to get ourselves right with God, but because he has already set us right in Jesus Christ. Justification precedes, and is the necessary basis of, actual transformation.

The Nature of Obedience: Sons, Not Slaves

Finally, the doctrine of justification transforms the nature of our obedience. We relate to God not as slaves, fearing the condemnation of an angry master, but as sons, confident in the love and acceptance of our Father.

This was the truth that changed Martin Luther's life. And two hundred years later, it changed the life of John Wesley. John Stott describes Wesley's post-graduate Oxford days when he was a member of a small religious group called the Holy Club:

> He was the son of a clergyman and already a clergyman himself. He was orthodox in belief, religious in practice, upright in his conduct and full of good works. He and his friends visited the inmates of the prisons and work-houses of Oxford. They took pity on the slum children of the city, providing them with food, clothing, and education. They observed Saturday as the Sabbath as well as Sunday. They went to church and to Holy Communion. They gave alms, searched the Scriptures, fasted and prayed. But they were bound in the fetters of their own religion, for they were trusting in themselves that they were righteous instead of putting their trust in Jesus Christ and in Him crucified. A few years later, John Wesley (in his own words) came to "trust in Christ, in Christ only for salvation" and was given an inward assurance that his sins had been taken away. After this, looking back to his pre-conversion experience, he wrote: "I had even then the faith of a *servant*, though not that of a son."[17]

There's the difference! Like Luther and Wesley, many people relate to God on the basis of duty and works, rather than sonship and grace. They trust in themselves, rather than Christ. But when we grasp that our acceptance with God is based on his grace given to us in Christ alone, the motivational center of gravity in our spirituality shifts. Now we are propelled not by guilt, but grace. We relate to him not as servants, but as sons.[18]

> *To see the law by Christ fulfilled*
> *To hear his pardoning voice*
> *Changes a slave into a child*
> *And duty into choice.*[19]

Do you realize the kind of confidence this wonderful truth can build into your relationship with God? My heart brims with joy and my eyes fill with tears when I reflect on God's gracious work for me in Christ. He has canceled the curse my sins deserved! Justice is satisfied and I am pardoned, accepted as righteous before the judge's—*my*

Father's—throne. The assurance of forgiveness granted to us through the cross is irrevocably life-changing.

Does the realization of what God has done for you in Christ cause your heart to burst with joy? Do you know with glad certainty that your sins are forgiven, that you stand before the throne of God robed in the flawless obedience and perfection of Jesus? When we grasp, or rather are grasped by, this grace, our whole approach to personal change is radically altered. We no longer pursue holiness to alleviate our guilt. Rather, we serve our Father with the freedom of children who delight to bear his likeness.

> *Mercy speaks by Jesus' blood;*
> *Hear and sing, ye sons of God;*
> *Justice satisfied indeed;*
> *Christ has full atonement made.*[20]

The Cure Has Begun

The Heart

Change that ignores the heart will seldom transform the life. For a while, it may seem like the real thing, but it will prove temporary and cosmetic.

—Paul David Tripp

Oscar Wilde's 1854 novel, *The Picture of Dorian Gray,* is a fascinating tale of a young man whose stunning good looks are matched only by his vanity and moral laxness. When he sees a portrait of himself that captures his beauty, he is jealous of the painting's permanence and says, "How sad it is! I shall grow old, and horrible, and dreadful. But this picture will remain always young . . . If it were only the other way! If it were I who was to be always young, and the picture that was to grow old! For that—for that—I would give everything!"[1]

His wish is granted. Over time, the face in the portrait begins to change, but Dorian Gray's outward youth and beauty remain. The narrative unfolds as Gray plunges head-first into a life of uninhibited extravagance and sensuality. His selfishness brings pain to others, even leading one young woman to take her own life. But Gray is relentless in his pursuit of pleasure. For eighteen years his youthful beauty never fades, while the portrait that hangs on the wall of his home slowly transforms into that of a hideous monster, mirroring the deepening depravity of Gray's soul.

Near the end of the book, the artist who painted the portrait implores him to turn from his corrupt lifestyle. In a fit of anger, Gray stabs the artist to death. Later, unable to bear the reflection of his deepening wickedness, Gray attempts to destroy the painting. Instead, it is he who is destroyed. Responding to his screams, his servants find the body of a repulsive monster, while the portrait has reverted to the handsome image of Dorian Gray.

Monstrous Hearts

Wilde's story is a powerful illustration, and brings to mind Jesus' scathing denunciation of those who were outwardly religious but inwardly corrupt.

> Woe to you, scribes and Pharisees, hypocrites! For you clean the outside of the cup and the plate, but inside they are full of greed and self-indulgence. You blind Pharisee! First clean the inside of the cup and the plate, that the outside also may be clean. Woe to you, scribes and Pharisees, hypocrites! For you are like whitewashed tombs, which outwardly appear beautiful, but within are full of dead people's bones and all uncleanness. So you also outwardly appear righteous to others, but within you are full of hypocrisy and lawlessness.
>
> —Matthew 23:25–28

Though the scribes and Pharisees wore a façade of righteousness, Jesus knew that behind their moral exterior was hidden a dark decadence of soul. Like Dorian Gray, they had an impressive exterior, but were monsters on the inside. They had monstrous hearts. We all do. In his spiritual autobiography, C. S. Lewis described how he found inside himself "a zoo of lusts, a bedlam of ambitions, a nursery of fears, a harem of fondled hatreds."[2] The same could be said of me. And of you.

Scripture repeatedly bears witness to the corruption and depravity of the human heart. "The Lord saw that the wickedness of man was great in the earth, and that every intention of the thoughts of his heart was only evil continually" (Gen. 6:5). "The heart is deceitful above all things, and desperately sick; who can understand it?" (Jer. 17:9). Paul's description of the human condition is true of us all until we are awakened by God's Spirit and changed by his grace. Human beings are darkened in mind, dead to God, and hardened in heart (Eph. 2:1–3, 4:18–19). Theologians call this the doctrine of "total depravity."[3] The problem, as Jonathan Edwards vividly describes it, is that our hearts have become small.

> Immediately upon the fall, the mind of man shrank from its primitive greatness and expandedness, to an exceeding smallness and contractedness . . . Sin, like some powerful astringent, contracted his soul to the very small dimensions of selfishness; and God was forsaken, and fellow-creatures forsaken, and man retired within himself, and became totally governed by narrow and selfish principles and feelings.[4]

We were created to be God's image-bearers in the world, designed to glorify and enjoy him forever and to love and serve our fellow human beings. Instead, we are focused on ourselves. We may look good on the outside, but inwardly we nurture evil in our sullied souls. As Derek Webb expressed in a recent ballad:

> *My life looks good I do confess*
> *You can ask anyone*
> *Just don't ask my real good friends*
> *'Cause they will lie to you*
> *Or worse they'll tell the truth*
>
> *'Cause there are things you would not believe*
> *That travel into my mind*
> *I swear I try and capture them*
> *But I always set them free*
> *It seems bad things comfort me*

Good Lord I am crooked deep down
Everyone is crooked deep down[5]

This massive distortion of soul, this corruption of heart must be the target in all spiritual transformation. Unless the heart changes, we don't change.[6]

What Is the Heart?

If our target in spiritual transformation is the heart, we should know what the heart *is*. When Scripture speaks of the heart, it does not refer to the blood-pumping organ in your chest. What is the heart?

The Heart Is the Source of Life

Proverbs 4:23 says, "Keep your heart with all vigilance, for from it flow the springs of life." The context of Proverbs 4 shows what these "springs" are:

> Put away from you crooked speech,
> and put devious talk far from you.
> Let your eyes look directly forward,
> and your gaze be straight before you.
> Ponder the path of your feet;
> then all your ways will be sure.
> Do not swerve to the right or to the left;
> turn your foot away from evil.
> —Proverbs 4:24–27

The springs of life include what we say with our mouths and do with our hands and feet. Our words, gaze, and ways are all determined by the heart.

The Heart Is "Command Central"

To put it another way, the heart is "command central" for the entire human personality: mind, heart, and will.[7] Johannes Behm defines the heart as: "the center of the inner life of man and the source or seat of all the forces and functions of soul and spirit."[8]

Using a different metaphor, Jesus taught the same truth. "The good person out of the good treasure of his heart produces good, and the evil person out of his evil treasure produces evil, for out of the abundance of the heart his mouth speaks" (Luke 6:45). As command central, the heart therefore is the source of our words and deeds.

I have a friend who says, "The tongue is the dipstick to the heart." Just as a dipstick reveals the quality and level of oil in a car engine, so words reveal what is in the heart. "Out of the abundance of the heart the mouth speaks." This is also true of our deeds. As Jesus says in another passage, "What comes out of a person is what defiles him. For from within, out of the heart of man, come evil thoughts, sexual immorality, theft, murder, adultery, coveting, wickedness, deceit, sensuality, envy, slander, pride, foolishness. All these evil things come from within, and they defile a person" (Mark 7:20–23).

We can illustrate the relationship between our words, deeds, and the heart like this.

Diagram 4.1: The Overflow of the Heart

Words and deeds flow out of the heart.

The Heart Is Active

David Powlison writes, "The human heart is an active verb. We do not 'have needs'; we 'do desires.'"[9] The heart is not merely an empty container that gets filled. It is not merely a "love tank" or "love bank" into which others make deposits and withdrawals. Nor is the heart passive, something that is only acted *upon*, but never *acts*. Affections and emotions are not like diseases that we *catch:* mumps, measles, chickenpox, flu. No, the heart *acts*. The heart *does*.[10]

The heart adores and aspires, craves and cries, desires, delights, and despairs. It is the source of all your musings, motivations, and murmurings. The heart has almost unlimited potential to act. All of its operations can be reduced to two basic categories, what Hebrews 4:12 calls "the *thoughts* and *intentions* of the heart." By these thoughts and intentions we think and will, contemplate and choose, imagine and intend.

The Heart Is the Organ of Worship

Because the heart is so active with its passions, affections, and desires, it is the organ with which we worship. Deuteronomy 11:16 warns, "Take care lest your heart be deceived, and you turn aside and serve other gods and worship them." Jesus says, "This people honors me with their lips, but their heart is far from me; in vain do they worship me, teaching as doctrines the commandments of men" (Matt. 15:8–9). Commenting on this passage, John Piper writes:

> Without the engagement of the heart, we do not really worship. The engagement of the heart in worship is the coming alive of the feelings and emotions and affections of the heart. Where feelings for God are dead, worship is dead. True worship must include inward feelings that reflect the worth of God's glory. If this were not so, the word hypocrite would have no meaning. But there is such a thing as hypocrisy—going through outward motions (like singing, praying, giving, reciting), which signify affections of the heart that are not there. "These people honor me with their lips, but their heart is far from me."[11]

Every heart worships something, either God or idols. We must realize that idols come in an endless variety of forms, not just statues of wood and stone. Scripture not only warns against bowing before images, but against idols of the heart (1 Thess. 1:9; Ezek. 14:3). Anything that holds the affections, desires, and longings of our hearts in disproportionate, inordinate ways is an idol. An idol is anything to which we attach the desires, expectations, affections, devotion, and dependence that properly belong to God. "The language of love, trust, fear, hope, seeking, serving—terms describing a relationship to the true God—is continually utilized in the Bible to describe our false loves, false trusts, false fears, false hopes, false pursuits, false masters."[12]

Even in ancient times wooden and stone idols were simply disguises for the idols of the heart. Venus (or Aphrodite), the goddess of love, disguised the idolizing of sex. Bacchus, the god of wine, camouflaged the inordinate desire for and dependence on alcohol. Narcissus, symbolizing self-worship, was punished for falling in love with his own reflection in a pool.

We are not so different. We worship the same things, just without the stone or wood disguises.

- Pornography has enshrined the worship of sex, importing it into countless lives via magazines and the internet. *Venus is still worshiped.*

- Drug and alcohol addictions are common fare, both outside and inside the church. *Bacchus is still worshiped.*

- In a culture gone to seed on self-esteem, the god of Self holds the highest throne of all. *Narcissus is still worshiped.*

We were created to worship the true and living God who created us, sustains us, and provides for us. This God is our lawgiver and judge. He reveals himself to us in his Word and through his Son. He loves and redeems us. We are all worshipers. We either worship him, or we worship idols of the heart. As Calvin said, "Man's nature, so to speak, is a perpetual factory of idols."[13] What do you crave more than God? Sexual pleasure? Money? Power? Approval? Comfort? Satisfaction for self?

Here's how you know what you worship. *You worship whatever controls you.* What is the True North of your heart, the resting place for the needle of your subconscious thoughts and desires? What is the object of your affections? What causes you to lose your composure, your cool, your inward peace and joy? What controls you?

It may be financial security, the luxury of "me time," or the seduction of sex. Or it may be God. As Jesus said, "No one can serve two masters, for either he will hate the one and love the other, or he will be devoted to the one and despise the other. You cannot serve God and money" (Matt. 6:24).

You worship whatever you serve.[14]

The Heart Is the Essential "You"

Third, the heart is the essential "you." "As in water face reflects face, so the heart of man reflects the man" (Prov. 27:19). You are what your heart is. This is why Scripture says, "man looks on the outward appearance, but the LORD looks on the heart" (1 Sam. 16:7). Therefore, to change *you*, your *heart* must change.

Jesus says in Luke 6:43–45: "For no good tree bears bad fruit, nor again does a bad tree bear good fruit, for each tree is known by its own fruit. For figs are not gathered from thorn bushes, nor are grapes picked from a bramble bush. The good person out of the good treasure of his heart produces good, and the evil person out of his evil treasure produces evil, for out of the abundance of the heart his mouth speaks."

Paul David Tripp's unpacking of this is classic:

Let's say I have an apple tree in my backyard. Each year its apples are dry, wrinkled, brown, and pulpy. After several seasons my wife says, "It doesn't make any sense to have this huge tree and never be able to eat any apples. Can't you do something?" One day my wife looks out the window to see me in the yard, carrying branch cutters, an industrial grade staple gun, a ladder, and two bushels of apples.

I climb the ladder, cut off all the pulpy apples, and staple shiny, red apples onto every branch of the tree. From a distance our tree looks like it is full of a beautiful harvest. But if you were my wife, what would you be thinking of me at this moment?

If a tree produces bad apples year after year, there is something drastically wrong with its system, down to its very roots. I won't solve the problem by stapling new apples onto the branches. They also will rot because they are not attached to a life-giving root system. And next spring, I will have the same problem again. I will not see a new crop of healthy apples because my solution has not gone to the heart of the problem. If the tree's roots remain unchanged, it will never produce good apples.

The point is . . . much of what we do to produce growth and change in ourselves and others is little more than "fruit stapling." It attempts to exchange apples for apples without examining the heart, the root behind the behavior. This is the very thing for which Christ criticized the Pharisees. Change that ignores the heart will seldom transform the life. For a while, it may seem like the real thing, but it will prove temporary and cosmetic.[15]

Too much of our religion is simply "fruit stapling." It is attaching something to our lives artificially instead of changing us deep down in the roots of our being, in our hearts. The result is that our behavioral change and attitudinal change is superficial and short-term. It doesn't last. Nor does it glorify God.

Getting to the Heart of Sin

All too often, strategies for pursuing holiness center on fruit-stapling instead of deep heart transformation. We try to live by lists: elaborate codes for moral behavior that tell us exactly what to do and not to do. Realizing the insufficiency of this approach, how do we actually get to the heart of sin?

Our discussion above about idolatry gets us close to the answer. But we need to place another concept alongside idolatry: the concept of *desires*. Powlison observes that:

If "idolatry" is the characteristic and summary Old Testament word for our drift from God, then "desires" (*epithumiai*) is the characteristic and summary New Testament word for the same drift. Both are shorthand for *the* problem of human beings . . . the New Testament merges the concept of idolatry and the concept of inordinate, life-ruling desires. Idolatry becomes a problem of the heart, a metaphor for human lust, craving, yearning, and greedy demand.[16]

We will never get to the heart of sinful behavior until we uncover the underlying desires of the heart that motivate us. Let me illustrate.

A couple of years ago, while planning for a mission trip to South Africa, I experienced an exaggerated amount of anxiety and stress. A friend had found the tickets for us and told me we would fly from South

Bend to Chicago to New York, and then from New York to Johannesburg, South Africa. It was a good deal, so I bought the tickets. Only two weeks later did I realize that we would be flying *in* from Chicago to the La Guardia airport in New York, but *out* to Johannesburg from JFK! We would only have a short amount of time to pick up our luggage, be transported to JFK, and check in for our international flight. My anxiety skyrocketed! You might think that the reason for this sinful worry was an underlying desire for control. But that wasn't it at all. I wasn't stressed about missing a flight. The truth is, I could care less about the inconvenience. My anxiety was rooted in my fear of losing respect from the team who was accompanying me. I was afraid of losing face. My sin was rooted in a desire: the desire for approval.

Here's another example. Holly and I once got in a fight over something really stupid—a movie. I had wanted to see this film for some time and had even bought an advance ticket to see the film on its opening night. I was excited! But after purchasing my ticket, some of our friends invited us to a cookout that night. We had just had our third child a few weeks before and Holly had been homebound for weeks. She understandably wanted to go to the cookout. I wanted to "stick to the plan" and go see the film. After all, I had already bought the ticket. When she gently tried to persuade me to change the plan, I erupted like a volcano. It was quickly clear that seeing this film was far too important to me. My desire for entertainment had become an idol. But perhaps the real idolatry underlying my anger was my desire to control my own schedule. I wanted to decide what I was going to do and when. I wanted my way. "What causes fights and quarrels among you? Don't they come from your desires that battle within you?" (James 4:1, NIV).

You and I will never make genuine progress in spiritual transformation until we address the idolatrous desires that lie at the root of our sinful behaviors. This is why Peter exhorts us, "As obedient children do not conform to the evil desires that you had when you lived in ignorance. But just as he who called you is holy, so be holy in all you do" (1 Peter 1:14–15, NIV). You will not be holy in your actions as long as you conform to evil desires. "Sin arises because we desire something more than we desire God. Overcoming sin begins by reversing this process: desiring God more than other things. The Bible calls this 'repentance.'"[17]

This means that when we are diagnosing our problems with sin we have to plow deep, to unearth the drives, motives, intentions and inclinations of the heart. We have to search out, with God's help and sometimes the help of others, the longings and cravings, the hopes and dreams, the pleasures and fears that drive us. Only when these are powerfully transformed by grace, will we really change.

Spurgeon once preached a sermon called "The Great Reservoir."[18] He likened the heart to a vast reservoir out of which flow many water sources. Spurgeon taught that if the reservoir is poisoned, only cleansing the water will do. Changing the pipes won't fix the problem. Neither will replacing the person who regulates the flow of water, or the engine that powers the machinery. And for a person to change, it will not suffice for her to merely change her principles or morals (the pipes), her understanding (the regulator of water flow), or her will (the engine). The only way to change a person is to cleanse the heart.

God Wants Our Hearts

Do you realize that God wants to own the affections of your heart? As Jesus said, "the hour is coming, and is now here, when the true worshipers will worship the Father in spirit and truth, for the Father is seeking such people to worship him" (John 4:23). The Father seeks those who worship him from the spirit—the heart.[19] Fruit-stapling certain behaviors to an outwardly moral life will not make us like Jesus. Christ is formed in us only as our hearts take the shape of his character. God will settle for nothing less than the deep affections of our hearts.[20] The good news is that what God demands from us, he will also give to us. Here are ten affections of the heart that God both requires, and gives.

Godly fear–This is a trembling yet joyful reverence and awe of our Holy Lord.

- Let all the earth fear the Lord; let all the inhabitants of the world stand in awe of him! (Ps. 33:8).

- Oh, fear the Lord, you his saints, for those who fear him have no lack! (Ps. 34:9; cf. Prov. 3:7; Eccl. 12:13; Phil. 2:12; Heb. 12:28).

Hope—Fear is to be mingled with biblical hope. This kind of hope is not a mere wish, but a confident expectation of good.

- Behold, the eye of the Lord is on those who fear him, on those who hope in his steadfast love (Ps. 33:18).
- Blessed is he whose help is the God of Jacob, whose hope is in the Lord his God (Ps. 146:5).
- But the Lord takes pleasure in those who fear him, in those who hope in his steadfast love (Ps. 147:11; cf. 1 Peter 1:3; 1 Thess. 5:8).

Desire—The Bible's commendation of desire for God is so important that Augustine said, "The whole life of a good Christian is a holy desire."[21]

- One thing have I asked of the Lord, that will I seek after: that I may dwell in the house of the Lord all the days of my life, to gaze upon the beauty of the Lord and to inquire in his temple (Ps. 27:4).
- As a deer pants for flowing streams, so pants my soul for you, O God. My soul thirsts for God, for the living God. When shall I come and appear before God? (Ps. 42:1–2).
- God, you are my God; earnestly I seek you; my soul thirsts for you; my flesh faints for you, as in a dry and weary land where there is no water (Ps. 63:1).
- Whom have I in heaven but you? And there is nothing on earth that I desire besides you (Ps. 73:25).

Joy—This is coupled with, and follows from, holy desire.

- Shout for joy in the Lord, O you righteous! Praise befits the upright (Ps. 33:1).
- Delight yourself in the Lord, and he will give you the desires of your heart (Ps. 37:4).

- Rejoice in the Lord always; again I will say, Rejoice (Phil. 4:4).
- In the way of your testimonies I delight as much as in all riches (Ps. 119:14).
- Then I will go to the altar of God, to God my exceeding joy, and I will praise you with the lyre, O God, my God (Ps. 43:4).

Hatred of evil–Negative affections are also necessary for the Godward heart.

- You who love the Lord, hate evil! (Ps. 97:10).
- I will not set before my eyes anything that is worthless. I hate the work of those who fall away; it shall not cling to me (Ps. 101:3).
- The fear of the Lord is hatred of evil. Pride and arrogance and the way of evil and perverted speech I hate (Prov. 8:13).

Brokenness over sin–I cannot truly hate evil without also mourning my sinfulness.

- The Lord is near to the brokenhearted and saves the crushed in spirit (Ps. 34:18).
- The sacrifices of God are a broken spirit; a broken and contrite heart, O God, you will not despise (Ps. 51:17).
- But this is the one to whom I will look: he who is humble and contrite in spirit and trembles at my word (Isa. 66:2).
- Blessed are those who mourn, for they shall be comforted (Matt. 5:4).

Gratitude–Gratitude in all things is closely related to an understanding of God's goodness and sovereignty.

- And let the peace of Christ rule in your hearts, to which indeed you were called in one body. And be thankful (Col. 3:15).
- Giving thanks always and for everything to God the Father in the name of our Lord Jesus Christ (Eph. 5:20).
- Give thanks in all circumstances; for this is the will of God in Christ Jesus for you (1 Thess. 5:18).

Compassion–As beneficiaries of God's great mercy and compassion, we are called to demonstrate the same.

* Put on then, as God's chosen ones, holy and beloved, compassion, kindness, humility, meekness, and patience (Col. 3:12).
* Blessed are the merciful, for they shall receive mercy (Matt. 5:7).
* He has told you, O man, what is good; and what does the Lord require of you but to do justice, and to love kindness [show mercy], and to walk humbly with your God? (Mic. 6:8).

Zeal–Our passions are to be defined by God's purposes.

* Do not be slothful in zeal, be fervent in spirit, serve the Lord (Rom. 12:11).
* [Jesus Christ] gave himself for us to redeem us from all lawlessness and to purify for himself a people for his own possession who are zealous for good works (Titus 2:14).
* When such zeal is lacking in his church, the Risen Christ is sickened and threatens to spit the church from his mouth. "I know your works: you are neither cold nor hot. Would that you were either cold or hot! So, because you are lukewarm, and neither hot nor cold, I will spit you out of my mouth . . . Those whom I love, I reprove and discipline, so be zealous and repent" (Rev. 3:15–16, 19).

Love–The Scriptures commend love as the supreme affection and the fountain of all other affections. Love fulfills the law and demonstrates true faith.

* You shall love the Lord your God with all your heart and with all your soul and with all your mind. This is the great and first commandment. And a second is like it: You shall love your neighbor as yourself. On these two commandments depend all the Law and the Prophets (Matt. 22:37–40).
* Owe no one anything, except to love each other, for the one who loves another has fulfilled the law (Rom. 13:8; cf. Gal. 5:14).

New Covenant, New Birth, New Hearts

These commands show that Christianity is not simply a matter of making right decisions or changing our behavior by willpower. There must be something deeper, more radical. We need heart transplants. The affections God demands can only arise from hearts made new, transformed by his grace. This is what God demands. This is what God promises to give.

In Deuteronomy, God commands his people to seek, love, serve, obey, and turn to him with all their hearts (Deut. 4:29; 6:5; 10:12; 11:13; 13:3; 26:16; 30:2, 10). But knowing the inability of his people to do this, he also commands them to circumcise their hearts, turning away from stubbornness (Deut. 10:16). Then, after prophesying Israel's eventual disobedience to the terms of God's covenant with them, God promises to gather them to himself again, and change their hearts, saying, "And the Lord your God will circumcise your heart and the heart of your offspring, so that you will love the Lord your God with all your heart and with all your soul, that you may live" (Deut. 30:6).

God promises to do *for* them what he has demanded *of* them. This promise foreshadows the promises of the new covenant that appear later in Jeremiah and Ezekiel.

> Behold, the days are coming, declares the Lord, when I will make a new covenant with the house of Israel and the house of Judah, not like the covenant that I made with their fathers on the day when I took them by the hand to bring them out of the land of Egypt, my covenant that they broke, though I was their husband, declares the Lord. But this is the covenant that I will make with the house of Israel after those days, declares the Lord: I will put my law within them, and I will write it on their hearts. And I will be their God, and they shall be my people.
>
> —Jeremiah 31:31–33

> I will make with them an everlasting covenant, that I will not turn away from doing good to them. And I will put the fear of me in their hearts, that they may not turn from me.
>
> —Jeremiah 32:40

> I will sprinkle clean water on you, and you shall be clean from all your uncleannesses, and from all your idols I will cleanse you. And I will give you a new heart, and a new spirit I will put within you. And I will remove the heart of stone from your flesh and give you a heart of flesh. And I will put my Spirit within you, and cause you to walk in my statutes and be careful to obey my rules.
>
> —Ezekiel 36:25–27

In several places the New Testament refers to the new covenant, circumcision of the heart, and spiritual cleansing. Jesus is called the "mediator of the new covenant" (Heb. 9:15, 12:24; cf. Heb. 8:1–13) and in the Passover meal with his disciples the night before his death he said, "This cup that is poured out for you is the new covenant in my blood" (Luke 22:20). Paul calls himself a "minister of the new covenant" (2 Cor. 3:6), explaining his ministry as the life-giving, veil-removing ministry of the Spirit that opens the eyes to behold the transforming glory of Christ in the gospel (2 Cor. 3:1–4:6). Three times he references the inward circumcision of the heart from Deuteronomy 30:6, calling it "circumcision . . . of the heart, by the Spirit" (Rom. 2:29), the "real circumcision" (Phil. 3:3), and "a circumcision made without hands" that is accomplished "by putting off the body of the flesh, by the circumcision of Christ" (Col. 2:11), that is, through union with Christ in his burial and resurrection (Col. 2:12).

Jesus' familiar words to Nicodemus about being born "from above" and born "of water and the Spirit" (John 3:3, 5) refer to the new covenant promise of spiritual cleansing from Ezekiel 36:25–27. Paul weaves the same concepts into his explanation of salvation.

> But when the goodness and loving kindness of God our Savior appeared, he saved us, not because of works done by us in righteousness, but according to his own mercy, by the washing of regeneration and renewal of the Holy Spirit, whom he poured out on us richly through Jesus Christ our Savior, so that being justified by his grace we might become heirs according to the hope of eternal life.
>
> —Titus 3:4–7

These passages demonstrate the depth of transformation we need and that God graciously provides for us through Jesus Christ. We need more than moral reformation and behavioral modification. We need inner cleansing, spiritual renewal, and new hearts, and God does that for us![22]

Though the full renovation of our hearts is an ongoing, lifelong process, God begins this work in the once-and-for-all, definitive event of new birth, or regeneration.[23] Regeneration, which Richard Lovelace calls "the beachhead of sanctification in the soul,"[24] is God's mysterious work of imparting new life to the soul.[25] Scripture uses many metaphors to describe this work of God, including **birth**—John 3:1–8; 1 Peter 1:3, 23; **creation**—2 Cor. 5:17; Eph. 2:10; 4:24, and **resurrection**—John 5:21; Eph. 2:1–7; Col. 2:12. Each of these metaphors remind us that regeneration is not something we can do for ourselves, but something God has to do for us. We can no more regenerate ourselves than a baby can conceive itself, a world create itself, or a corpse raise itself to life. As John Piper writes, "God is the great Doer in this miracle of regeneration."[26]

These metaphors also teach us that regeneration produces change. It is the creation of light in our hearts (2 Cor. 4:6), being born again to a living hope (1 Peter 1:3), the infusion of new life to those who were spiritually dead (Eph. 2:5), resulting in the practice of righteousness, a love for others, and a faith in Christ which overcomes the world (1 John 2:29; 3:9; 4:7; 5:1, 4, 18). To quote Lovelace:

> Regeneration is the re-creation of spiritual life in those who are dead in trespasses and sins (Eph. 2:1). It occurs in the depths of the human heart, at the roots of consciousness, infusing new life which is capable of spiritual awareness, perception and response, and is no longer "alienated from the life of God" (Eph. 4:18).[27]

No one has described this more beautifully than Charles Wesley in his lyrical description of the experience of new birth in his well-known hymn, "And Can it Be":

> *Long my imprisoned spirit lay*
> *Fast bound in sin and nature's night*

> *Thine eye diffused a quickening ray*
> *I woke, the dungeon flamed with light*
> *My chains fell off, my heart was free*
> *I rose went forth and followed thee!* [28]

This is the beginning of God's glorious work in us. He takes our stony hearts, monstrous and deformed by sin as they are, and replaces them with new hearts. He cleanses us from idols by his Word (Ezek. 36:25; Eph. 5:26), sanctifies and indwells us by his Spirit (1 Cor. 6:11; 2 Thess. 2:13; 1 Peter 1:2; Rom. 8:9; 1 Cor. 3:16; 2 Cor. 1:22; Gal. 4:6), creates us anew in Christ Jesus (2 Cor. 5:17; Eph. 2:10), grants us the gifts of repentance and faith (Acts 5:31; 2 Tim. 2:25; Phil.1:29), and renews the image of God within us (Col. 3:10; Eph. 4:24). God gives what he demands. As Augustine prayed more than 1,500 years ago, "Give me the grace to do as you command, and command me to do what you will! . . . when your commands are obeyed, it is from you that we receive the power to obey them." [29]

Undragoned by Grace

In the opening chapter of C. S. Lewis's Narnian adventure, *The Voyage of the Dawn Treader,* we are introduced to Eustace Scrubb. "There was a boy called Eustace Clarence Scrubb, and he almost deserved it," [30] Lewis writes. You don't have to read long before you realize that Eustace is a spoiled and selfish brat. At one point in the story, Eustace and the other characters are on an island with much work to do to repair their ship, the *Dawn Treader.* Lazy and selfish Eustace doesn't want to help, so he sneaks away to sleep in the woods. There he discovers a dragon's lair, full of treasure, that he greedily begins planning to use for himself. But something happens to Eustace in the dragon's cave. He falls asleep. When he awakens, he is shocked to see the breath of a dragon before him and a dragon's clawed feet to his left and right. At first he thinks a dragon has entered the cave, but then, to his utter astonishment and dismay, he discovers that he has turned into a dragon! As Lewis says, "Sleeping on a dragon's hoard with greedy, dragonish thoughts in his heart, he had become a dragon himself." [31]

What happens to Eustace afterwards is amazing. Becoming a dragon is a very humbling experience for him, and he lives in this state for six days. Then one night, Eustace is "more miserable than ever," and a lion comes to him and commands him to follow it into the mountains. The lion, of course, is Aslan, who leads Eustace the dragon to the top of a mountain where there is a garden. In the midst of the garden is a large well, like a huge bath, with marble steps going down into it and the clearest water Eustace had ever seen. The lion tells the "dragon-that-had-been-Eustace" that he may go in only after he undresses. Eustace thinks that he cannot undress, because, being a dragon, he has no clothes. But then he realizes that just as snakes shed their skin, perhaps he can shed his scaly exterior. So, he starts scratching. Scales start coming off all over the place, and then his whole skin peels off just as if he were a banana. But when the skin is all off, he realizes that he is still hard and scaly like a dragon. So, he thinks, there is another suit of scales underneath the first and he peels away a second layer of scales. But there is still another scaly skin underneath that one, and then another, until finally Eustace realizes that no matter how deep he goes, there is always a scaly skin underneath.

At that moment, Aslan says, "You will have to let me undress you." At first, Eustace is afraid of the lion's claws. But his desperation is greater than his fear, so he lays down flat on his back and lets the lion go to work. The first tear is so deep that Eustace thinks the lion has torn to his very heart. It hurts worse than anything Eustace has ever felt. But he is delighted that the skin is finally off. Then Aslan throws him into the water so that he is bathed, and afterwards dresses him in new clothes. Finally, Eustace is un-dragoned![32]

Before you can fight sin and pursue holiness, you must be un-dragoned. Sin's penalty must be removed and its power broken. You cannot change yourself any more than Eustace, the dragon, could peel away the many layers of scales. Only God can pull that old skin away, wash you, and dress you in new clothes.

At the end of that particular chapter, Lewis writes:

> It would be nice and fairly nearly true, to say that "from that time forth Eustace was a different boy." To be strictly accurate, he began to be a

different boy. He had relapses. There were still many days when he could be very tiresome. But . . . the cure had begun.[33]

If you are a Christian, that is true of you. You have begun to be a different person. You may have relapses, but the cure has begun.

5

Closing the Gap

Sanctification

Sanctification can be ours only by means of the resources of Christ, brought to us through the Holy Spirit as he takes what is Christ's, reveals it to us, and thus conforms us more and more into his likeness, from one degree of glory to another, as we gaze on the glory of the Lord.

—Sinclair Ferguson

Holly and I were married on a lovely summer day under a lush canopy of fresh flowers. She was radiant, stunning, beautiful. The sanctuary was packed with five hundred friends and family. The moving, Christ-exalting ceremony was conducted by my dad, who is also a pastor. This is just my opinion, but I'm pretty sure it was the most beautiful wedding in history.

Prior to that day, I had read several books on marriage. I was familiar with all the relevant passages of Scripture. And Holly and I had received helpful premarital counseling from a wise and mature

Christian couple. But after the wedding, although we were now married, signifying a categorical change in status before God and man, I actually knew very little about how to be a husband. I loved Holly very much and genuinely desired to meet her needs and pursue her happiness. But becoming in practice who I am in position has been a longer process! In fact, I am still learning to close the gap between my legal status and my actual character.

Something similar is true of us all as Christians. Because we are united to Christ by faith, God has given us a new status and identity. As we saw in chapter 3, we are counted righteous through faith in Christ. God relates to us not as sinners, but as saints; not as slaves, but as sons. But learning to live true to our new identity is a process. There is a gap between our position and our practice. Spiritual formation is concerned with closing that gap.

Already Holy: Our Position

Scripture describes every believer in Jesus as already holy, or sanctified. Theologians often call this our *definitive* or *positional sanctification*. When the New Testament writers addressed believers as "saints," this is the reality they had in mind.

For example, in writing to the Corinthians, a church that in many ways was quite *un*saintly, Paul addresses them as, "those sanctified in Christ Jesus, called to be saints together" (1 Cor. 1:2; cf. 1 Cor. 6:11). Despite serious ongoing sin in that congregation, Paul saw their sanctification as something fully settled, an established and unchanging fact, accomplished in the past and effective for the present and the future. In Christ, we are *already* sanctified.[1]

Pursuing Holiness: Our Progress

But of course, as the Corinthians amply demonstrated, and as Paul affirmed, it is possible for "saints" to commit serious sins. In fact, there exists in each of us a gap between definitive sanctification and the actual outworking of holiness in everyday life. Though we are already saints—already holy—Scripture calls us to *pursue* holiness, to flesh it out in daily practice (e.g., see 2 Cor. 7:1; Heb. 12:14; 1 Peter 1:15–16). Since we have been set apart as God's people in Christ and through the

Spirit, we are now to live as his holy people.[2] We are called to close the gap that separates who we are in position from who we are in practice. This is what we call *progressive sanctification.*

The aim of this book is to help close the gap. But the gap is not closed by moving on from the gospel to something else or by adding anything to the gospel. You and I will experience deep and lasting change only as the Holy Spirit progressively applies to our hearts a more solid, practical, and thorough understanding of what God has accomplished for us through the death and resurrection of Christ.[3] Sanctification, like justification, is dependent on our union with Jesus Christ by faith.

In this chapter, I want to focus first on the gospel resources that are ours through union with Christ, and then discuss how we should apply these resources to our lives as we learn to live in sync with the gospel.

Positional Sanctification: Our Gospel Resources through Union with Christ

First of all, let's consider the resources that belong to us through our union with Christ. My purpose here is to encourage you by outlining as clearly as possible how your new status in Christ has irreversibly revoked the authority of sin in your life. We can be assured of actual progress in dealing with specific sinful attitudes and behaviors in our lives (which, let's admit, we all still struggle with), only because in Christ we really *are* liberated from sin's tyrannical rule.

"Shall we continue in sin?"

One of the key sections of Scripture on this topic is Romans 6. Prior to this point in the book of Romans, Paul has exulted in the glorious grace of God. His emphasis has been on how that grace freely justifies the ungodly—through the obedience and righteousness of Christ credited to us by faith alone. Paul's conclusion is that though we were weak and ungodly sinners who were enemies of God, God demonstrated his love for us by sending Christ to die for us. God has justified us by the blood of his Son, thus reconciling us to himself. "Where sin increased, grace abounded all the more" (Rom. 5:20).

But then Paul raises an objection: "What shall we say then? Are we to continue in sin that grace may abound?" (Rom. 6:1). If grace abounds where there is a lot of sin, why not throw off restraint and sin all the more? Should we adopt the attitude expressed by the twentieth-century poet W. H. Auden who quipped, "I like committing crimes. God likes forgiving them. Really the world is admirably arranged?"[4]

To put a really fine point on it, if we're freely saved by sheer grace, then why should we worry about ongoing sin in our lives at all? "Are we to continue in sin that grace may abound?" Paul answers with a resounding no! "By no means! How can we who died to sin still live in it?" (v. 2). Paul revolted at the suggestion that a believer could continue to "live in" sin. The thought was impossible!

But what does Paul mean by "live in sin"? Christians, after all, are certainly not completely sinless! If you are like me, you still find yourself struggling against sin on a daily basis. And on occasion, sadly, there isn't even that much struggle. So, does that mean I am not a true Christian? What does Paul mean?

In studying Romans 6, I have found Douglas Moo's comments most helpful. He writes:

> "Living in sin" is best taken as describing a "lifestyle" of sin—a habitual practice of sin, such that one's life could be said to be characterized by that sin rather than by the righteousness God requires. Such habitual sin, "remaining in sin" (v. 1), "living in sin" (v. 2), is not possible, as a constant situation, for the one who has truly experienced the transfer out from under the domain, or tyranny, of sin. Sin's power is broken for the believer, and this *must* be evident in practice (see also James 2:14–26; and perhaps 1 John 3:6, 9). Yet the nature of Christian existence is such that the believer can, at times, live in such a way that is inconsistent with the reality of what God has made him in Christ . . . Therefore, while "living in sin" is incompatible with Christian existence and impossible for the Christian as a constant condition, it remains a real threat. It is this threat that Paul warns us about in verse 2.[5]

So, while Paul grants that believers still struggle with sins, hence his exhortations in verses 12 and 13 of this chapter *not* to sin, he wants us to know that the power of sin to rule our lives is utterly and decisively broken for all who are joined to Christ.

But *how* is the power of sin broken? Paul answers in the following verses. His argument hinges on two realities: first, the story of the gospel, in which Christ died to sin and was raised from the dead in new life; and second, how the gospel rewrites our stories, rendering what is true of Christ as also true of us. Let's take each in turn.

The Gospel Story

First, notice how Paul recounts the events of the gospel—the death and resurrection of Christ—with reference to the issue of sin. Understanding Romans 6:9–10 will help us follow the overall argument: "We know that Christ, being raised from the dead, will never die again; death no longer has dominion over him. For the death he died he died to sin, once for all, but the life he lives he lives to God." What does this mean? In what sense did Christ die to sin?

The breadth of Scripture agrees that Jesus was sinless. As Hebrews says, he was "holy, harmless, undefiled, separate from sinners" (Heb.7:26, KJV). So, when Paul says that Christ died to sin, he doesn't mean that he died for any personal sins of his own. Yet, Christ came as one of us. He identified himself with sinful human beings and lived "in the likeness of sinful flesh" (Rom. 8:3).

When Jesus died on the cross, sin did its worst to him. "The wages of sin is death" (Rom. 6:23); therefore, Jesus paid those wages once and for all. By dying in our place, he came under sin's tyranny and overthrew it.[6] And in his death, Jesus destroyed Satan, the one who had the power of death (Heb. 2:14). He overcame the strong arm of the enemy and took the sting out of death's tail. In effect, when Jesus died, sin and death died with him!

But he didn't only die, he rose again. "Christ was raised from the dead by the glory of the Father . . . We know that Christ being raised from the dead will never die again; death has no more dominion over him" (Rom. 6:4, 9). In his resurrection, the effectiveness of Jesus' triumph over death was complete. Death could not hold him. *He is alive!*

The Gospel Rewrites Our Stories

But what does this have to do with you and me? How does this change our relationship to the tyrannical dominion of sin? If we are unsaved and therefore separated from Christ, it doesn't change anything. As Calvin wrote, "We must understand that as long as Christ remains outside of us, and we are separated from him, all that he has suffered and done for the salvation of the human race remains useless and of no value to us."[7] But Paul's point is that Christ is not outside of us and we are not outside of him! We are joined to Christ, therefore we (like him) have "died to sin" (Rom. 6:2). What is true of him is true of us! The gospel story rewrites our stories. That is why sin's dominion in our lives has been thwarted. As Charles Wesley said in one of his hymns, "He breaks the power of canceled sin, he sets the prisoner free. His blood can make the foulest clean, his blood atoned for me."[8]

As you read through Romans 6:3–10, notice how Paul connects our story to the gospel story. We were baptized[9] into his death and raised to walk in newness of life. His death counts as ours, and since he died to sin, the sway of sin in our lives has been broken. The power of his resurrection gives us life, both now and in the future. The pattern of the gospel—the death and resurrection of Christ—determines the pattern of our lives (see diagram 5.1). This is what the seventeenth-century English Puritan Walter Marshall called "The Gospel Mystery of Sanctification."[10]

Death	Resurrection
Christ died (vv. 9–10)	Christ was Raised. (vv. 4, 9)
Christ died to sin (vv. 8–10)	Christ lives to God (v. 10)
We are joined to Christ in his death. (vv. 3–7)	We are joined to Christ in his resurrection. (vv. 4, 5, 8)
Therefore, we have died to sin. (v. 2)	Therefore, we are alive to God and walk in newness of life. (vv. 4, 11)

Diagram 5.1: Our Union with Christ in His Death and Resurrection

All our progress in actual change depends on this new relationship to Christ. He is in us and we are in him. In Christ, we have died to sin and are now alive to righteousness (v. 11).

This truth permeates the New Testament. Ephesians describes how we have been made alive, raised, and seated with Christ (Eph. 2:5–6). In Galatians, Paul says, "I have been crucified with Christ. It is no longer I who live, but Christ who lives in me. And the life I now live in the flesh I live by faith in the Son of God, who loved me and gave himself for me" (Gal. 2:19b–20). In language similar to Romans 6, Colossians says we have "been buried with [Christ] in baptism" and "raised with him through faith in the powerful working of God, who raised him from the dead" (Col. 2:12). Paul then shows how dying and rising with Christ determines our thinking and actions (Col. 3:1ff).

Through union with Christ, you are righteous (having been justified), new (regenerated), and holy (definitively sanctified). In this unbreakable union with Christ we are given a new history, a new identity, and a new destiny.

- We are given a new *history*, because his past counts as our past: his perfect life and obedient death is credited as ours. His death to the ruling power of sin counts as ours, securing our freedom from sin's tyranny.
- We are given a new *identity*, because when we are joined to Christ, God sees us in his Son. In fact, we become saints, children of God, and heirs with Christ.
- We are given a new *destiny*, because in the resurrection of Christ, the age to come has dawned. His resurrection guarantees that we will be raised from the dead as well, and, in fact, empowers us to live in newness of life in the here and now.

Jesus has not just given us a ticket to heaven. He has changed our essential identity. He has irrevocably altered the effect of our past on our present and future by causing his death and resurrection to count as ours. We really are new creatures, even as we press on by God's grace to become more holy.

The point is that sanctification (freedom from the *dominion* of sin), no less than justification (freedom from the *guilt* of sin), comes through faith in Christ alone.[11] *Everything* we need for life and godliness is found in him! Transformation can happen in no other way.

The gospel reminds us that Christ himself is the one and only human being who has perfectly imaged the holy character of God. He is the pioneer of our salvation, the new Adam, and therefore, the head of the new creation. We can only reflect the image of God as we become like Christ. And we can only become like him if we are *in* him. As Sinclair Ferguson rightly says:

> Perfect humanity, perfect holiness, is first of all expressed in him . . . The nature of sanctification is that it is true God-likeness. But true God-likeness in human form is Christ-likeness. Since Christ-likeness is the full expression of the image of God in man, true sanctification is true humanness. The only resources for such sanctification are in Christ. Our sanctification is Christ's sanctification of himself in our humanity progressively applied to and realized in us through the ministry of the Holy Spirit . . . Sanctification can be ours only by means of the resources of Christ, brought to us through the Holy Spirit as he takes what is Christ's, reveals it to us, and thus conforms us more and more into his likeness, from one degree of glory to another, as we gaze on the glory of the Lord (2 Cor. 3:18).[12]

You and I will experience deep and lasting change only as the Holy Spirit applies the resources of the gospel to our hearts and lives. The gospel tells us that we are already freed from sin as a ruling power. The gospel also points us to Christ as the pattern for holiness; he is the quintessentially sanctified human being. And the gospel promises that the riches of Christ, applied to our hearts, will effectively produce progressive change in our lives.

Union with Christ Is the Basis, Not the Goal of Holiness

This biblical perspective stands in conflict with traditions that view holy living as the *prerequisite to*, rather than the *result of*, union with Christ. For example, some writers in the mystical and contemplative traditions view union with Christ as the goal of spiritual formation. From this perspective, union with Christ is an experiential reality that is attained as the struggling Christian passes through a series of stages via a rigorous pattern of spiritual disciplines. But gospel-driven spiritual formation is exactly the opposite. Our union with Christ is not the *goal* of holiness, but its *basis*.[13] It is not something to be achieved through human effort, but something we have received through grace.

Do you realize that through union with Christ, *you* are righteous, new, and holy? To use theological terms, you have been justified, regenerated, and sanctified. True to his work on your behalf, God now calls you to grow in righteousness, newness, and holiness. Your position in Christ— your new identity—now determines your practice (see diagram 5.2).

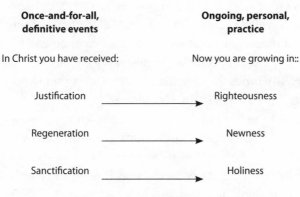

Once-and-for-all, definitive events	Ongoing, personal, practice
In Christ you have received:	Now you are growing in::
Justification	Righteousness
Regeneration	Newness
Sanctification	Holiness

Diagram 5.2: Your Position in Christ Determines Your Practice

In Christ, we are already saints! We do not work to achieve this status. It is ours in Christ. Of course, we still must apply effort and engage in disciplines as we pursue greater holiness. But, as we learned in chapter 3, we pursue holiness not *for* grace, but *from* grace. We are changed as we cooperate with God's grace in Christ by applying the resources of Christ to our lives, thus progressively closing the gap between our position in Christ and our practice as his disciples. This leads to the second concern of this chapter—to discuss how to live in sync with the gospel, as we apply these gospel resources to our lives in our pursuit of progressive sanctification.

Progressive Sanctification: Applying the Resources of the Gospel to Our Lives

We learn how to apply the gospel to our lives in our pursuit of holiness from the second half of Romans 6. We can summarize Paul's instructions in three essential, liberating commands.

1. Count on It!

The first thing Paul commands us to do is *count on the reality of what is true of us in Christ*. "So you also must consider yourselves dead to sin and alive to God in Christ Jesus" (Rom. 6:11). Notice that this verse doesn't command us to die to sin or put sin to death. That does come later (Rom. 8:13), but it isn't the focus here.[14] Paul is telling us to recognize our death to sin *in Christ* as an already accomplished fact! This explains what Paul means when he says, "We know that our old self was crucified with him in order that the body of sin might be brought to nothing, so that we would no longer be enslaved to sin" (Rom. 6:6). We shouldn't make the mistake of equating the old self (or "old man," KJV) with the remainders of indwelling sin which must be mortified. The old man is already crucified.[15]

Don't miss the glory of this: *If you are in Christ, your fundamental identity has been changed.* Your identity is not defined by the sins of your past, but by the righteousness and obedience of Jesus Christ. You are not a liar, thief, adulterer, or idolater. Though you may have committed any or all of these sins, this is not who you are. The old you is dead—crucified with Christ. Now joined to Christ, you are a saint—a person set apart from sin, and belonging to God.

Think of John Newton, the author of the hymn "Amazing Grace." Prior to his conversion, Newton was a slave trader in West Africa—a godless, ruthless man. But when he came to faith in Christ, he was deeply transformed. After his conversion, Newton wrote, "Though . . . [I am] not what I ought to be, not what I might be, not what I wish or hope to be, and not what I once was—I think I can truly say with the apostle, 'By the grace of God I am what I am.'"[16] This is true of every Christian. Though you are not yet as much like Jesus as you someday will be, you are not the same person you once were. You have a new identity because of your union with Christ. You are dead to sin and alive to God. Living in sync with the gospel begins with counting on this reality.[17]

2. Don't Let Sin Reign

Since we are dead to sin and alive to God in Christ Jesus, *we must not allow sin to control our actions*. As we are exhorted in Romans

6:12, "Let not sin therefore reign in your mortal bodies, to make you obey their passions."[18] This second command injects a dose of reality into our thinking. Though the old self is crucified, this doesn't mean the battle with sin is over. Sin still wages war against your soul, assaulting your thoughts and senses with passions demanding acquiescence. The old slave master still insists on your obedience! But you mustn't let sin rule.

This exhortation raises an important question: does the believer still have a sinful nature? The answer depends on how "sinful nature" is defined. It is clear that the believer still contends against the flesh. "The desires of the flesh are against the Spirit, and the desires of the Spirit are against the flesh, for these are opposed to each other, to keep you from doing the things you want to do" (Gal. 5:17). So we still contend with sinful desires. I think this is also what Paul means in Romans 7, when he says, "I find it to be a law that when I want to do right, evil lies close at hand. For I delight in the law of God, in my inner being, but I see in my members another law waging war against the law of my mind and making me captive to the law of sin that dwells in my members" (Rom. 7:21–23).[18] On a similar note, Peter exhorts us to "abstain from the passions of the flesh, which wage war against your soul" (1 Peter 2:11). So, yes—the believer still struggles against the sinful inclinations, passions, and the desires of the flesh.

Some teachers, however, view the flesh (or "old" or "sinful" nature) as a static, unchanging principle within the believer that constantly struggles against the Spirit (or "new" or "regenerate" nature) for control in a believer's life. The flesh and the new nature are like a pair of junkyard dogs (a black dog versus a white dog, as the illustration usually goes) locked in a fierce, lifelong battle. Whichever one you feed wins. From this perspective, the Christian is something of a Jekyll and Hyde, a conflicted being with two personalities vying for mastery in his heart. Living in holiness depends on constantly counteracting the "old nature" with the power of the Spirit. As long as the believer is filled with the Spirit, the power of sin is counteracted—and the Christian can live a "victorious" (or "higher" or "deeper") life, *completely* free from all conscious and willful sin. On the other hand, believers who continue to struggle with sin are living in "defeat" because they pursue holiness in "the energy of the flesh," rather than abiding in Christ and being filled with the Spirit.[19]

But this teaching fails in two ways. First, it fails to grasp the extensive scope of transformation that results from union with Christ. Implicit to this view of sanctification is the possibility that a true believer could live in habitual dominion to sin. But that would deny the radical change experienced by all who are joined to Christ.[20] As we learned earlier in this chapter, all believers are united to Christ in his death and resurrection. The black dog (or, to revert to theological language, "the old man") is dead! Therefore all believers are freed from sin's slavery and walk in newness of life.[21] But, second, this teaching also fails to recognize that even mature and "spiritual" believers will continue to fight against sin throughout their lives. On one hand, we claim too little if we assert that believers can live in unbroken bondage to habitual sin. But on the other hand, we claim too much if we think we have achieved the kind of victory that removes us from the arena of struggle.

The truth is that though all believers will continue to contend with the remnants of indwelling sin, sin is not a power equal in influence to the Holy Spirit.[22] Genuine and sustainable change is not only possible, but guaranteed by God's grace. A Christian's inner nature and personal identity as a human being have been fundamentally altered.[23] We are no longer slaves of sin! The passions of sin do not reflect who we are in Christ. As 2 Corinthians 5:17 says, "if anyone is in Christ, he is a new creation. The old has passed away; behold, the new has come."

But to live in line with your new identity, you must say "no!" to the passions of sin.[24] "For the grace of God has appeared, bringing salvation for all people, training us to *renounce* ungodliness and worldly passions, and to live self-controlled, upright, and godly lives in the present age" (Titus 2:11–12). Sin still dwells within—but it has no authority to master you. Don't let it control you!

3. Yield to Your New Master

How then are we to deal with our remaining sinful passions? While I'll return to deal with this question more thoroughly in chapter 7, Paul's answer in this passage is quite clear: *we must yield ourselves to God, rather than sin.* In verse 13 of Romans 6 he tells us, "Do not present your members to sin as instruments for unrighteousness, but present yourselves to God as those who have been brought from death to life, and your members to God as instruments for righteousness."

Get the imagery in this verse. Paul envisions a battlefield with warlords, warriors, and weapons. The battlefield is the body. The warriors are passions and desires. The weapons these warriors wield are our "members," which probably refer to both physical body parts and our natural capacities as human beings.[25] The warriors will serve one of two possible warlords: Sin or God. Do not let Warlord Sin reign in the battlefield of the body! Don't hand over your capacities as a human being as weapons for serving Warlord Sin. Rather, yield yourselves to God and use your members as weapons for righteousness.[26] And notice how verse 13 motivates us by appealing once again to our position in Christ: we are to do all this "as those who have been brought from death to life."

Verses 15–20 spell this out in terms of slavery.[27] Paul says that we are the slaves of whichever master we obey—either sin, which leads to death, or obedience, which leads to righteousness. We will either be slaves to sin who are "free" from righteousness or slaves of righteousness who are free from sin (v. 18, 20). Verses 21–23 then spell out the respective ends of these two kinds of slavery. Slavery to sin ends in death, but slavery to God yields the fruit of holiness and leads to eternal life. As Paul summarizes in verse 23, "the wages of sin is death, but the free gift of God is eternal life in Jesus Christ our Lord." But we are all slaves to one master or the other. Ultimate freedom is an illusion. As the legendary folk-rock singer Bob Dylan says, we've all "Gotta Serve Somebody." Believe it or not, that's good theology! Freedom from one master always entails service to another. All the various expressions of human sinfulness are rooted in an alternative slavery.

Some people are enslaved to *money*, and as Scripture says, "The love of money is a root of all kinds of evil" (1 Tim. 6:10). Discontent, greed, covetousness, luxurious living, waste, dishonesty, stealing, cheating, economic oppression of the poor—these are just a few of the fruits growing from this root.

Others are enslaved to *sex*. The results? Guilt, dysfunctional interpersonal relationships, illegitimate births, abortion, STDs, pornography, lust, adultery, broken marriages, rape, the abuse of women and children.

Still others are enslaved to *power*, with the outgrowth of ambition, pride, conceit, the desire for control, and abusive relationships.

One of the common denominators in all of these slaveries is their dehumanizing effect. The more a person is enslaved to money, sex, or power, the less likely she is to be a well-adjusted human being within the nexus of relationships to God, people, and the world that makes for a joyful life. But Jesus came to free us from the tyranny of money, sex, and power. Christ leads his followers down the path of generosity and contentment, chastity and marital fidelity, servant-hood and humility. Is this restrictive? Yes. But it's also liberating.[28]

Jesus is sometimes resisted because his lordship seems so restrictive. People may speak disparagingly of the rugged moral requirements of being a disciple of Jesus and declare themselves freed from his standards. But who is truly free? The person who throws off moral restraint in the quest for money, sex, and power, or those who enjoy freedom from the ravages of sin as they yield to the mastery of Jesus and willingly serve others with humility, chastity, and generosity? *You've gotta serve somebody.* The truest freedom is found in a new kind of slavery—slavery to Christ. C. S. Lewis remarked that "the hardness of God is kinder than the softness of men, and his compulsion is our liberation."[29] In the words of English poet John Donne:

> *Yet dearly I love you, and would be loved fain,*
> *But am betrothed unto your enemy*
> *Divorce me, untie, or break that knot again;*
> *Take me to you, imprison me, for I*
> *Except you enthrall me, never shall be free,*
> *Nor ever chaste, except you ravish me.*[30]

The good news is that if you are joined to Christ you have been set free from sin's dominion. The bondage to sin is broken! "But thanks be to God, that you who were once slaves of sin have become obedient from the heart to the standard of teaching to which you were committed, and, having been set free from sin, have become slaves of righteousness" (Rom. 6:17–18). The reign of sin is thwarted! "Sin will not be lord of those who have been captured by God's grace through the gospel."[31]

All We Need Is in Christ Alone

The main takeaway from this chapter is that everything we need for the pursuit of spiritual transformation is found in Christ alone. John MacArthur, in his excellent book *Our Sufficiency in Christ*, tells three rather unusual stories, that are (I think) all true and all illustrate this truth. First, there is the story about two brothers in New York City who were sons of a famous doctor. Both were bachelors, but well educated and lived on the luxurious family estate left to them by their father. But they were forgotten over time, because they were recluses. In 1947 the police got an anonymous phone tip that someone had died in the mansion. What the police found were two corpses in a house full of junk—140 tons of garbage! The brothers had been stockpiling the trash for years, collecting everything, throwing away nothing. Though they were immensely wealthy, they had lived in a squalid dump.

The second story is about William Randolph Hearst, a famous and wealthy newspaper publisher who read about several pieces of art he wanted to add to his collection. He sent his agent all over the world looking for the items. Months later, the agent returned and reported that the items had finally been found: in one of Hearst's warehouses! He had purchased the items years before.

The third story is about a poor man who went on a cruise. He saved all that he could to go on the cruise, but had no money left for food. So, he took a suitcase full of peanut butter sandwiches. But as he watched the porters carry trays of delicious, luxurious food, he almost went crazy. After several days he begged for a plate of food, promising the porter to do anything to earn the meal. The porter informed him that if he had a ticket, he could eat as much as he wanted. The food came with the cruise![32]

Each of these stories could serve as parables for believers who look to someone other than Christ and something other than the gospel to change them, satisfy them, and make them new. Wealthy, they live in the squalid trash of sin, rather than enjoy the treasure of Christ and his glory. Hungry, they try to fill their souls with the peanut butter sandwiches of self effort, thinking that they need to add something to God's grace in order to enjoy the fullness of life in Christ. Like William Randolph Hearst, they are on a quest for something that is already theirs!

The gospel tells us that we have everything we need in Christ. His death is ours; we are therefore freed from sin. His resurrection is ours; we thus walk in newness of life. We don't need to add anything to what Christ has done for us. We simply need to believe the gospel and apply it more deeply to our lives.

As John Calvin wrote in this rhapsodic, worshipful passage in the *Institutes*:

> We see that our whole salvation and all its parts are comprehended in Christ [Acts 4:12]. We should therefore take care not to derive the least portion of it from anywhere else. If we seek salvation, we are taught by the very name of Jesus that it is "of him" [1 Cor. 1:30]. If we seek any other gifts of the Spirit, they will be found in his anointing. If we seek strength, it lies in his dominion; if purity, in his conception; if gentleness, it appears in his birth. For by his birth he was made like us in all respects [Heb. 2:17] that he might learn to feel our pain [cf. Heb. 5:2]. If we seek redemption, it lies in his passion; if acquittal, in his condemnation; if remission of the curse, in his cross [Gal. 3:13]; if satisfaction, in his sacrifice; if purification, in his blood; if reconciliation, in his descent into hell; if mortification of the flesh, in his tomb; if newness of life, in his resurrection; if immortality, in the same; if inheritance of the Heavenly Kingdom, in his entrance into heaven; if protection, if security, if abundant supply of all blessings, in his Kingdom; if untroubled expectation of judgment, in the power given him to judge. In short, since rich store of every kind of good abounds in him, let us drink from this fountain, and from no other.[33]

PART TWO

THE PATTERN
OF PERSONAL CHANGE

This book is about change. We have learned that God's goal in changing us is to restore his image within us by replicating the character of his Son in our lives, through the power of his Spirit.

In Part One we learned that God accomplishes his transforming purpose in us through the gospel. The implications of the gospel for spiritual formation are profound. Through Christ and his work for us, we are justified, counted righteous before God, and therefore pursue holiness not *for* grace, but *from* grace. The doctrine of justification by faith steadies our feet on the path to holiness, preserving us from the precipice of legalism.

But we are not only justified, we are sanctified: set apart by God for holiness through our union with Jesus Christ. We are freed not only from sin's penalty, but also its power. The curse of sin has been canceled and its bondage has been broken. In other words, we really are changed—transformed. Through the indwelling of the Spirit in our hearts, God has established a beachhead for his ongoing work in our lives.

In Part Two of this book, we will discover how these definitive, once-and-for-all events (justification and sanctification) get worked out in the actual pursuit of holiness. We will learn that holiness is both threatening and beautiful and that to pursue holiness requires both unrelenting effort in putting sin to death and unfailing trust in the Spirit's work of molding us into the image of Christ.

But the gospel doesn't get left behind as we press on to holiness. No, the gospel beckons us forward and sweetens the difficulties on the narrow way with the promise of deep satisfaction and joy as we grow in conformity to and communion with our Savior.

Martin Luther said it well, and his words are fitting as we embark on the next leg of our journey:

> This life, therefore, is not righteousness, but growth in righteousness; not health, but healing; not being, but becoming; not rest, but exercise. We are not yet what we shall be, but we are growing toward it. The process is not yet finished, but it is going on. This is not the end, but it is the road. All does not yet gleam in glory, but all is being purified.[1]

6

Captivated by Beauty

Holiness

Holiness is nothing but the implanting, writing, and realizing of the
gospel in our souls.

—John Owen

Holiness is a word that pops up often in church services. When we
gather to worship and begin to sing, we often employ lyrics that celebrate God's holiness, thank him for declaring us holy, and ask him for
greater measures of personal holiness.

But do we actually understand what we are singing? Do we really
long for holiness? What *is* holiness? "How little people know who think
holiness is dull. When one meets the real thing . . . it is irresistible,"
remarked C. S. Lewis in one of his letters.[1]

Irresistible? Really? Are you drawn by the magnetic pull of holiness?
What is Lewis talking about?

What comes to your mind when you encounter the word "holiness"? Is your imagination flooded by Old Testament images of winged seraphic creatures, flashes of lightning, or blood sacrifices consumed by fire from heaven? Do the faint echoes of awe, guilt, or fear reverberate in your soul? Perhaps you associate holiness with long skirts, no makeup, the boycott of face cards or movie theaters, or other standards of dress or conduct.

Maybe you think of holy spaces, places, or objects such as shrines, temples, and altars. Or perhaps you see holiness as an impossible ethical ideal, a level of Christian living that is desirable but unattainable. Most people probably don't think of holiness at all, unless they are at church, and even then the concept may be fuzzy, amorphous, and obscure.[2]

In contrast to our muddled thinking about holiness, and in language even more flamboyant than C. S. Lewis's, Jonathan Edwards wrote:

> Holiness is a most beautiful and lovely thing. We drink in strange notions of holiness from our childhood, as if it were a melancholy, morose, sour and unpleasant thing; but there is nothing in it but what is sweet and ravishingly lovely.[3]

Is holiness really irresistible, beautiful, sweet, and ravishingly lovely? People describe their lovers with these words in sonnets and love songs, but holiness? Edwards probably thought of passages in Scripture that exhort us to "worship the Lord in the *beauty* of holiness" (1 Chron. 16:29; Ps. 29:2; 96:9, KJV).

On the other hand, there is something that is threatening, even terrifying, about holiness. This is what the German Lutheran scholar, Rudolph Otto, called the *"mysterium tremendum,"* the awful mystery of holiness. Otto described this as "the hushed, trembling, and speechless humility of the creature in the presence of—whom or what? In the presence of that which is a *mystery* inexpressible and above all creatures."[4] This association is certainly biblical. When human beings encountered God's holiness in Scripture, their response was *always* one of awe, fear, or dread.

So, is holiness beautiful? Or dreadful? Or both?

The purpose of this chapter is to help us understand holiness. We will discover what holiness is, how it is fully realized in Christ, and how God calls us to holiness and uses the gospel to produce it in our lives.

The Nature of Holiness

Novelist Flannery O'Connor once said, "To the hard of hearing you shout, and for the almost blind you draw large and startling figures."[5] She did this in her fiction, often ending her stories with unusual and even shocking twists that force the moral of the story upon her readers.

Our gracious God knows we are almost blind and hard of hearing. And in Scripture, he shouts and draws large, startling pictures to help us understand his holy nature. These pictures reveal two basic characteristics about God's holiness, which we could call his *otherness* and his *moral perfection.*

God's Otherness

The first occurrence of the word "holy" in Scripture is in the second chapter of Genesis. Having completed the six days of creation, God rests from his creation work on the seventh day. Verse 3 says, "God blessed the seventh day and made it holy." The phrase "made it holy" is a single verb in Hebrew[6] which means to consecrate, separate, or set apart. God set apart the seventh day from the other six, making it unique.[7] The next occurrence of the verb conveys a similar meaning. After instituting the Passover meal in the inaugural event of Israel's deliverance from slavery in Egypt, God instructs Moses, "Consecrate to me all the firstborn. Whatever is the first to open the womb among the people of Israel, both of man and of beast, is mine" (Ex. 13:2). The word "consecrate" is the same word we saw in Genesis 2:3. God is commanding Moses to set apart the firstborn children and animals in Israel for himself. The noun form of this word[8] expresses the same idea; it means that which is "set apart" or "consecrated" to God.

God himself is set apart from all others. "Who is like you, O Lord, among the gods? Who is like you, majestic in holiness, awesome in glorious deeds, doing wonders?" (Ex. 15:11). To put it simply, God is in a class all by himself. God is *other* than we are. He is called the Holy

One of Israel (Ps. 89:18), has a holy name and dwells in a holy place (Isa. 57:15; Ps. 99:3; Deut. 26:15; cf. Ps. 20:6; 24:3). His Spirit is holy (Ps. 51:11) and he does holy works (Ps. 105:42) and makes holy promises (Ps. 145:17). God does everything for the sake of his holy name (Ezek. 36:22). Psalm 89:35 says that God swears by his holiness "because that is a fuller expression of himself than anything else."[9]

But God also sets apart for himself various people, places, and things. When Moses heard God speak from the burning bush, he was on holy ground (Ex. 3:5). God chose Israel to be a holy nation, set apart as his special people (Ex. 19:6). The garments of Aaron, the high priest, were holy garments (Ex. 28:2, 4). The priests made holy sacrifices on a holy altar (Ex. 29:37) in a holy place, while the ark of the testimony was kept in the Most Holy Place (Ex. 26:33–34). Even the furniture and utensils used within the tabernacle were holy (Ex. 30:27–29). Because Jerusalem housed the temple, it was known as God's holy city (Isa. 52:1). Anything set apart for God's special use was holy.

This, then, is the first picture of holiness: the *otherness* of God, which moves him to consecrate persons and things for himself.

God's Moral Perfection

Closely connected to the idea of consecration is that of ethical purity and moral perfection. As we saw above, God is other than we are. But this otherness is not merely metaphysical. It is also moral. God is unique in the perfection and purity of his character. As the prophet Habakkuk said, the Holy One is "of purer eyes than to see evil and cannot look at wrong" (Hab. 1:12–13).

This moral dimension to God's holiness consists in the excellence of his nature, the integrity of his justice, and the purity of his wisdom. As the seventeenth-century theologian, Stephen Charnock said, God's holiness is the glory of his perfections:

> As his power is the strength of [his perfections], so his holiness is the beauty of them. As all would be weak, without almightiness to back them, so all would be uncomely without holiness to adorn them . . . [holiness] is the rule of all his acts, the source of all his punishments. If every attribute of the Deity were a distinct member, purity would be the form,

the soul, the spirit to animate them. Without it, his patience would be an indulgence to sin, his mercy a fondness, his wrath a madness, his power a tyranny, his wisdom an unworthy subtlety. It is this gives a decorum to all.[10]

Holiness, then, is not merely one of many attributes of God. It is the sum and substance of all the attributes. All of God's perfections are holy perfections. Holiness is the beauty, the splendor, the "fearful symmetry,"[11] of God's infinitely flawless character. But even with our best attempts to define God's holiness, words fail. To use the words of A. W. Tozer, "God's holiness is not simply the best we know infinitely bettered. We know nothing like the divine holiness. It stands apart, unique, unapproachable, incomprehensible and unattainable. The natural man is blind to it. He may fear God's power and admire His wisdom, but His holiness he cannot even imagine."[12]

God's utterly self-consistent holiness demands a corresponding purity in those created in his holy image. Moral perfection is the condition for a relationship with God. "Who shall ascend the hill of the Lord? And who shall stand in his holy place?" asks the psalmist (Ps. 24:3). The answer is found in the strict ethical requirements which follow. Because God is holy, only those who have clean hands, pure hearts, and honest lips can stand in his presence (Ps. 24:4–6; cf. Ps. 15:1–5). God's holiness demands ours. In Leviticus 20:7, the Lord told Moses to say to the Israelites, "Consecrate yourselves, therefore, and be holy, for I am the Lord your God" (cf. Lev. 11:44–45; 19:2; 1 Peter 1:16).

Yet we are human, inherently sinful, placing all of us in a deep moral crisis. Our God is holy, and we are not. When we see our sinfulness in the light of God's holy character, we tremble.

When God gave his law to Israel at Sinai, the people of Israel "saw the thunder and the flashes of lightning and the sound of the trumpet and the mountain smoking, the people were afraid and trembled and stood far off and said to Moses, 'You speak to us, and we will listen; but do not let God speak to us lest we die' " (Ex. 20:18–19). Isaiah the prophet, perhaps the most righteous man of Israel in his day, was reduced to psychological shambles, when he saw "the Lord sitting upon a throne, high and lifted up," surrounded by winged seraphim, who covered their faces as they cried, "Holy, holy, holy is the Lord of hosts; the whole earth is full of his glory!" (Isa. 6:1–5).

Job, despite his initial confidence as a plaintiff desiring audience before the Almighty's throne (Job 23:1–7), lost all self-esteem when he heard the living Lord speak. In self-abhorrence, he confessed, "I had heard of you by the hearing of the ear, but now my eyes see you; therefore I despise myself, and repent in dust and ashes" (Job 42:5–6). Reflecting on these kinds of biblical stories, Calvin wrote of the "dread and wonder with which Scripture commonly represents the saints as stricken and overcome whenever they felt the presence of God." He concluded that, "man is never sufficiently touched and affected by the awareness of his lowly state until he has compared himself with God's majesty."[13]

The emotions of awe, dread, and fear are appropriate responses to God, because he is holy and we are not. He is pure, clean, righteous, and true. We are soiled with guilt and deceit. His character is holy. Ours isn't. This realization should give us pause when approaching our God.

The more we gaze upon God, the more we are forced to acknowledge that the unqualified perfection set before us as an unchanging standard is utterly unapproachable. We have to do with a God of transcendent holiness. This rightly evokes in our hearts the responses of awe and dread.

Fully Realized Human Holiness

If God's holiness is his transcendent otherness, his infinite moral perfection which demands a corresponding perfection of purity in us—which we desperately lack—then we, like Isaiah, are "undone." We are faced with what R. C. Sproul calls, "the trauma of holiness."[14] God is holy and we are not. Surely it is impossible, isn't it, for holiness and humanity to coexist?

But Scripture provides another picture—a picture of incarnate holiness, immanent holiness, drawing near to us in the person of Jesus.

Everything about Jesus' life was fragranced with the aroma of holiness. Prior to Jesus' miraculous conception, an angel appeared to his mother Mary saying, "The Holy Spirit will come upon you, and the power of the Most High will overshadow you; therefore the child to be born will be called holy— the Son of God" (Luke 1:35). John the Baptist, the herald and forerunner of Jesus, pointed to him as one who would baptize "with the Holy Spirit and fire" (Luke 3:16). Demons, possessing insight more keen than Jesus' own companions, recognized him as "the Holy One of God" (Luke 4:34). Peter proclaimed Jesus as the "Holy and Righteous One" (Acts 3:14), and the early disciples acknowledged Jesus to be God's "holy servant" (Acts 4:27, 30). Like "a lamb without blemish or spot" Christ ransomed us for God (1 Peter 1:18–19) by offering himself "without blemish to God" (Heb. 9:14). He is our great high priest, "holy, innocent, unstained, separated from sinners, and exalted above the heavens" (Heb. 7:26). He was "declared to be the Son of God in power according to the Spirit of holiness by his resurrection from the dead, Jesus Christ our Lord" (Rom. 1:4). In raising Jesus, God did not let his Holy One see corruption (Acts 2:27).

The greatest and clearest picture of holiness in Scripture is this Jesus of whom we sing and teach and preach. It's not that the example of Jesus added any dimension to the character of God, but that every aspect of Jesus' life exuded the beauty and splendor of God's moral perfection and ethical purity *in human form*. Though he experienced the full scope of temptation, he remained completely sinless (Heb. 4:15). Jesus literally embodied what Sinclair Ferguson calls "fully realized human holiness."[15]

In his fully realized human holiness, Jesus shows us what we were made for. The beauty of his moral flawlessness is irresistibly attractive and resonates in our hearts. Perhaps this is one reason why children loved Jesus and felt safe in his arms: they sensed his intrinsic goodness and purity.

Yet his untarnished perfection is also threatening, even terrifying. In Mark 4, when Jesus was in a fishing boat with his disciples during a dangerous storm, the disciples were understandably frightened. But when Jesus stilled the wind and waves with mere words, his fearful disciples became terrified! They had come face to face with his transcendence. This is also why Peter, having glimpsed the majesty of his Lord displayed in a miraculous catch of fish, cried out, "Depart from me, for I am a sinful man, O Lord" (Luke 5:8).

There is something about holiness that provokes both of these responses: attraction and alarm, delight and dread. Augustine expressed this combination of emotions when he wrote:

> What is that light whose gentle beams now and again strike through to my heart, causing me to shudder in awe yet firing me with their warmth? I shudder to feel how different I am from it: yet in so far as I am like it, I am aglow with its fire.[16]

Augustine's words explain why we are so conflicted in our feelings about holiness. We shudder, because of our sin. We are not holy, so we feel threatened by the dissimilarity between our hearts and our holy God. Yet at the same time, we are aglow with the fire of the Holy One, because holiness is what we were made for.

As we have seen in previous chapters, the good news is that God credits Christ's perfection to all who trust in him. Ultimately, Jesus alone can ascend the hill of the Lord and stand in his holy place. But we stand there with him. His obedience is ours. His perfection counts for us. Christ is our holiness, our sanctification (1 Cor. 1:30).

God's Purpose to Make Us Holy

Our salvation was secured by the substitutionary work of Christ for us. He is our perfect representative, our sinless substitute. By faith, we are declared righteous in Christ. As we saw in chapter 4, in Christ we are given a new history, identity, and destiny. But this has radical, far-reaching implications for our present lives. God not only works for us, but in us. He not only counts us as holy, he purposes to make us holy—by calling us to holiness and by applying the gospel to our hearts to produce holiness within us.

Called to Holiness

In the Old Testament, Israel's call to holiness was rooted in God's holy character and redemptive grace. In Leviticus, for example, the Lord says, "You shall be holy to me, for I the Lord am holy and have separated you from the peoples, that you should be mine" (Lev. 20:26). Notice that the command ("you shall be holy to me") is based both on

God's holiness ("for I the Lord am holy") and his gracious initiative in making Israel his people ("and have separated you from the peoples, that you should be mine"). God declares himself to be the Lord who sanctifies his people seven times in Leviticus (Lev. 20:8; 21:8, 15, 23; 22:9, 16, 32). And only after he has first sanctified his people, does he then command them to sanctify themselves.

> So you shall keep my commandments and do them: I am the Lord. And you shall not profane my holy name, that I may be sanctified among the people of Israel. I am the Lord who sanctifies you, who brought you out of the land of Egypt to be your God: I am the Lord.
>
> —Leviticus 22:31–33

The New Testament picks up the theme of holiness with the same language. Peter says, in 1 Peter 2, we are "a holy priesthood" (v. 5) and "a holy nation, a people for [God's] own possession" (v. 9). And, lifting language straight out of Leviticus, he reshapes the call to holiness around Christ.

> Therefore, preparing your minds for action, and being sober-minded, set your hope fully on the grace that will be brought to you at the revelation of Jesus Christ. As obedient children, do not be conformed to the passions of your former ignorance, but as he who called you is holy, you also be holy in all your conduct, since it is written, "You shall be holy, for I am holy."
>
> —1 Peter 1:13–16

Paul also connects every aspect of our salvation to holiness, from the gracious purpose of God's eternal plan, to the cross work of Christ, to the application of his work in our lives by God's Spirit.

- **Election**—In Ephesians 1:4, he looks backward to God's gracious election, explaining that God chose us in Christ, "before the foundation of the world, that we should be holy and blameless before him."
- **The Cross**—Then in Ephesians 5, he says Christ loved the church as his bride and gave himself up for her, "that he might sanctify

her, having cleansed her by the washing of water with the Word, so that he might present the church to himself in splendor, without spot or wrinkle or any such thing, that she might be holy and without blemish" (Eph. 5:25–27; cf. Col. 1:22).

- **The Work of the Spirit**—Paul also thanks God for choosing people to be saved through the "sanctification of the Spirit and belief in the truth" and calling them to this salvation through the gospel (2 Thess. 2:13–14).

- **God's call**—Believers are called "in holiness" (1 Thess. 4:7) and "to a holy calling" (2 Tim. 1:9).

- **New Creation**—Even the concept of new creation is linked to holiness, as Paul reminds us that the new man is "created after the likeness of God in true righteousness and holiness" (Eph. 4:24).

This brings us back to the unifying theme of this book—the restoration of the image of God within us. In his classic book, *Holiness: Its Nature, Hindrances, Difficulties, and Roots*, J. C. Ryle said, "True holiness . . . is something of 'the image of Christ,' which can be seen and observed by others in our private life and habits and character and doings."[17] Spiritual formation, rightly understood, is about the outworking of God's transforming grace as he conforms us to the image of Christ by the power of his Spirit through the renewing of our minds (Rom. 8:29; 2 Cor. 3:18; Rom. 12:1–2).

The glorious image of Christ, his "fully realized human holiness," is the pattern and goal of our transformation. Sanctification is God's gracious work in setting us apart for the realization of this divine purpose. As Sinclair Ferguson says:

"To sanctify" means that God repossesses persons and things that have been devoted to other uses, and have been possessed for purposes other than his glory, and takes them into his own possession in order that they may reflect his own glory. . . . Underlying all is the motif of expressing this divine image: being holy as he is holy. . . . Sanctification means being restored to the glory-image of God by being made like Jesus Christ. . . . Christlikeness is the end in view; sanctification is the transformation which produces it.[18]

Applying the Gospel in the Pursuit of Holiness

So, God calls us to holiness or Christlikeness. But how does he actually make us holy? *Only through the gospel.* The essential conviction of this book is that only by the intentional application of the gospel to our hearts and lives do we increasingly become like Jesus. "Holiness," said John Owen, "is nothing but the implanting, writing, and realizing of the gospel in our souls."[19] But how does this actually work?

Holiness is not mere morality, but the deep, personal transformation of the soul *through* the renewal of the mind in the truth of the gospel. When Paul refers to the stunning contrast between what we once were and who we now are, he grounds the dramatic change we have experienced in our personal appropriation of Christ. We see this in Ephesians 4 as Paul urges his readers not to live as unbelievers who are calloused in soul and have "given themselves up to sensuality, greedy to practice every kind of impurity." Why? Because, "that is not the way you learned Christ!" (vv. 19–20). Paul continues,

> Assuming that you have heard about him and were taught in him, as the truth is in Jesus, to put off your old self, which belongs to your former manner of life and is corrupt through deceitful desires, and to be renewed in the spirit of your minds, and to put on the new self, created after the likeness of God in true righteousness and holiness.
>
> —Ephesians 4:21–24

To urge us to live distinct and separate lives, Paul reminds us of the implications of the message we embraced when we learned, heard about, and were taught in Christ. We were taught to put off the old self—the old human nature, the personality dominated by sin, inherited from our original father, the first man, Adam. This nature belonged to our former way of life and was characterized by ongoing corruption.

But we were also taught to be renewed in the spirit of our minds. We need inner renewal because our minds are so deeply infected with the deceit of evil (cf. vv. 17–18, 22). Transformation is impossible apart from our internalization of gospel truth.[20]

If you own a computer, you've probably had at least one awful experience with a virus. Your computer has been hacked. A virus has contaminated your system. Spy-ware is compromising your information. A Trojan horse is interfering with your programs. Once you've experienced this electronic nightmare, you know that the only way to combat future infections is regularly to download new virus definitions and scan your computer for threats. If you don't do this, your computer will get infected and eventually lock down or crash. Our minds are much the same. Sin has infected our thinking with viruses, worms, and Trojan horses. Our minds are sabotaged by false patterns of thinking, by deceitful desires, and by images, information, and ideologies that distort reality, compromise truth, and lead to futility. The only way to be freed from this deception is to be continually renewed[21] with the truth of the gospel.

And Paul further says that we were taught to put on the new self. If the old self refers to the old, corrupt nature, which is inherited from and patterned after the first man, then the new self refers to the new nature, given to us in the new creation work of God. The new self is human nature renewed, patterned after the perfect, holy humanity of Jesus, the last man. It is the new nature and new identity granted to us by God, the new man re-created in his perfect image.[22]

Putting Off the Old, Putting On the New

Now notice how the gospel works itself out in Christian living in both negative and positive ways. Negatively, in putting off the old; and positively, in putting on the new. As mentioned in previous chapters, God's work in our lives has both once-and-for-all, definitive aspects, but also ongoing, practical, developmental aspects. We see this pattern here as well. Putting off and putting on happens *decisively* when we come to Christ in faith. But the *outworking* of this basic pattern in personal life continues, as Paul builds on this gospel foundation with the brick and mortar of ethical instruction (Eph. 4:25–32). In just seven verses, he presents a series of practical exhortations that address the everyday sins of telling lies, getting angry, stealing, speaking sinfully, and harboring bitterness.

Each of these exhortations includes both positive and negative counterparts. Paul tells us to put away falsehood, but also to speak the truth to one another (v. 25). We are to be angry—implying that some forms of anger are appropriate—but not to be sinfully angry (v. 26). Thieves are no longer to steal. Rather, they must earn an honest wage and give to those in need (v. 28). Instead of using corrupt language, we are to build up others, conveying grace with our words (v. 29). Finally, we must put away the corrosive attitudes of bitterness and anger, and cultivate kindness and forgiveness in their place (vv. 31–32).

And notice how all of Paul's exhortations are reinforced with gospel-laden reasons. Paul not only tells what to do, he tells us *why*. He motivates us with gospel-rich reminders of why we should live as he tells us to. We should speak truth, rather than lie, because we are members of the same body (v. 25). We are to steer clear of sinful anger, lest we give the devil a foothold in our lives (vv. 26–27). Former thieves are to work hard in order to give to those in need (v. 28). Our words will give grace to others, when we remember we are sealed with the Spirit and seek not to grieve him with our speech (vv. 29–30). The forgiveness we have already received in Christ is the supreme motivation for forgiving others (vv. 31–32).

The goal is never simply refraining from sin, but actively replacing sin with righteousness as we are consciously motivated by the gospel. The restoration of God's image within us always has both these negative and positive dimensions. We must put off the old *and* put on the new—put sin to death *and* grow in grace. This is the invariable pattern of Scripture. Theologians call these negative and positive dimensions to holiness "mortification" and "vivification." While it's not important to remember these terms, it is essential to grasp the biblical concepts. This is how the gospel is realized and written in our souls.

As we saw in chapter 4, the pattern was set in the death and resurrection of Christ. Through faith in him, we share in his death and resurrection. We have died to sin and now live in newness of life (Rom. 6). But that pattern of death and resurrection is worked out in our lives in the disciplines of mortification and vivification. Killing sin and growing in grace summarize the biblical prescription for a holy life. This is how the gospel is applied to our hearts in the pursuit of holiness (see diagram 6.1).[23]

Death	Resurrection
We died with Christ (Rom. 6:2–4)	We walk in newness of life (Rom. 6:4)
Put off the old man (Col. 3:9)	Put on the new man (Col. 3:10)
Cleanse yourself from defilement of body and spirit (2 Cor. 7:1)	Bring holiness to completion in the fear of God (2 Cor. 7:1)
Don't be conformed (Rom. 12:2)	Be transformed (Rom. 12:2)
Crucify the flesh (Gal. 5:24)	Walk in the Spirit (Gal. 5:25)
Renounce ungodliness and worldly passions (Titus 2:12)	Live sober, righteous, and godly lives in the present age (Titus 2:12)
Lay aside every weight and sin (Heb. 12:1)	Run the race set before us (Heb. 12:1)
Do not be conformed to the passions of your former ignorance (1 Peter 1:14)	But as he who called you is holy, you also be holy in all your conduct (1 Peter 1:15)
Mortification: Kill your sins	**Vivification: Grow in grace**

Diagram 6.1: Living Out the Pattern of the Gospel

Have you seen the play or the film *My Fair Lady*? It's the story of an English phonetics professor, Dr. Henry Higgins, and a cockney-accented flower girl named Eliza Doolittle. Higgins bets a friend that he can transform the uncultured Miss Doolittle into a lady suitable for London's high society. What a transformation it is! Eliza is taught to speak properly, trained in etiquette and manners, and given a new wardrobe. By the end of the story the grimy-faced, uneducated flower girl has morphed into a beautiful lady who passes for royalty.

God does something similar in our lives (although, unlike Henry Higgins, with loving and gracious motives!). He strips away the grime and filth of our old life and adorns us with a new set of clothes—new ways of thinking, speaking, and living. He befits us as royalty, to live as heirs of his kingdom!

This is the practical outworking of being renewed in the spirit of our minds. The fruit of personal change grows from hearts renewed in the gospel. Holiness is the lifestyle of the new creation—not the prerequisite to becoming the new creation. *Holiness is nothing but the implanting, writing, and realizing of the gospel in our souls.*

"Oh, This Pleasing Pain!"

David Brainerd was the missionary to Native Americans whose life is known to us because of Jonathan Edwards' diligence in editing Brainerd's diaries to produce *The Life and Diary of David Brainerd*. Brainerd was a melancholy young man who struggled with sickness, loneliness, and harsh working and living conditions. His greatest struggles were with the corruption remaining within his own afflicted heart. But Brainerd pursued hard after God and holiness, giving himself relentlessly to ministry among the Indians (dozens were saved) and to prayer, fasting, and study. Brainerd called his passion for more holiness a "pleasing pain."

> When I really enjoy God, I feel my desires of him the more insatiable and my thirstings after holiness the more unquenchable; . . . Oh, for holiness! Oh, for more of God in my soul! Oh, this pleasing pain! It makes my soul press after God . . . Oh, that I might not loiter on my heavenly journey![24]

Pleasing pain? This strikes us as an oxymoron—a contradiction in terms. How can pain bring pleasure? Yet this is what Brainerd felt. The pursuit of holiness was pleasing, because Brainerd was irresistibly attracted to the beauty of holiness. But it was painful as well, because of his ongoing struggles with sin.

This is our experience as well, when we are pursuing true holiness. We feel a mixture of emotions. Fear and trembling, as we consider the transcendent perfection of our holy God, is mingled with delight in the beauty of holiness. Pain, in the agonizing process of putting sin to death, but gladness in gospel-driven growth in grace. Longing for more of God in our souls, and rest in knowing God's love revealed in the cross of Christ.

7

Killing Sin

Mortification

Be killing sin, or sin will be killing you.
—John Owen

"The tiger ate her hand. It slowly proceeded to eat the rest of her arm." That's how Vikram Chari described the horrifying spectacle that he and his six-year-old son witnessed at the San Francisco Zoo on December 22, 2006, when a Siberian tiger named Tatiana attacked her keeper.

For those who work with wild animals, the bloody assault was a reminder of what they already know but don't always remember—the creatures they've become so accustomed to can turn on them at any moment. "'If you're not afraid of it, it will hurt you,' said animal behaviorist Dave Salmoni. 'You can't get the wild out of a cat because he's in a cage.'"[1]

Lots of us think we can tame sin, but like a tiger, sin turns and masters us at the first opportunity. You cannot get the wild out of sin simply by caging it. We may think we have evil under control, that we have tamed sin, rendering it harmless enough to share a peaceful, mutual coexistence. But sin will never be domesticated. It is wolf, not dog; piranha, not goldfish. Evil is untamable. It is our enemy—opposed to us in every way. At every moment, sin is wired to destroy.

The analogy with wild animals breaks down, however, for sin can be far more subtle in its destructive intentions than a slashing claw or crushing jaws. Sin regularly assaults us, though we often fail to notice. Sin knows us well and quietly gnaws away at our faith and affections.

We can therefore never be tolerant or open-minded about our sin. We are called to aggressively hate our sin—to despise it, reject it, deplore it, starve it, and make every effort to kill it. As the seventeenth-century pastor and theologian John Owen said, "Be killing sin or it will be killing you."[2]

That's what this chapter is about—understanding and implementing the biblical call to kill sin.

Theologians call this duty of killing sin *mortification*. Mortification is not a word we often use. We are familiar with several related words—such as mortuary (a funeral home) or mortician (a funeral director). When people use the word "mortify," they usually mean to humiliate or shame someone. But that is not what theologians mean by "mortification." When it comes to sin, to mortify means to kill.

Mortification Misunderstood

It is easy to misunderstand the doctrine of mortification. Why? Because it is hard to accept the depravity of our souls, and our need to continually put sin to death. When we drift from this reality, the true nature of mortification can become unclear. The following statements will help counter some of the common misconceptions about mortification.

Mortification Does Not Produce Perfection

Our desire to be perfectly sinless is a good thing. It is God's desire for us as well. He wants it so much that he sacrificed his Son to achieve it. While perfect holiness is what we ultimately desire and press toward, it is not possible to completely rid ourselves of indwelling sin in this life. Mortification doesn't completely eradicate sin from our hearts. The principle of sin dwells within us, even after we become believers. "For the desires of the flesh are against the Spirit, and the desires of the Spirit are against the flesh, for these are opposed to each other, to keep you from doing the things you want to do" (Gal. 5:17). Scripture characterizes the Christian life as a walk, a fight, and a race. We are *moving in the direction* of increasing holiness and Christlikeness, but not without regular battles along the way. While we press on for the prize, we haven't reached it yet (Phil. 3:12–14). We should strive to make as much progress on that journey as we can, all the while knowing that until our work here is done and we receive the full reward that Christ purchased for us at the cross, we will never "arrive" at perfection.

Mortification Is Not Furthered by Asceticism

The word "asceticism" derives from the Greek word *askesis* (exercise). It refers to a system of spiritual disciplines chiefly focused on renouncing the world and the flesh as part of the great struggle against the devil.[3] As we will learn in chapter 10, spiritual disciplines do play an important role in the pursuit of holiness. But asceticism wrongly assumes that sin is coextensive with the created world, and so prescribes poverty (the renunciation of wealth), celibacy (the renunciation of marriage), and other forms of extreme self-denial as the means of spiritual growth. The idea is that the more we deny our physical nature, the more "spiritual" we will become.

Scripture strongly warns against this approach. Paul cautioned Timothy that some people would depart from the faith "by devoting themselves to deceitful spirits and teachings of demons . . . who forbid marriage and require abstinence from foods that God created to be received with thanksgiving" (1 Tim. 4:1–3). Scripture never teaches that the material creation is intrinsically evil. Food is good. Sex, within marriage, is also good (cf. Heb. 13:4). "For everything created by God is good, and nothing is to be rejected if it is received with thanksgiving, for it is made holy by the word of God and prayer" (1 Tim. 4:4–5). Colossians warns against those who say, "'Do not handle, Do not taste, Do not touch.'" Paul says that "these have indeed an appearance of wisdom in promoting self-made religion and asceticism and severity to the body, but they are of no value in stopping the indulgence of the flesh" (Col. 2:21–23).

So, when Scripture teaches us to put sin to death (Rom. 8:13; Col. 3:5) and crucify the flesh with its passions and desires (Gal. 5:24), it doesn't mean that we must take vows of poverty, abstain from sexual relations within marriage, or live in a monastery. God's created world is good. The problem does not lie within the material world or our physicality as human beings, but in the corruption of our hearts.

Mortification Is More Than Behavior Modification

It is possible to change what we do, even reducing the frequency of certain sins, without actually becoming more pure in heart.[4] Diet and exercise can reduce sloth and gluttony, for example, but the underlying sin of self-indulgence may remain. The office worker who stops visiting pornographic websites on his company computer for fear of losing his job has probably just replaced sins of lust with sins of pride. To mortify sin *will* bring about behavioral change, but mortification is more than behavioral modification.

Mortification's Meaning

As we saw in the last chapter, the biblical prescription for living a holy life can be summarized in two complementary responsibilities: killing sin (mortification) and growing in grace (vivification). The clearest biblical language about mortification is found in Romans 8, Colossians 3, and Galatians 5.

> So then, brothers, we are debtors, not to the flesh, to live according to the flesh. For if you live according to the flesh you will die, but if by the Spirit you *put to death the deeds of the body*, you will live. For all who are led by the Spirit of God are sons of God.
>
> —Romans 8:12–14

> *Put to death therefore what is earthly in you*: sexual immorality, impurity, passion, evil desire, and covetousness, which is idolatry. On account of these the wrath of God is coming. In these you too once walked, when

you were living in them. But now you must *put them all away*: anger, wrath, malice, slander, and obscene talk from your mouth. Do not lie to one another, seeing that you have *put off the old self with its practices* and have put on the new self, which is being renewed in knowledge after the image of its creator.

—Colossians 3:5–10

And those who belong to Christ Jesus have *crucified the flesh with its passions and desires*.

—Galatians 5:24

Simply put, mortification is killing sin. This includes putting to death both sinful actions (deeds) and the sinful motivations (passions and desires) which produce them. But this language of putting to death does not suggest finality. There is nothing we can do in this life to bring sin to a *complete* end. The imagery of mortification is intended, rather, to communicate the vehemence, enmity, and total-war mentality we must have toward sin.

Mortification is not a once-for-all act, like justification. It is an inseparable component of our ongoing transformation, which as we have learned, is a *process* that continues throughout our lives. We "put sin to death," therefore, whenever we consciously recognize sin for the implacable enemy it is, habitually fighting its impulses, and weakening its power in our lives—a little bit at a time, day after day, every day, for the rest of our lives.

Ten Ways to Kill Sin

Killing sin, crucifying the flesh, is no easy affair. It involves the habitual rejection of sinful desires, motives, thoughts, and habits in our lives. If we are to kill sin we must oppose it consistently. We must habitually fight its impulses and make every effort to weaken its power over us. The following ten strategies are not exhaustive, but I believe they will be helpful.

1. Yield Yourself to God

As we saw in chapter 5, Paul teaches us that one of the first steps in fighting against sin is surrendering to God.

> Let not sin therefore reign in your mortal body, to make you obey its passions. Do not present your members to sin as instruments for unrighteousness, but present yourselves to God as those who have been brought from death to life, and your members to God as instruments for righteousness.
>
> —Romans 6:12–13

He specifies in this passage that we are to hand over both our *selves* and our *bodies* to God. Just to be clear, he notes that we are to hand over our *members*—that is, every individual part of the body, without exception. Paul repeats the exhortation in Romans 12: "I appeal to you therefore, brothers, by the mercies of God, to present your *bodies* as a living sacrifice, holy and acceptable to God, which is your spiritual worship" (Rom. 12:1). But we can never really yield our bodies to God without first surrendering our very selves.

This is particularly challenging in our self-centered culture. Many Christians have absorbed, even embraced, our culture's obsession with self. As David Wells writes:

> Much of the Church today, especially that part of it which is evangelical, is in captivity to idolatry of the self. This is a form of corruption far more profound than the lists of infractions that typically pop into our minds when we hear the word *sin*. We are trying to hold at bay the gnats of small sins while swallowing the camel of self.[5]

We will never make much progress in the war against sin until we have first dethroned self. It was for good reason that John Calvin, in his *Institutes*, placed self-denial first among his instructions in "The Sum of the Christian Life." Calvin shows that self-denial is essential if we are to have a right attitude toward others, love our neighbors, be devoted fully to God's will, trust only in God's blessing, and bear adversity in a God-honoring way. "He alone has duly denied himself who has so totally resigned himself to the Lord that he permits every part of his life to be governed by God's will."[6]

The denial of self-rule for God's rule is square one in the fight against sin. As Jesus himself said, "If anyone would come after me, *let him deny himself* and take up his cross and follow me" (Mark 8:34). Putting sin to death starts here.

2. Accept That the Battle Never Ends

Killing sin is a constant duty that will require lifelong battle. In Romans 8:12–13, Paul says "we are debtors, not to the flesh, to live according to the flesh. For if you live according to the flesh you will die, but if by the Spirit you put to death the deeds of the body, you will live." It's not obvious in the English translation, but all the verbs here emphasize an active, ongoing effort. In other words, "if by the Spirit *you are putting to death* the deeds of the body, you will live."

Owen captured the point well when he said: "You must always be at it while you live; do not take a day off from this work; always be killing sin or it will be killing you."[7] We must never let up the fight. Sin is always pounding away at us, "always acting, always conceiving, and always seducing and tempting."[8]

This is not to say that genuine progress cannot be made in overcoming specific sins. A believer can stop lying and is expected to. Christians are commanded and expected to refrain from sinful anger, stealing, impure and ungracious speech, attitudes of malice and bitterness, and all forms of sexual impurity. We once were children of darkness; now we are children of light. God expects us to live true to our new identity (Eph. 4:25–5:8). Nevertheless, the Christian is never off-duty when it comes to killing sin. "I find it to be a law that when I want to do right, evil lies close at hand" (Rom. 7:21). There is no cease-fire in this war.[9]

3. Take God's Side Against Your Sin

Third, you must learn to always take God's side against your sin. This is implied in yielding ourselves to God; but we must be conscious and consistent in *acting on* the inclinations toward holiness and *acting against* the inclinations toward sin. "The duty of mortification consists in a constant taking part with grace, in its principles, actings, and fruits, against the principles, actings, and fruits of sin."[10]

Every day we are faced with split-second choices. When provoked by mistreatment, will I indulge my anger and retaliate with angry words of my own? A cold shoulder? A dirty look? Or will I respond in love, with gentleness and grace?

When confronted with a sexually provocative image, will I indulge in lustful thoughts? Or turn away and seek to fill my mind with the pure pleasures of God? Will I pray for the people represented in these images, eternal beings made in the image of God? Or will I reduce them to objects of desire for my own sinful pleasure?

When weighted with responsibilities, will I run through every worrisome and self-reliant scenario, imagining preventions, escapes, options? Or will I cast my anxious thoughts on the Lord and prayerfully make my requests known to him, trusting in his wise and merciful providence to rightly order the circumstances of my life?

The only way to mortify sin is to act with increasing consistency on the right inclinations instead of the wrong ones. This is the discipline of ongoing repentance. As John Stott writes:

> The first great secret of holiness lies in the degree and the decisiveness of our repentance. If besetting sins persistently plague us, it is either because we have never truly repented, or because, having repented, we have not maintained our repentance. It is as if, having nailed our old nature to the cross, we keep wistfully returning to the scene of its execution. We begin to fondle it, to caress it, to long for its release, even to try to take it down again from the cross. We need to learn to leave it there. When some jealous, or proud, or malicious, or impure thought invades our mind we must kick it out at once. It is fatal to begin to examine it and consider whether we are going to give in to it or not. We have declared war on it; we are not going to resume negotiations. We have settled the issue for good; we are not going to re-open it. We have crucified the flesh; we are never going to draw the nails.[11]

4. Make No Provision for the Flesh

Which flame is harder to extinguish, that of a match, or a forest fire? And does a forest fire ever begin at full power? Never. Fires start small, then get bigger.

Paul tells us, "But put on the Lord Jesus Christ, and make no provision for the flesh, to gratify its desires" (Rom. 13:14). This verse is about lighting fewer matches, and being careful to snuff out the lit ones before the flames increase. In practice this means not exposing yourself to things—websites, magazines, or movies, for example—that are likely to bring strong temptation.

Making no provision for the flesh also involves rejecting the first inclinations of sin. In rejecting the urge to snap back in sarcasm at a hurtful word, or indulge the lustful thought or glance, we extinguish the match in those first few seconds. If we don't, we may soon have a raging fire on our hands. Owen wisely warns, "*Rise mightily against the first sign of sin. Do not allow it to gain the smallest ground.*"[12]

Sin is subtle. It always sneaks up on us in soft-soled slippers. But once it takes hold it will drag us as far as it can. "Every time sin rises to tempt or entice, it always seeks to express itself in the extreme. Every unclean thought or glance would be adultery if it could; every covetous desire would be oppression; and every unbelieving thought would be atheism. It is like the grave that is never satisfied."[13]

We must, therefore, be ruthless with sin. This was Jesus' point when he said:

> And if your hand causes you to sin, cut it off. It is better for you to enter life crippled than with two hands to go to hell, to the unquenchable fire. And if your foot causes you to sin, cut it off. It is better for you to enter life lame than with two feet to be thrown into hell. And if your eye causes you to sin, tear it out. It is better for you to enter the kingdom of God with one eye than with two eyes to be thrown into hell, "where their worm does not die and the fire is not quenched."
>
> —Mark 9:43–48

These are frightening words that have been misconstrued by some as a demand for literal self-mutilation. But, as one commentary notes,

> this was not a demand for physical self-mutilation. [Rather] in the strongest manner possible Jesus speaks of the costliest sacrifices. For the sake of the unconditional rule of God the members of the body must not be placed at the disposal of sinful desire. The sinful member must be renounced in order that the whole body be not cast into hell. Conversely, concern for the preservation of a hand, a leg or a foot must not lead a man to denial of the sovereignty of God or his allegiance to Jesus.[14]

Jesus is teaching us to be radical in dealing with sin. We have to burn the bridges that lead us into sin.

One bridge I had to burn was watching James Bond movies. I had always enjoyed the exotic locales, suspenseful plots, and cool gadgets of the 007 films. But about ten years ago, when watching a Bond film with my wife, Holly, I became really uncomfortable with the many sexual innuendos and scantily clad women. We turned the movie off and later that evening God's Spirit impressed me with the thought, "Brian, you are a Christian. These movies have no place in your life." I vowed never to watch a Bond movie again. I knew this was a bridge to be burned.

The bridges you need to burn will probably be different than mine. But ask yourself: What are you allowing in your life that is clearly leading you into temptation or sin? Cut it off. Let it go.

5. Use Your Spiritual Sword

As Romans 8:13 says, we must put sin to death "by the Spirit." But how do we do that? How does the Spirit help us put sin to death? Consider Ephesians 6:17, "Take ... the sword of the Spirit, which is the word of God." Linking Romans 8 and Ephesians 6 together, we see that one way the Spirit helps us kill sin is with his sword, the Scriptures. As someone once said, "Either this Book will keep you from sin, or sin will keep you from this Book."

The psalmist agreed,

How can a young man keep his way pure?
By guarding it according to your word.
With my whole heart I seek you;
let me not wander from your commandments!
I have stored up your word in my heart,
that I might not sin against you.
—Psalm 119:9–11

We need to follow the example of Jesus when he was tempted by Satan in the wilderness. Do you remember how Jesus responded to each temptation? "It is written!" (Matt. 4:1–11). He quoted Scripture; he used the Spirit's sword.

Before Holly and I moved to Indiana, we lived in the "Big Country" of West Texas, out in the sticks with the coyotes, armadillos, and rattlesnakes. When our first spring rolled around, I taught Holly how to use a shotgun, in case she ever saw a snake when I wasn't home. One day, when I had driven to the Dallas-Fort Worth airport to pick up a friend, Holly was mowing the yard and ran over a snake before she even saw it. When she spotted the snake, she initially thought it was a toy. Reaching down to pick it up, she realized it was both moving and real. She immediately called me on the cell phone, frantic. I walked her through loading and preparing to shoot the gun (my previous instructions evidently having been insufficient). When she was ready to fire, she asked me to stay on the line as she set the phone down. I heard a huge noise as the gun went off, and a moment later Holly was back on the line screaming hysterically, "I missed it! I missed it!" Holly didn't finish mowing the yard that day. My unfortunate wife just didn't have enough skill with her weapon to kill the snake!

Many believers sadly fail to defeat temptation because they lack sufficient skill with their spiritual weapon, the Word of God. When we do not avail ourselves of Scripture, we will have few resources for fighting sin when it appears unannounced. How skilled are you with your sword?

6. Aim at the Heart

Remembering the focus of chapter 4, we must aim at the heart. Sin is a heart matter, not just a problem of behavior. Stomping on the fruit of sin—the sinful behavior itself—won't kill the tree. Jesus repeatedly focuses our attention on the heart. As Jesus said, "The good person out of the good treasure of his heart produces good, and the evil person out of his evil treasure produces evil, for out of the abundance of the heart his mouth speaks" (Luke 6:45).

Consider also Jesus' stinging words in Matthew 23: "Woe to you, scribes and Pharisees, hypocrites! For you clean the outside of the cup and the plate, but inside they are full of greed and self-indulgence. You blind Pharisee! First clean the inside of the cup and the plate, that the outside also may be clean" (vv. 25–26). If we focus only on sinful behavior and not on the motives and desires that generate the behavior, we will become hypocrites and fail to grow in holiness.

7. Replace Sin with Grace

Repentance involves not just turning *from*, but turning *to*. As we saw in chapter 6, holiness demands both "putting off" and "putting on." We must not only *put off* sin, we must *put on* grace. The negative must be replaced with the positive.

Owen shows that this is "the great way of the mortification of sin":

This, therefore, is the first way whereby the Spirit of God mortifieth sin in us; and in a compliance with it, under his conduct, do we regularly carry on this work and duty,—that is, *we mortify sin by cherishing the principle of holiness and sanctification in our souls, labouring to increase and strengthen it by growing in grace, and by a constancy and frequency in acting of it in all duties, on all occasions, abounding in the fruits of it. Growing, thriving, and improving in universal holiness, is the great way of the mortification of sin.* The more vigorous the principle of holiness in us, the more weak, infirm, and dying will be that of sin. The more frequent and lively are the actings of grace, the feebler and seldomer will be the actings of sin. The more we abound in the "fruits of the Spirit," the less we shall be concerned in the "works of the flesh." And we do deceive ourselves if we think sin will be mortified on any other terms.[15]

So, an effective and practical way to apply this to the sins you are fighting, is to determine to kill each specific sin by cultivating the particular virtue which best counters it. Counter greed by cultivating contentment and generosity. Give more money away. Wage war on pride by practicing humility. Be quick to confess when you're wrong. Kill lust by loving others in selfless purity. When tempted to leer at someone of the opposite sex, turn your eyes and pray for them instead. Crucify self-centeredness by serving those around you. Volunteer to do the dishes or put up the laundry–even if it's not your turn!

In John Bunyan's allegorical *Holy War*, the members of Diabolus's horde who had subverted the rule of Emmanuel in the city of Mansoul are put on trial. Their names are Mr. Atheism, Mr. Hard-heart, Mr.

False-peace, Mr. No-truth, Mr. Pitiless, and Mr. Haughty. Bunyan, who clearly understood the counteracting effect of corresponding virtues, named some of the members of the jury: Mr. Belief, Mr. True-heart, Mr. Upright, Mr. See-truth, Mr. Good Work, and Mr. Humble. The only way truly to get rid of vice—and not just temporarily deflect it—is to displace it with virtue.[16]

What are your areas of greatest temptation? What are some specific things you can do, not merely to avoid committing those sins again, but to weaken sin's hold? How will you replace your sinful thought patterns and behaviors with those that are virtuous and Christlike?

8. Stay in Community

Battles are best fought by armies, not individuals. One of our strategies in putting sin to death must be to stay close to other Christians. "Two are better than one, because they have a good reward for their toil. For if they fall, one will lift up his fellow. But woe to him who is alone when he falls and has not another to lift him up!" (Eccl. 4:9–10).

Another passage presents an even sterner warning. "Take care, brothers, lest there be in any of you an evil, unbelieving heart, leading you to fall away from the living God. But exhort one another every day, as long as it is called 'today,' that none of you may be hardened by the deceitfulness of sin" (Heb. 3:12–13). The implications of this statement are staggering. The writer assumes that one means God uses to keep people from falling away from him is mutual, daily exhortation. Perseverance in the faith is a community project.

Believers need one another. *You* need fellow Christians. You can't do it alone. As Joshua Harris writes, "Lone Rangers are Dead Rangers."[17] So stay in community. Live out the "one another" commands in the context of your local church. Build strong friendships with believers who will encourage and pray for you. Learn to confess your faults to them (James 5:19). Let your brothers and sisters in Christ help you kill your sin.

9. Look to the Cross

Even more importantly, we must look to the cross. Without this all other strategies will ultimately fail. "There is no death of sin without the death of Christ"[18] said Owen. This cross-centered approach to killing sin is clear in Scripture. Before Paul speaks of putting to death the deeds of the body in Romans 8:13, he reminds us that:

> There is therefore now no condemnation for those who are in Christ Jesus. For the law of the Spirit of life has set you free in Christ Jesus from the law of sin and death. For God has done what the law, weakened by the flesh, could not do. By sending his own Son in the likeness of sinful flesh and for sin, he condemned sin in the flesh, in order that the righteous requirement of the law might be fulfilled in us, who walk not according to the flesh but according to the Spirit.
>
> —Romans 8:1–4

Let's trace the argument. The righteous requirement of the law can be fulfilled in us, only because we are in Christ Jesus, absolved from guilt and condemnation, and freed from the law of sin and death, through the sin-defeating death of God's Son.

Paul goes on in this passage to point out that, since we now live according to the Spirit, rather than the flesh, we have our minds set on the Spirit. The Spirit of God dwelling within us proves we belong to Christ and that our bodies will be resurrected like his. Therefore, we are not to live as debtors to the flesh. Instead we are to put to death the misdeeds of the body, by the power of God's Spirit (vv. 5–13).

A similar dynamic is at work in Colossians 3 and Romans 6. In Colossians 3, the apostle points us back to the fact that we have been raised with Christ, that we have died, that our life is hidden with Christ in God, and that when Christ appears, we will also appear with him in glory. Paul is reminding us of our union with Christ in the gospel realities of his death, burial, resurrection, and exaltation. Only then does he tell us to put sin to death (vv.1–5). And in Romans 6:9–13, as we saw in chapter 5, the power to say no to sin comes from Christ's decisive defeat of sin in his death.

Over and over again, when the Bible commands us to put sin to death, it does so in the context of Christ's victory over the very sins we battle. Because of the death and resurrection of Jesus, we fight from a position of victory. Therefore, as Owen reminds us:

Set your faith upon Christ for the killing of your sin. His blood is the great sovereign remedy for sin-sick souls ... By faith fill your heart with a right consideration of the provision that God has made in the work of Christ for the mortification of your sins.[19]

But the cross is also what progressively frees the affections of our hearts from the enticements of sin. Paul said, "But far be it from me to boast except in the cross of our Lord Jesus Christ, by which the world is crucified to me, and I to the world" (Gal. 6:14). Commenting on this verse, Owen writes:

Set your affections on the cross of Christ. This is eminently effective in frustrating the whole work of indwelling sin. The apostle gloried and rejoiced in the cross of Christ. His heart was set on it. It crucified the world to him, making it a dead and undesirable thing (Gal. 6:14). The baits and pleasures of sin are all things in the world, "the lust of the flesh, the lust of the eyes, and the pride of life." By these sin entices and entangles our souls. If the heart is filled with the cross of Christ, it casts death and undesirability on them all, leaving no seeming beauty, pleasure, or comeliness in them. Again, Paul says, "It crucifies me to the world and makes my heart, my affections, and my desires dead to all these things. It roots up corrupt losts and affections, and leaves no desire to go and make provision for the flesh to fulfill its lusts." Labour, therefore, to fill your hearts with the cross of Christ.[20]

10. Depend on the Spirit

Finally, as we look to the cross in our efforts to put sin to death, we must also remember that the power of the cross is only available to us through the Spirit of Christ. Remember Paul's words in both Romans 8 and Galatians 5: "For if you live according to the flesh you will die, but if *by the Spirit* you put to death the deeds of the body, you will live" (Rom. 8:13). "But I say, walk *by the Spirit*, and you will not gratify the desires of the flesh" (Gal. 5:16). While our constant effort is necessary and required, we clearly cannot defeat sin in our own strength. "Mortification from a self-strength, carried on by ways of self-invention, to the end of a self-righteousness, is the soul and substance of all false religion in the world."[21]

This is true because only the Spirit can truly convict the heart of the evil and danger of sin. "A man may easier see without eyes, speak without a tongue, than truly mortify one sin without the Spirit."[22] Only the Spirit can reveal to us the fullness of Christ and establish in our hearts the confident expectation of triumph through him.[23]

Life Out of Death

C. S. Lewis's *The Great Divorce* is a fantasy about a busload of shadowy, hellish ghosts who are given an excursion into the solid borderland of Heaven. Here, the tangible weight of God's glory is evident in every blade of grass, and fruit so heavy the ghosts can scarcely lift a single piece. Each phantom is given opportunity to stay in the borderland and develop the capacities for savoring the higher joys of Heaven. But one by one, they choose to return to the Gray City (Hell) rather than loose themselves of the passions, desires, and sins that enslave them.

All except for one, a wraith who is afflicted with lust, which is embodied as a red lizard that sits on his shoulder, whispering seductive lies. A strong, fiery angel offers to kill the lizard but the wraith produces every reason imaginable for allowing it to live. He fears the pain of the angel's blazing hand. He imagines that the destruction of his lust will be his personal undoing as well. Finally, he agrees to let the angel seize the lizard and break its neck. When the reptile is destroyed, the shadowy wraith suddenly becomes solid, while the dead lizard morphs into a vibrant stallion. With unbounded joy, the new man mounts his steed and rides into the heavenly country.[24]

This is a picture of what can happen when we are diligent in putting sin to death. The battle is not *against* our joy and happiness, but *for* our maximum pleasure, pleasure in God. The fight may be painful. It will involve giving up evil things that are presently dear to us. But when the battle is finished and the sin is mortified, God brings life—new, transforming, unexpectedly wonderful, joyful life—out of death. The old and tired is put off, the fresh and new is put on. God changes weakness into strength. He transforms our broken desires into something larger, more beautiful, and more powerful than we could ever have imagined. And in the power and goodness of those desires, God takes us places we didn't think we could go.

8

Growing in Grace

Vivification

Holiness is the healthy growth of morally misshapen humans toward
the moral image of Jesus Christ, the perfect man.

—J. I. Packer

As a boy, I liked the story of *Peter Pan*. I was familiar with the animated
Disney version from a young age, and enjoyed the book by J. M. Barrie.
Cut-throat pirates, wild Indians, the Lost Boys, Fairies, a flying ship,
the villainous Captain Hook—what's not to like? I even appreciated
Steven Spielberg's movie *Hook*. But as an adult I came to realize that
this tale about Neverland is not simply a fantasy. It's also a tragedy, the
story of a boy who refused to grow up.

In fact, the rejection of adult responsibility was an underlying theme
in Barrie's original stage play and novel, the opening line of which reads,
"All children, except one, grow up."[1] Today, psychologists recognize
the tragedy inherent in the story of Peter Pan, one made more acute

because Barrie was not quite right; there are other Peter Pans among us. Since the publication of *The Peter Pan Syndrome: Men Who Have Never Grown Up* by Dr. Dan Kiley in 1983, "Peter Pan syndrome" has become a pop-psychology label applied to socially immature adults. The phenomenon is not a rare one. Think of the forty-year-old male who is so obsessed with the playoffs or so energized about his videogame system that he neglects his wife and children. Variations on the Peter Pan tragedy happen every day.

Believers who do not mature spiritually are similarly tragic. "The child who acts as a man is a monstrosity; the man who acts as a child is a tragedy. If this is true in nature, how much more in Christian behaviour."[2] Healthy Christians grow up.

Growing Up

The previous chapter focused on putting sin to death, but as we saw there, mortification is not the same as spiritual growth. Scripture commands us not only to put off, but to put on. The Father not only prunes the branches that abide in the vine, he expects them to bear fruit (John 15:1–2, 16). Peter exhorts us to "put away all malice and all deceit and hypocrisy and envy and all slander" *and* "like newborn infants [to] long for the pure spiritual milk, that by it [we] may grow up to salvation." Later he urges believers to "grow in the grace and knowledge of our Lord and Savior Jesus Christ" (1 Peter 2:1–2; 2 Peter 3:18).

The goal of spiritual formation is not simply to refrain from sin! God intends so much more for you. His goal is to restore his image within you by making you more and more like Jesus. Spiritual growth involves the growth of grace in your soul as you mature in likeness to Christ. J. C. Ryle described the process well:

> When I speak of growth in grace I only mean increase in the degree, size, strength, vigour and power of the graces which the Holy Spirit plants in a believer's heart. I hold that every one of those graces admits of growth, progress, and increase. I hold that repentance, faith, hope, love, humility, zeal, courage and the like may be little or great, strong or weak, vigorous or feeble, and may vary greatly in the same man at different periods of his life. When I speak of a man growing in grace, I mean

simply this—that his sense of sin is becoming deeper, his faith stronger, his hope brighter, his love more extensive, his spiritual-mindedness more marked. He feels more of the power of godliness in his own heart. He manifests more of it in his life. He is going on from strength to strength, from faith to faith, and from grace to grace.[3]

The purpose of this chapter is to cultivate spiritual maturity by examining how we grow in grace, a process that theologians call "vivification."

Learning to Walk

Holly and I have three children, Stephen, Matthew, and Susannah. Each one of them has been slow in learning to walk. The children of many of our friends began walking at ten or twelve months, but not ours. Our three are quite verbal, however, picking up words and phrases quickly. Does this mean they will be better communicators than athletes? It wouldn't be a surprise—both Holly and I are sadly lacking in coordination! That's okay. Not everyone can be quick on their feet.

But what's okay in human development is not nearly so okay in the Christian life. Like my children, believers usually learn to "talk" before they can "walk." They pick up Christian lingo quickly. Even as new converts, Christians can often spout Bible verses, debate theology, and pray in Christianese. Learning to walk in obedience, however, is a slower process. And genuine spiritual growth is not measured in how well we talk, but in how faithfully we walk with Jesus.

The word *walk* is an important one in Scripture, for it stands "at the center of Paul's ethical thinking."[4] In Ephesians, Paul describes our behavior prior to salvation as *walking* in trespasses and sins (Eph. 2:1). A few verses later, he says we are created in Christ Jesus to *walk* in good works (Eph. 2:10). The last three chapters of Ephesians are structured around five uses of the word *walk*.

- We should *walk* in a manner worthy of God's call, by relating to one another with humility, gentleness, patience, forbearance, and love (4:1–2).

- We should "no longer *walk* as the Gentiles do, in the futility of their minds," since we have put off the old self and put on the new (4:17–24).

- We should be imitators of God and *walk* in love as Christ loved us (5:1–2).

- We should *walk* in light, since we are children of light, not darkness (5:8).

- We should look carefully how we *walk*, being wise, not unwise (5:15).

The metaphor of walking teaches us three important things about spiritual growth. It is a lifelong, active, imitation of Jesus.

Lifelong. First, *walk* underscores the lifelong nature of spiritual growth. This is a recurring emphasis in this book. Spiritual formation doesn't happen over a long weekend, but through the course of many months and years. The Christian life is not a hundred-yard dash, but the journey of a lifetime.

Active. Second, growing in grace requires our participation and effort. As Dallas Willard writes, "Grace is opposed to earning, but not to effort."[5] We are saved by grace, not meritorious works. But that doesn't mean we are passive in our transformation. Children must learn to walk as they develop and mature into healthy adults. So must we.

Imitation. Third, Jesus is the example we follow. We imitate Jesus by walking in love (Eph. 5:2; cf. Rom. 6:4; Col. 2:6; 1 John 2:6). His life is the pattern for ours. For a moment, think of a dance instead of a walk, a dance gracefully choreographed to music. You can only learn the moves by imitating the choreographer. Spiritual formation is similar. As new believers, we don't know the right moves. Even as we begin to learn them, we can't execute them smoothly. We're not sure on our feet yet. We don't really know how to dance. We need to continue imitating the one who knows the dance perfectly and can execute it without flaw. This is Jesus, who has perfectly choreographed the Christian life for us. As we imitate him and copy his steps, we learn to dance . . . to walk as he walked.

"Holiness is the healthy growth of morally misshapen humans toward the moral image of Jesus Christ, the perfect man," writes J. I. Packer.[6]

This again echoes the theme of this book: spiritual transformation is the restoration of the image of God within us as we increasingly become like Jesus.

The Pattern of Spiritual Transformation

How does God get us up on our feet and moving in the right direction? What are some of the basic elements we need to understand in order to walk more like Jesus? Two related passages of Scripture give us the answer.

> I appeal to you therefore, brothers, by the mercies of God, to present your bodies as a living sacrifice, holy and acceptable to God, which is your spiritual worship. Do not be conformed to this world, but be *transformed* by the renewal of your mind, that by testing you may discern what is the will of God, what is good and acceptable and perfect.
>
> —Romans 12:1–2

> And we all, with unveiled face, beholding the glory of the Lord, are being *transformed* into the same image from one degree of glory to another. For this comes from the Lord who is the Spirit
>
> —2 Corinthians 3:18

In these verses, Paul provides us with five essential elements which make up spiritual transformation: the goal, the motive, the cost, the process, and the power. Each element is important. We must have the right goal, if we're to know what we're striving for. We also need to be rightly motivated in our pursuit, while at the same time fully understanding and embracing the cost. An understanding of the process is also essential, if we're to fully cooperate with it. And, of course, we must be resourced with power, or we'll get nowhere.

The Goal: The Image of Christ

As we saw in chapter 1 and have repeatedly emphasized throughout this book, the goal of spiritual transformation is conformity to the character of Christ. We see this in 2 Corinthians 3:18: We "are being transformed into the same image from one degree of glory to another." This is God's eternal purpose. As Romans 8:29 says, God has "predestined us to be conformed to the image of his Son." He wants to make us more and more like Jesus in his spotless holiness, humble service, radiant joy, and self-giving love.

The Motive: The Mercies of God

Next, consider the motive, which Paul declares with the phrase, "the mercies of God." This again takes us back to the thrust of this book. All genuine spiritual transformation is driven by the gospel.

Sometimes Paul's letters are somewhat evenly divided between an exposition of the gospel and encouragement to his readers to live differently because of the gospel. But in the book of Romans, the first eleven chapters (out of sixteen) are almost entirely one great and glorious exposition of the gospel. Then we come to the first phrase of the first verse of chapter 12, which includes a "therefore" encompassing all that came previously. After eleven complete chapters explaining and extolling the glories of the gospel, how does Paul summarize it all in a single phrase? "Therefore, by the mercies of God."

Paul is saying that the gospel is ultimately about God's mercies[7] lavished on us in Christ, even when we were enemies to God (Rom. 5:10). God has justified us freely in Christ (Rom. 3:24), liberated us from sin's slavery (Rom. 6:6–7), and indwelt us by his Spirit (Rom. 8:9, 13–17). God did not even spare his own Son, but gave him up for us (Rom. 8:32). This level of mercy and grace, this stunning demonstration of unwavering commitment to those whom he loves, assures us that God will give us everything we need. What amazing mercy! Only the ravishing taste of such mercy and grace can change us.

The Cost: Present Your Bodies as Living Sacrifices

The only fitting response to this lavish mercy is a life devoted to worship. Paul says, "I appeal to you therefore, brothers, by the mercies of God, to present your bodies as a living sacrifice, holy and acceptable to God, which is your spiritual worship" (Rom.12:1). If we're captivated by the wonder of God's mercy, we will yield all we are in worshipful sacrifice to him.

The command to present our bodies to God vividly portrays unqualified surrender. Here, *present* means to yield or hand something over to another. Paul uses this word earlier in Romans when he commands us to yield ourselves, and the members of our bodies, to the Lord as instruments for righteousness (Rom. 6:13, 16, 19). Why does Paul emphasize the *body*? Because everything I do in seeking to walk as Christ walked involves my body. God doesn't have me unless he has my body.

To describe the nature of our bodily worship, Paul hijacks Old Testament language, terms like "sacrifice," "holy," and "acceptable to God." In the Old Testament, of course, these words referred to literal sacrificial animals, which were required to be healthy, spotless, and blemish-free. In a powerful, even shocking, adaptation of such language, Paul fills these words with new meaning. We no longer worship by killing animals. But in an equally extreme and decisive approach in our worship, we devote our own living, breathing bodies in active, unreserved service to God.

Everything we do in the body is meant to be worship: eating, sleeping, walking, driving, working, talking, cooking, singing, exercising, typing, making love—all of it. "So, whether you eat or drink, or whatever you do, do all to the glory of God" (1 Cor. 10:31). Spiritual transformation is not restricted to a religious compartment of life, while leaving the rest of what we do—the "secular"—untouched and unchanged. God wants all of us, soul and body, all the time. He intends to lift every aspect of our lives up into worship.[8] This requires, of course, complete and total surrender: nothing less than the full, unreserved abandonment of all our desires, prerogatives, ambitions, and personal rights. Such self-surrender is the only way to make real progress in the Christian life. If you hold on to some vestige of self-will, following Jesus will feel intolerably difficult—a moral and spiritual regimen that seems impossible to follow. But this gets right to the heart of one of the great differences between the demands of morality and the way of Jesus. As C. S. Lewis put it, "Christianity is both harder and easier."

> In fact, we are very like an honest man paying his taxes. He pays them all right, but he does hope that there will be enough left over for him to live on. Because we are still taking our natural self as the starting point.
>
> As long as we are thinking that way, one or other of two results is likely to follow. Either we give up trying to be good, or else we become very unhappy indeed. For, make no mistake: if you are really going to

try to meet all the demands made on the natural self, it will not have enough left over to live on. The more you obey your conscience, the more your conscience will demand of you. And your natural self, which is thus being starved and hampered and worried at every turn, will get angrier and angrier. In the end, you will either give up trying to be good, or else become one of those people who, as they say, "live for others" but always in a discontented, grumbling way—always wondering why the others do not notice it more and always making a martyr of yourself. And once you have become that you will be a far greater pest to anyone who has to live with you than you would have been if you had remained frankly selfish.

The Christian way is different: harder, and easier. Christ says "Give me All. I don't want so much of your time and so much of your money and so much of your work: I want You. I have not come to torment your natural self, but to kill it. No half-measures are any good. I don't want to cut off a branch here and a branch there, I want to have the whole tree down. I don't want to drill the tooth, or crown it, or stop it, but to have it out. Hand over the whole natural self, all the desires which you think innocent as well as the ones you think wicked—the whole outfit. I will give you a new self instead. In fact, I will give you Myself: my own will shall become yours."[9]

Do you see the difference? Morality demands that we be good, but Christ demands much more. He demands that we give him all. That makes Christianity seem really hard. And, in a way, it is. But it's also easy, because Christ also gives us a new self. He transforms us so that his will becomes ours. But devoting our whole selves to him, body and soul, in a life of surrendered worship, is the first step.

The Process: Renewing the Mind

Spiritual transformation is a process of inner renewal that involves the total reorientation of our minds and hearts. This is one of the key differences between true Christ-centered change and mere religion. God is interested in more than our external conformity to a set of rules. He wants to make us new on the inside. The change he desires goes much deeper than behavior. Our minds must be renewed.[10]

Deep, lasting change requires me to attend to how this present age impacts my thinking. As Paul says: "Do not be conformed to this world, but be transformed by the renewal of your mind" (Rom. 12:2). Rather than conforming to the mind-set of the fallen world around me, I must be renewed in the core of my being. The capacity to discern and embrace God's will for healthy, God-honoring humanity depends on the transformation of my thoughts and affections. God changes me not by manipulating my choices or forcing my will, but by restoring my heart and renovating my mind. The implications for spiritual formation are profound. J. I. Packer observes:

> Man was made to know good with his mind, to desire it, once he has come to know it, with his affections, and to cleave to it, once he has felt its attraction, with his will; the good in this case being God, his truth and his law. God accordingly moves us, not by direct action on the affections or will, but by addressing our mind with his word, and so bringing to bear on us the force of truth . . . Affection may be the helm of the ship, but the mind must steer; and the chart to steer by is God's revealed truth.[11]

This means we are *transformed* as our minds are *informed*. Since this is true, it is vital to saturate our minds with the truth of the gospel. Jesus said as much, when he prayed to his Father, "Sanctify them in the truth; your word is truth" (John 17:17). Only when the truth is renewing our minds, will we be transformed, and thus be equipped "by testing [to] discern what is the will of God, what is good and acceptable and perfect" (Rom. 12:2).

As believers, we long for a resource that will help us grow. We want to discern God's will and follow it. So we look to counselors, seminars, and books in our quest for the magic bullet, the secret of change, the key to victory. But the most important resource—the truth of the gospel—is at arm's reach. We only have to appropriate it in our lives. Spiritual growth is not about moving on from where we began—the gospel. It's about growing deeper in the gospel. Or, rather, getting the gospel deeper into us. As Richard Lovelace writes:

Growth in *faith* is the root of all spiritual growth and is prior to all disciplines of works. True spirituality is not a superhuman religiosity; it is simply true humanity released from bondage to sin and renewed by the Holy Spirit. This is given to us as we grasp by faith the full content of Christ's redemptive work: freedom from the guilt and power of sin, and newness of life through the indwelling and outpouring of his Spirit.[12]

The Power: The Spirit of the Lord

This can raise a reasonable question: Is the responsibility for growth left in my hands? If the gospel is what changes me and it's up to me to apply it, does this cast me back upon myself? Look again at what Paul says, this time in 2 Corinthians 3:18: "And we all, with unveiled face, beholding the glory of the Lord, are being *transformed* into the same image from one degree of glory to another. *For this comes from the Lord who is the Spirit.*" The agent of transformation is the Spirit of the Lord. The power comes from him.

This is the necessary balance to the previous point. Spiritual growth depends on saturating our minds with truth, but transformation is not merely a cognitive process. It is personal and supernatural. "Spiritual life is produced by the presence and empowering of the Holy Spirit, not simply by the comprehension of doctrinal propositions or strategies of renewal."[13]

So, does that mean there is nothing for us to do? Not at all. For Paul also commands us to "walk by the Spirit" (Gal. 5:16, 22), and "be filled with the Spirit" (Eph. 5:18).[14] There is, you see, a dynamic interplay between God's work and ours. The Spirit empowers all of our obedience, yet it is still our responsibility to "keep in step with the Spirit" (Gal. 5:25, NIV).

Once again, Paul's words help us:

> Therefore, my beloved, as you have always obeyed, so now, not only as in my presence but much more in my absence, work out your own salvation with fear and trembling, for it is God who works in you, both to will and to work for his good pleasure.
>
> —Philippians 2:12–13

This exhortation captures the interaction. We are given responsibility: "work out your own salvation" (v. 12). But we are *not* left on our own.

The command to work out our salvation is grounded in God's promise to work in us. This work of God is on two levels: our motivations and our actions.

To Will: Motivations. "For it is God who works in you, both *to will* and to work for his good pleasure" (v. 13). To "will" is to desire, determine, or resolve. The original word embraces both the affections and volitions of the human personality: God works on our desires and choices. John MacArthur suggests that God uses two things to work on our wills: holy discontent and holy aspirations.[15] He makes us dissatisfied with our sinfulness and inspires spiritual longings for something better. He changes the motivational structures of our hearts. J. I. Packer calls this "life supernaturalized at the motivational level,"[16] for any desire within us for true holiness has come from God, not ourselves.

To Work: Actions. "For it is God who works in you, both to will and *to work* for his good pleasure" (v. 13). To "work" means to operate, effect, or do. God gives us not only new desires but also the ability to carry them out. This is why Paul teaches us to pray that God would fulfill our "resolve for good and every work of faith by his power" (2 Thess. 1:11).

So, we have a responsibility. We must work out our own salvation. We must obey. We must put sin to death, fight the good fight of faith, grow in grace, and pursue holiness. Yet we can only obey God *as we are empowered by the grace of his Spirit.* "God's work in salvation, in Paul's view, never absorbs or invalidates man's work, but arouses and stimulates it and gives it meaning."[17] Consider several other passages that show this dynamic tension.

> But by the grace of God I am what I am, and his grace toward me was not in vain. On the contrary, I worked harder than any of them, though it was not I, but the grace of God that is with me.
>
> —1 Corinthians 15:10

> It is no longer I who live, but Christ who lives in me. And the life I now live in the flesh I live by faith in the Son of God, who loved me and gave himself for me.
>
> —Galatians 2:20

> Him we proclaim, warning everyone and teaching everyone with all
> wisdom, that we may present everyone mature in Christ. For this I toil,
> struggling with all his energy that he powerfully works within me.
> —Colossians 1:28–29

In each of these passages believers are active. Paul worked hard, lived by faith in Christ, proclaimed the gospel, and toiled for the maturity of others. Yet in each case, God and his grace played the decisive role. The Christian life is not either-or, but both-and. We work *and* God works. The two go together. God equips us with everything good that we may do his will, working in us what is pleasing in his sight through Jesus Christ (Heb. 13:21). This is why I use the word "dynamic" to describe how grace operates in our lives. Growth is not automatic. You and I *must* cooperate. But even our cooperation and effort is dependent on God's grace.[18]

Jonathan Edwards captured the biblical balance well:

> In efficacious grace we are not merely passive, nor yet does God do some,
> and we do the rest. But God does all, and we do all. God produces all,
> and we act all. For that is what he produces, *viz.* our own acts. God is
> the only proper author and fountain; we are the only proper actors. We
> are, in different respects, wholly passive, and wholly active.[19]

This is hope-giving, liberating, and energizing. Reflecting on the interplay between God's grace and my responsibility encourages me not to sit back in passivity. I have a role to play. But it also keeps me from despair, for my spiritual growth isn't ultimately dependent on my unaided efforts. God is committed to my growth in grace and is working in my heart.

Five Characteristics of Spiritual Growth

The mystery of the Christian life, then, is the mystery of how God's Spirit works in us and through us. His role is to regenerate us, cleanse us, renew us, fill us, transform us, and strengthen us.[20] Our role is to keep in step with him. "If we live by the Spirit, let us also walk by the Spirit" (Gal. 5:25). The following passage and its surrounding context provides a clear picture of what walking by the Spirit looks like and suggests several important insights about the nature of spiritual growth.

> For you were called to freedom, brothers. Only do not use your freedom as an opportunity for the flesh, but through love serve one another. For the whole law is fulfilled in one word: "You shall love your neighbor as yourself." But if you bite and devour one another, watch out that you are not consumed by one another. But I say, walk by the Spirit, and you will not gratify the desires of the flesh. For the desires of the flesh are against the Spirit, and the desires of the Spirit are against the flesh, for these are opposed to each other, to keep you from doing the things you want to do. But if you are led by the Spirit, you are not under the law. Now the works of the flesh are evident: sexual immorality, impurity, sensuality, idolatry, sorcery, enmity, strife, jealousy, fits of anger, rivalries, dissensions, divisions, envy, drunkenness, orgies, and things like these. I warn you, as I warned you before, that those who do such things will not inherit the kingdom of God. But the fruit of the Spirit is love, joy, peace, patience, kindness, goodness, faithfulness, gentleness, self-control; against such things there is no law. And those who belong to Christ Jesus have crucified the flesh with its passions and desires. If we live by the Spirit, let us also walk by the Spirit. Let us not become conceited, provoking one another, envying one another.
>
> —Galatians 5:13–26

My purpose isn't to give a detailed explanation of these two lists (the works of the flesh and the fruit of the Spirit), but to briefly discuss five characteristics of spiritual growth which emerge from a study of this passage.[21]

1. Spiritual Growth Is Relational

First, *spiritual growth always happens in a relational context.* Did you notice how this passage is framed with "one another" commands? Paul commands us to serve one another through love (v. 13) and warns us to not devour one another or become conceited, provoking and envying one another (vv. 15, 26). Many of the virtues he lists as fruit of the Spirit have a strong relational dimension—love, patience, kindness, goodness, and gentleness. "Spiritual growth is not something that is normally expected to take place in isolation from other believers."[22] So how are your relationships with others? Are you serving others in love? Do you demonstrate patience and gentleness to your spouse and children? Are you kind to strangers? Genuine transformation will always affect how we treat others.

2. Spiritual Growth Involves Conflict

On the other hand, we also learn that *spiritual growth involves conflict*. It never happens in ideal conditions. Expect a fierce contest between the Spirit and the flesh (Gal. 5:16–17). Conflict is normal in Christian experience. No one walks in the Spirit without waging warfare against unruly passions and desires (cf. 1 Peter 2:11). The flesh with its passions and desires must be nailed to the cross (v. 24). The Spirit leads us to put sin to death (Rom. 8:13–14). Though the mortification of sin isn't the same as positive growth in grace, we will never outgrow our need for it this side of glory.

3. Spiritual Growth Is Inside Out

Third, *spiritual growth happens from the inside out*. Spiritual growth is organic, not mechanical; fruit is grown, not built. The "fruit of the Spirit" (v. 22) is positioned in clear contrast to the "works of the flesh" (v. 19). Why doesn't Paul say "the *works* of the Spirit"? Why call it fruit? Because, like fruit, a character formed by the Spirit can only be grown from the inside out. It can't be legislated. As one commentary notes, the term "works,"

> already has definite overtones in this letter. It refers to what man can do, which, in the case of the works of the law (2:16; 3:2, 5, 10), has already been shown to be inadequate. The fruit of the Spirit, on the other hand, suggests that which is a natural product of the Spirit rather than of man, made possible by the living relationship between the Christian and God (cf. 2:20; John 15:1–17).[23]

Think of it like this: there's a huge difference between a Christmas tree and a living tree. You can hang artificial fruit on a Christmas tree, but that doesn't make it alive. But a living tree produces fruit by the slow process of photosynthesis, as chlorophyll uses sunlight to convert water and carbon dioxide into carbohydrates that supply nutrients to the plants. Bearing spiritual fruit is a similar process, dependent on the Spirit's work of applying the gospel to our hearts in order to transform our lives.

4. Spiritual Growth Is Symmetrical

A fourth observation: *spiritual growth is symmetrical.* The text doesn't say "fruits," but "fruit." The nine qualities, which follow, grow together. "The singular form stresses that these qualities are a unity, like a bunch of grapes instead of separate pieces of fruit, and also that they are all to be found in all Christians."[24] This implies that you can't discern genuine spiritual growth by the presence of only one or two positive character traits.

Following the first Great Awakening, Jonathan Edwards considered this principle an essential test in judging the reality of one's personal experiences:

> In the truly holy affections of the saints is found that proportion which is the natural consequence of the universality of their sanctification. They have the whole image of Christ upon them: they have "put off the old man, and have put on the new man" entire in all his parts and members. "It has pleased the Father that in Christ all fullness should dwell": there is in him every grace; he is full of grace and truth: and they that are Christ's, do of his fullness receive, and grace for grace (John 1:14, 16); i.e. there is every grace in them, which is in Christ: "grace for grace"; that is, grace answerable to grace: there is no grace in Christ, but there is its image in believers to answer it: the image is a true image; and there is something of the same beautiful proportion in the image, which is in the original; there is feature for feature, and member for member. There is symmetry and beauty in God's workmanship.[25]

If this is true then, as Tim Keller says, "you are really only as spiritually mature as your weakest trait."[26] This should give us pause and provoke serious self-examination. Perhaps you claim spiritual health because you are gentle with other people; but is this gentleness balanced with the courage to be faithful in lovingly confronting sin (Gal. 6:1–2)?

Maybe you are unusually self-disciplined. But are you patient and kind to others? Is your discipline rigid and stoic or vibrant with the Spirit's joy? On the other hand, you may be a very happy person. But if you have no patience in adversity, perhaps your "joy" results from a sanguine personality, rather than the Spirit's work. When transformation is real, God goes to work on all the defects in our character, leading us to put all sin to death. Our imitation of Christ will not be perfect, but neither will we pick and choose in our obedience. Genuine spiritual growth is balanced, symmetrical growth.

I don't know about you, but this causes me to realize how far I have to go. Measured by this standard, I'm still a toddler in my walk with Christ—much like a child taking small steps on wobbly legs, only to fall on his backside again and again. While I want to be like Jesus, I still have so far to go.

5. Spiritual Growth Is Supernatural

But you and I shouldn't despair, because the final principle takes us back to the work of the Spirit once more and gives us hope: *spiritual growth is supernatural.* As Packer writes, "holy habits, though formed . . . by self-discipline and effort, are not natural products. The discipline and effort must be blessed by the Holy Spirit, or they would achieve nothing."[27]

I have a casual appreciation for classical music and a particular admiration for Beethoven's Ninth Symphony. Every time I listen to it, I am moved by its magnificent beauty. I admire Beethoven's talent. But to suggest that I could compose a symphony just as majestic is ridiculous. Admiration is one thing; imitation is another. Sometimes we feel the same way about following Jesus. We admire the perfection of his holy humanity—but imitate him? This seems out of reach. But what if someone discovered a way of replicating Beethoven's genius in me? What if I could have Beethoven himself composing and conducting music through my hands? Then I *could* write a symphony!

This is the role the Spirit plays in our lives! He lives inside of us as the "Spirit of Christ" (Rom. 8:9). Jesus lived the exemplary Spirit-filled life. As we saw in chapter 6, he is the example of "fully realized human holiness."[28] His character is precisely what God aims to produce in us. The Lord Jesus is our pattern. And his Spirit, sent into our hearts, is the agent who works from the inside out to reproduce this pattern in our lives.[29] We will not grow if we are left to ourselves. We must depend on the Spirit. Since this is true, let us heed the counsel of Richard Lovelace:

> We should make a deliberate effort at the outset of every day to recognize the person of the Holy Spirit, to move into the light concerning his presence in our consciousness and to open up our minds and to share all our thoughts and plans as we gaze by faith into the face of God. We should continue to walk throughout the day in a relationship of communication and communion with the Spirit mediated through our knowledge of the Word, relying upon every office of the Holy Spirit's role as counselor mentioned in Scripture. We should acknowledge him as the illuminator of truth and of the glory of Christ. We should look to him as teacher, guide, sanctifier, giver of assurance concerning our sonship and standing before God, helper in prayer, and as the one who directs and empowers witness.[30]

Everything depends on the Spirit.

Growing Down

Are you discouraged as you consider your present level of spiritual maturity? Are you stumbling in your walk with Jesus? Are you in greater need now than when you began this book? As painful as it may be, this awareness is actually a sign of health. G. C. Berkouwer rightly observed that "the life of sanctification proceeds in weakness, temptation, and exposure to the powers of darkness."[31] This is normal spiritual growth.

C. S. Lewis once wrote that "when a man is getting better, he understands more and more clearly the evil that is still left in him." Surely this is why Paul, near the end of his life, confessed himself the foremost of sinners (1 Tim. 1:15). However, as Lewis went on to say, "When a man is getting worse, he understands his own badness less and less. A moderately bad man knows he is not very good; a thoroughly bad man thinks he is alright."[32] Knowing you are not all right is a good indication that you are on the road to recovery. Spiritual maturity leads us to greater humility. The process of growing up turns out to be a process of growing down.

John Newton, author of the well-loved hymn "Amazing Grace," discovered this as well. In lyrics that echo the story of Jonah, Newton wrote:

> *I asked the Lord that I might grow*
> *In faith, and love, and every grace,*
> *Might more of his salvation know,*
> *And seek more earnestly his face.*
>
> *I hoped that in some favoured hour*
> *At once He'd answer my request,*
> *And by His love's constraining power*
> *Subdue my sins, and give me rest.*
>
> *Instead of this, He made me feel*
> *The hidden evils of my heart;*
> *And let the angry powers of hell*
> *Assault my soul in every part.*
>
> *Yea more, with His own hand*
> *He seemed intent to aggravate my woe;*
> *Crossed all the fair designs I schemed,*
> *Blasted my gourds, and laid me low.*
>
> *"Lord why is this," I trembling cried,*
> *"Wilt thou pursue thy worm to death?"*
> *"'Tis in this way," the Lord replied,*
> *"I answer prayer for grace and faith."*
>
> *"These inward trials I employ,*
> *From self and pride to set thee free*
> *And break thy schemes of earthly joy,*
> *That thou may'st find thy all in Me."*[33]

If the pace of your growth in Christ is slower than you would like, don't be too discouraged. Let your sense of need drive you to his feet. Seeing your need to grow up is the first step to actually doing so.

The Quest for Joy

Motivation

> The power of sin's promise is broken by the power of God's. All that God promises to be for us in Jesus stands over against what sin promises to be for us without him.
>
> —John Piper

How good is your grip on the doctrine of sin? If you've made it this far in the book, you probably recognize and accept that you are a sinner. You acknowledge, along with Paul, that despite your underlying desire to be holy you still want some things you should not want, think some things you should not think, like some things you should not like, say some things you should not say, and do some things you should not do. All this sinful thinking and acting is bound up with your desire for some kind of satisfaction, some taste of happiness. Me, too. You and I sin because we believe it will make us happier, even if only for a moment.

You could then easily conclude that there must be something wrong with happiness. You might even think that wanting to be happy, or seeking satisfaction for yourself, are suspicious, questionable activities—flirtations with the unholy, self-indulgence run amok. How can you have a heart that races after joy without also racing after sin? Holiness, after all, requires self-denial, doesn't it?

Yes, it does. But consider this. Have you ever heard a well-intentioned Christian leader say, "God is more concerned with your holiness than your happiness"? In a sense, this is true. God certainly places a high premium on holiness. But the problem lies in what this statement implies. The balanced, biblical reality is that the pursuit of holiness and the quest for joy are not at odds. The two goals are really one.

The Holy Pursuit of Joy

So, everyone longs for happiness. And believers in Jesus thirst for holiness. But holiness and happiness are not mutually exclusive. God is not a cosmic killjoy who is indifferent to the joy of his children! To suggest that God doesn't want us to be happy rips the heart out of biblical commands such as "Delight yourself in the LORD, and he will give you the desires of your heart" (Ps. 37:4) and "Make a joyful noise to the LORD, all the earth! Serve the LORD with gladness! Come into his presence with singing!" (Ps. 100:1–2).

God is concerned with both our holiness and our joy. On one hand, God knows we can never find true and lasting happiness apart from holiness, because holiness is the pure oxygen that happiness breathes. Without holiness, joy suffocates, withers, and dies. Sin kills joy. But when we cherish righteousness and detest sin, joy will flourish and grow. As Scripture says of Jesus, "You have loved righteousness and hated wickedness; therefore God, your God, has anointed you with the oil of gladness beyond your companions" (Heb. 1:9). In the words of Thomas Brooks, an English pastor in the seventeenth century, "Holiness differs nothing from happiness but in name. Holiness is happiness in the bud, and happiness is holiness at the full. Happiness is nothing but the quintessence of holiness."[1]

On the other hand, the quest for joy is one of the primary motivations for pursuing holiness. Over and over, Scripture appeals to our desire for joy and satisfaction by promising blessing for those who seek Christ. And Scripture repeatedly warns that misery will come to those who refuse Christ and choose sin instead. Seeking satisfaction outside of a relationship with God simply won't work. As C. S. Lewis wrote:

> God made us: invented us as a man invents a machine. A car is made to run on petrol, and it would not run properly on anything else. Now God designed the human race to run on Himself. He Himself is the fuel our spirits were designed to burn, or the food our spirits were designed to feed on. There is no other. That is why it is just no good asking God to make us happy in our own way without bothering about religion. God cannot give us happiness and peace apart from Himself, because it is not there. There is no such thing.[2]

Only as we seek our satisfaction in God will we begin to break free from the gravitational pull of sin's lower pleasures. In the words of Matthew Henry, "The joy of the Lord will arm us against the assaults of our spiritual enemies and put our mouths out of taste for those pleasures with which the tempter baits his hooks."[3]

My Journey into Joy

Discovering the power of joy in Christ has been a life-changing journey for me. There have been several crucial steps along the way.

The seeds of this discovery are in my journals from 1995. An entry on Psalms 23 and 34, recorded on May 28, 1995 says: "The Lord is my shepherd, I shall not want (23:1)—O fear the Lord ye His saints; for there is no want to them that fear him . . . they that seek the Lord shall not want any good thing (34:9–10). How often do I come back to these verses—their essence is contentment. Satisfaction. No wants . . . I'm not there."

That summer, I began to unearth little nuggets of joy in the old hymns I had grown up singing, but never really understood. I remember being struck with these lyrics:

> *Jesus is all I wish or want,*
> *for Him I pray, I thirst, I pant;*
> *Let others after earth aspire,*
> *Christ is the treasure I desire.*

> *Possessed of Him, I ask no more;*
> *He is an all sufficient store;*
> *To praise Him all my powers conspire–*
> *Christ is the treasure I desire.*[4]

One of John Newton's lesser-known hymns also became very meaningful to me. One verse says,

> *Content with beholding His face,*
> *My all to His pleasure resigned,*
> *No changes of season or place*
> *Would make any change in my mind:*
> *While blessed with a sense of His love,*
> *A palace a toy would appear;*
> *All prisons would palaces prove,*
> *If Jesus would dwell with me there.*[5]

These hymns were pointing me to pleasure that was qualitatively different from the short-lived satisfaction I found in other things. This was a happiness that transcended my circumstances. But I was caught on the horns of a dilemma: while I wanted to be happy and sometimes glimpsed the joy of knowing God, another part of me thought that the more spiritual I became, the less dependent I should be on emotionally fulfilling experiences of God. An unhealthy asceticism was lurking in my theology.

The Meditations of a Christian Hedonist

Then I discovered John Piper's book *Desiring God: The Meditations of a Christian Hedonist.* The title aroused my interest, but I was unprepared for the radical vision of the Christian life I would find in its pages. "Christian hedonism," explains Piper, "is a philosophy of life built on the following five convictions:

1. The longing to be happy is a universal human experience, and it is good, not sinful.
2. We should never try to deny or resist our longing to be happy, as though it were a bad impulse. Instead, we should seek to intensify

this longing and nourish it with whatever will provide the deepest and most enduring satisfaction.

3. The deepest and most enduring happiness is found only in God. Not from God, but in God.

4. The happiness we find in God reaches its consummation when it is shared with others in the manifold ways of love.

5. The extent that we try to abandon the pursuit of our own pleasure, we fail to honor God and love people. Or, to put it positively: The pursuit of pleasure is a necessary part of all worship and virtue. That is:

> The chief end of man is to glorify God by
> enjoying Him forever.[6]

Piper summarizes these convictions in the single sentence, "God is most glorified in me, when I am most satisfied in Him."[7] When I began to understand this, everything came into focus. I finally learned not only that satisfaction *can* be found in God, but that I am *commanded* to be satisfied in God and should make that satisfaction my lifelong pursuit. My biggest problem, therefore, is not that I desire happiness, when I should be doing my duty.[8] My biggest problem is that I am willing to settle for "the two-bit, low-yield, short-term, never-satisfying, person-destroying, God-belittling pleasures of the world,"[9] *instead* of infinite joy in Christ! But a refusal to settle for anything inferior to the joy of Christ, is what glorifies God.

> God's quest to be glorified and our quest to be satisfied reach their goal in this one experience: our delight in God, which overflows in praise. For God, praise is the sweet echo of His own excellence in the hearts of His people. For us, praise is the summit of satisfaction that comes from living in fellowship with God.
>
> The stunning implication of this discovery is that all the omnipotent energy that drives the heart of God to pursue His own glory also drives Him to satisfy the hearts of those who seek their joy in Him.[10]

My world was changing.

God Is Enough to Satisfy God!

Piper's books pushed me towards the Puritans. One of the first books I read was Thomas Brooks's short exposition of Lamentations 3:24, "'The Lord is my portion,' says my soul, 'therefore I will hope in him.'" The title is *An Ark for All God's Noahs In a Gloomy Stormy Day or The Best Wine Reserved Till Last or The Transcendent Excellency of a Believer's Portion Above All Earthly Portions Whatsoever.* (We may joke about the length of Puritan book titles, but perhaps their verbosity reflected overflowing passion for God and a deep appreciation of Scripture.) The book shows that God is a better portion—a better inheritance—than any pleasure or possession we could ever find outside of Christ. Brooks showed that God is:

Present

Immense

All-sufficient

Absolute, needful, and necessary

Pure and universal

Glorious, happy, and blessed

Peculiar

Universal

Safe and secure

Suitable

Incomprehensible

Inexhaustible

Soul-satisfying

Permanent, indefinite, never-failing, everlasting

An Incomparable Portion![11]

From Brooks I saw not only that I *should* be satisfied in God, but that I *could* be! One paragraph struck my mind like lightning and thundered in my heart with joy:

Certainly, if there be enough in God to satisfy the spirits of just men made perfect, whose capacities are far greater than ours; and if there be enough in God to satisfy the angels, whose capacities are far above theirs; if there be enough in God to satisfy Jesus Christ, whose capacity is unconceivable and unexpressable; yea, if there be enough in God to satisfy himself, then certainly there must needs be in God enough to satisfy the souls of his people. If all fullness, and all goodness, and infiniteness will satisfy the soul, then God will. There is nothing beyond God imaginable; and therefore the soul that enjoys him, cannot but be satisfied with him. God is a portion beyond all imagination, all expectation, all apprehension, and all comparison; and therefore he that hath him cannot but sit down and say, I have enough.[12]

Reading Lewis, Piper and Brooks helped me start paying attention to biblical words like "portion" and "blessed" and "joy." I began to see these words for what they really are—powerful descriptions of the pleasures found in knowing God through Jesus Christ. And I discovered that this kind of joy in God, when steadily cultivated and ardently pursued, is powerful enough to bring increasing freedom from the competing but destructive pleasures of sin.

Christian Motivation

Perhaps you have lingering reservations about the desire for happiness being an appropriate motive for pursuing holiness. It's one thing to appeal to C. S. Lewis, John Piper, or the Puritans. But what does Scripture say?

Consider the teaching of Jesus. He called his disciples to a standard of righteousness far beyond that of the Pharisees, the religious elite of the day (Matt. 5:20). Yet his appeals to holy living were laced with promises of blessedness and satisfaction. The beatitudes (Matt. 5:3–11) are promises of blessing given to the true citizens of the kingdom. Nine times Jesus says, "Blessed (Greek, *makarios,* happy) are . . . " The characteristics which follow (poverty of spirit, mourning, meekness, hunger and thirst for righteousness, mercy, purity of heart, peacemaking, and being persecuted) remind us that Jesus *doesn't* promise temporal prosperity or comfort. But the promises of present joy ("Blessed *are*" . . . "for theirs *is* the kingdom of heaven") and future reward ("for they *shall be* comforted . . . inherit the earth . . . be satisfied . . . receive mercy . . . be called the sons of God," etc.) remind us that true riches belong to those who live under his saving reign.

In Matthew 6, Jesus teaches us about genuine piety. Again, he appeals to our desire for God's blessing. We are to give to the needy (Matt. 6:2–4), pray (vv. 5–15) and fast (vv. 16–18) not for the praise of men, but trusting the promise that "the Father who sees in secret will reward" us (vv. 4, 6, 18). In verses 19–20, Jesus teaches us to lay up treasures in heaven and not on earth, because treasures on earth do not last (moth and rust destroy and thieves break in and steal), but treasures in heaven do. Choose the lasting treasure!

Reflect also on these parables Jesus told about the kingdom:

> "The kingdom of heaven is like treasure hidden in a field, which a man found and covered up. Then in his joy he goes and sells all that he has and buys that field.
>
> "Again, the kingdom of heaven is like a merchant in search of fine pearls, who, on finding one pearl of great value, went and sold all that he had and bought it."
>
> —Matthew 13:44–46

When we think of these parables, we often (and appropriately) emphasize the *cost* of the kingdom. We must sell all to get the treasure in the field. But notice the rest of what Jesus says: the man in the first parable sold everything to buy the field with the hidden *treasure* because of his *joy!* He didn't feel he was sacrificing to purchase this field. Because it held treasure, the field was a bargain—having value well beyond the price paid. Similarly, because the pearl had *great value,* the merchant sold everything to buy it. Yet we sometimes think of following Christ, seeking the kingdom, and pursuing holiness only in terms of the cost. We forget the *treasure.* And in so doing, we emasculate discipleship of joy.

Self-denial and Satisfaction

But what about the call to deny ourselves and take up the cross? Bearing the cross doesn't sound like pleasure! What about "the cost of discipleship"? What about Dietrich Bonhoeffer: "When Christ calls a man, he bids him come and die"?[13]

Yes, there is a cost to following Jesus. I agree with Bonhoeffer's words. But that isn't everything he said. In *The Cost of Discipleship*, he also wrote, "The yoke and the burden of Christ are his cross. To go one's way under the sign of the cross is not misery and desperation, but peace and refreshment for the soul, it is the highest joy."[14] Peace, refreshment for the soul, the highest joy. This is what we gain when we embrace the cost of following Jesus.

More importantly, this also reflects the teaching of Jesus. This is what we learn from our Lord:

- We should go through the narrow gate and travel the hard way because we desire *life* (Matt. 7:13–14).
- We should take Christ's easy yoke and light burden in order to find *rest for our souls* (Matt. 11:28–30). As Augustine famously prayed, "You made us for yourself, and our hearts find no peace till they rest in you."[15]
- Those who leave all for Christ receive *eternal life* (Matt. 19:29–34).
- The call to discipleship is rooted in the desire to *save* or *find your life* (Matt. 16:24–26).

Jesus repeatedly motivates us with promises of reward, rest, life, and salvation. "If anyone would come after me, let him deny himself and take up his cross and follow me. For whoever would save his life will lose it, but whoever loses his life for my sake will find it" (Matt. 16:24–25). Jesus is saying to his disciples: "Don't throw your life away. Don't waste it! Save it! Keep it! Find it!" But how are they to do that? By losing it. This is what missionary and martyr Jim Elliot meant when he said, "He is no fool who gives what he cannot keep to gain what he cannot lose."[16]

Christians too often blunder in reading these texts. We move the exclamation point away from motivation to duty. We so emphasize poverty of spirit, mourning, meekness, hunger, being merciful, purity, the call to be peacemakers, and suffering persecution, that we lose sight of the promises of happiness, joy, and satisfaction.

The transforming truth I learned from John Piper, and ultimately from Scripture, is that my biggest problem is *not* that I desire to be happy when I ought to be more concerned about doing my duty. This is not Jesus' diagnosis of human need. My biggest problem is my blindness to the source of true joy. I need opened eyes and a renewed heart so that I will desire what is truly satisfying!

In one of the most life-changing paragraphs I have ever read, C. S. Lewis said:

> The New Testament has lots to say about self-denial, but not about self-denial as an end in itself. We are told to deny ourselves and to take up our crosses in order that we may follow Christ; and nearly every description of what we shall ultimately find if we do contains an appeal to desire. If there lurks in most modern minds the notion that to desire our own good and earnestly to hope for the enjoyment of it is a bad thing, I submit that this notion has crept in from Kant and the Stoics and is no part of the Christian faith. Indeed, if we consider the unblushing promises of reward and the staggering nature of the rewards promised in the Gospels, it would seem that Our Lord finds our desires not too strong, but too weak. We are half-hearted creatures, fooling about with drink and sex and ambition when infinite joy is offered us, like an ignorant child who wants to go on making mud pies in a slum because he cannot imagine what is meant by the offer of a holiday at the sea. We are far too easily pleased![17]

The greatest hindrance to our deep transformation and spiritual growth is the smallness of our desire. We trifle with the "mud pies" of lust and greed, when we could enjoy a "holiday at the sea" or, to use biblical language, "pleasures at God's right hand forevermore" (Ps. 16:11). We are content to play with Monopoly money when we could have eternal treasure. We desperately try to drink from broken cisterns, while neglecting the Fountain of Living Waters (Jer. 2:11–13).

Divine Promises, Fleeting Pleasures, Expulsive Power

So, the motivation for pursuing holiness is the desire for deep and lasting happiness *in God*.[18] Genuine transformation is empowered by the promise of "solid joys and lasting pleasures that none but Zion's children know."[19] That is why God has filled his Word with promises. As Peter writes, God has "granted to us his precious and very great promises, so that through them [we] may become partakers of the divine nature" (2 Peter 1:4). Or consider these words from Paul:

> Since we have these promises, beloved, let us cleanse ourselves from every defilement of body and spirit, bringing holiness to completion in the fear of God.
>
> —2 Corinthians 7:1

This is a command to pursue holiness; but notice the motivation preceding the command: "since we have these promises." What promises? Go back a few verses. In 2 Corinthians 6:14–15, the apostle urges the Corinthians to pursue the purity of their worship and fellowship by resisting any compromise with idolatry. "Do not be unequally yoked with unbelievers," he says (v. 14). Then he recalls the Old Testament to remind the Corinthians of their incredible privileges as God's special people.

> What agreement has the temple of God with idols? For we are the temple of the living God; as God said, "I will make my dwelling among them and walk among them, and I will be their God, and they shall be my people. Therefore go out from their midst, and be separate from them, says the Lord, and touch no unclean thing; then I will welcome you, and I will be a father to you, and you shall be sons and daughters to me, says the Lord Almighty."
>
> —2 Corinthians 6:16–18

These are the great promises of the new covenant. We are God's temple, God's dwelling place, God's family. He is our God and Father who dwells among us. These three new covenant promises embrace the wealth of all God has promised to be and do for us in Christ. His presence, his provision, his protection—all of it is right here.

How to Turn Away from Fleeting Pleasures

One of the most compelling biblical examples of how faith in God's promises empowers holiness is found in the story of Moses as told in Hebrews 11.

> By faith Moses, when he was grown up, refused to be called the son of
> Pharaoh's daughter choosing rather to be mistreated with the people
> of God than to enjoy the fleeting pleasures of sin. He considered the
> reproach of Christ greater wealth than the treasures of Egypt, for he
> was looking to the reward.
>
> —Hebrews 11:24–26

The writer to the Hebrews presents Moses as an example of faith.
Faith is characterized by the conviction that God will reward those
who seek him. "And without faith it is impossible to please him, for
whoever would draw near to God must believe that he exists and that
he rewards those who seek him" (Heb. 11:6). It is *impossible* to please
God if you seek him out of any other motive than the desire for reward.
We do not seek God as his benefactors, thinking we can reward him.
We are always the beneficiaries of his grace.

Notice the decisions and actions Moses' faith produced. We see him
both refusing and choosing. By faith Moses "refused to be called the
son of Pharaoh's daughter." Imagine the implications of this! Moses
had been raised in the household of Pharaoh. He was "instructed in
all the wisdom of the Egyptians, and he was mighty in his words and
deeds" (Acts 7:22). He was a prince in Egypt, possibly a high-ranking
government official. As part of the royal family, he had luxury at his
fingertips: the choicest food, the richest accommodations, the most
beautiful women. And he turned his back on all of it. He "refused to be
called the son of Pharaoh's daughter *choosing* rather to be mistreated
with the people of God than to enjoy the fleeting pleasures of sin"
(vv. 24–25).

How could he do this? Why did he consider "the reproach of Christ
greater wealth than the treasures of Egypt"? Verse 26 answers: *"For he
was looking to the reward."* Moses was empowered by the promise of a
superior satisfaction. "By faith he left Egypt, not being afraid of the anger
of the king, *for he endured as seeing him who is invisible*" (v. 27). He was
captivated by a greater beauty, a more enduring treasure, a more satisfying
pleasure than Egypt could offer. To quote John Piper once more:

> Faith is not content with "fleeting pleasures." It is ravenous for joy.
> And the Word of God says, "In Thy presence is fullness of joy; in Thy

right hand there are pleasures forever" (Ps. 16:11). So faith will not be sidetracked into sin. It will not give up so easily in its quest for maximum joy.[20]

That is faith: Believing that God, and all he promises to be for us in the gospel, is more satisfying than sin. Faith is the powerful conviction that joy in Jesus is so superior to the fleeting pleasures of sin that I am compelled to choose the eternal over the temporal and the Savior over sin, even if I suffer.

"The Expulsive Power of a New Affection"

In a sermon famously titled, "The Expulsive Power of a New Affection," Thomas Chalmers said:

> There are two ways in which a practical moralist may attempt to displace from the human heart its love of the world—either by a demonstration of the world's vanity, so that the heart shall be prevailed upon simply to withdraw its regards from an object that is not worthy of it; or, by setting forth another object, even God, as more worthy of its attachment, so that the heart shall be prevailed upon not to resign an old affection, which shall have nothing to succeed it, but to exchange an old affection for a new one . . . the only way to dispossess [the heart] of an old affection is by the expulsive power of a new one.[21]

To put it simply, there are two ways to convince someone to stop eating Big Macs. You can either show him the documentary *Supersize Me!* in an attempt to show the detrimental effect of fast food on one's health, or you can give him a high quality *filet mignon,* sizzling hot, fresh off the grill. Both methods are appropriate, but it is much easier to give up fast food when there is a more appetizing alternative. As Milton Vincent writes:

> On the most basic of levels, I desire fullness, and fleshly lusts seduce me by attaching themselves to this basic desire. They exploit the empty spaces in me, and they promise that fullness will be mine if I give in to their demands. When my soul sits empty and is aching for something to fill it, such deceptive promises are extremely difficult to resist.

Consequently, the key to mortifying fleshly lusts is to eliminate the emptiness within me and replace it with fullness; and I accomplish this by feasting on the gospel . . . As I perpetually feast on Christ and all of His blessings found in the gospel, I find that my hunger for sin diminishes and the lies of lust simply lose their appeal. Hence, to the degree that I am full, I am free.[22]

Fighting Sin with the Promises of God

So, the desire for happiness is the motivation for pursuing holiness. God's promises of satisfaction in Christ appeal to this motive over and again. But this doesn't imply that you can somehow become immune to temptation or completely freed from the battle against sin. No, understanding the motivation for holiness *relocates the battle*. It reminds us that the lifelong battle for holiness is a battle for our affections fought on the terrain of our hearts. Holiness is not just the *quest* for joy; it is the *fight* for joy.

How, then, does this work on a practical level? How do God's promises help us in the actual battle against specific sins? Let's see how God's promises—what John Piper calls "future grace"—empower us for battle against three common sins.[23]

Greed

How do God's promises effectively combat the seductive power of greed? The Psalmist fought covetousness by praying that God would turn his heart toward the Word. "Incline my heart to your testimonies, and not to selfish gain!" (Ps. 119:36). Notice that this is a battle for right desires and inclinations, fought on the battleground of the heart.

Consider Jesus' words and notice how he points us to the promise of God's pleasure in giving us the kingdom.

"Fear not, little flock, for it is your Father's good pleasure to give you the kingdom. Sell your possessions, and give to the needy. Provide yourselves with moneybags that do not grow old, with a treasure in the heavens that does not fail, where no thief approaches and no moth destroys. For where your treasure is, there will your heart be also."

—Luke 12:32–34

Similarly, the writer to the Hebrews countered covetousness with the wonderful promise of our Lord's presence: "Keep your life free from the love of money, and be content with what you have, for he has said, 'I will never leave you nor forsake you'" (Heb. 13:5). We can be free from love of money and content with what we have because the Lord promises his abiding presence. The presence and faithfulness of Christ is more satisfying than money!

In contrast, ponder the sad life of Guy De Maupassant, the nineteenth-century French author and father of the modern short story. De Maupassant was famous and affluent. His stories were widely read and he lived on an extravagant yacht. Having rejected religion as a young man however (he purposely got himself expelled from seminary), he became increasingly fearful of death. He also suffered from syphilis— a sexually transmitted disease which, left untreated, can unravel the mind. By age forty-one, De Maupassant was considered insane. He died two years later. In spite of his wealth and success, his own words became his epitaph: "I have coveted everything and taken pleasure in nothing."[24]

Anxiety

What about anxiety? Can the promises of God help us trudge out from the boggy mire of fretful thoughts, everyday anxiety, and compulsive worry? Jesus thought so, for three times in Matthew 6 he commands his disciples to not be anxious (vv. 25, 31, 34). But he not only forbids worry, he supplies us with ammunition for fighting the battle. He reminds us that our heavenly Father who feeds the birds and clothes the fields also cares for us (vv. 26–30). Indeed, God knows our needs before we even ask (v. 32, cf. v. 8). And he promises to meet our earthly needs, if we seek the kingdom of God and his righteousness first (v. 33).

In Philippians 4, we are again urged to struggle against anxiety through the cultivation of thankful prayer, with the promise that "the peace of God, which surpasses all understanding, will guard [our] hearts and [our] minds in Christ Jesus" (Phil. 4:6–7).

Several months ago, as I was preparing to preach on this passage, I thought it would be helpful to read what someone who did not live in my century said about it. It's one thing for me or some twenty-first-century pastor or scholar to comment, "Don't be anxious about anything—just pray." But I wanted to read what someone who really suffered had to say. So, remembering that John Calvin was a man who suffered much, I pulled out his commentary on Philippians. Calvin had an almost intolerable work load, usually preaching or lecturing more than thirty times a month, in addition to his other pastoral duties. He was married to a chronically ill wife whom he outlived by fifteen years. They had three children, all of whom died at birth or in infancy. And he suffered ongoing persecution throughout most of his adult life. And here are Calvin's words:

> In these words he exhorts the Philippians . . . to cast all their care upon the Lord. For we are not made of iron, so as to be unshaken by temptations. But our consolation, our relief, is to . . . unload into the bosom of God everything that harasses us.[25]

Consolation and relief are found as we unload our anxieties on God.

Lust

How do the promises of God work against lust? Consider again the word of Jesus: "Blessed are the pure in heart, for they shall see God" (Matt. 5:8). It is the compelling vision of God's beauty that enables us to resist the temptations of illicit sexual desire. This was the discovery that transformed Augustine, whose *Confessions* have become a classic of spiritual literature. As a young man he had been warned by his godly Christian mother that sex outside of marriage was sinful and destructive. But as soon as he hit the city, he dove headfirst into what he later called a "hissing cauldron of lust," becoming involved with a woman who was to be his mistress for fifteen years.

When Augustine was almost thirty, God began to stir something in his heart through the teaching of a local Christian pastor. He was thrilled with a new awareness of God, but he also found himself tortured and torn between his lust and the new beauty he was discovering in God. In an attempt to set things straight, he broke off the relationship with his mistress. He was planning to marry a Christian woman, but the sexual addiction was so strong that he was soon in another illicit sexual relationship.

The decisive moment came when he was thirty-two. After hearing of the holiness and purity of another Christian disciple, he retired alone to a garden and was converted while reading Paul's words in Romans, "Not in reveling and drunkenness, not in lust and wantonness, not in quarrels and rivalries. Rather, arm yourselves with the Lord Jesus Christ; spend no more thought on nature and nature's appetites" (Rom. 13:13–14). He later wrote of the effect these words had upon him: "I had no wish to read more and no need to do so. For in an instant, as I came to the end of the sentence, it was as though the light of confidence flooded into my heart and all the darkness of doubt was dispelled."[26] The light had broken in. His life was changed. He never went back to his sexual idolatries. He had found a greater joy, a superior pleasure, in Jesus.

How sweet it was all at once to be rid of those fruitless joys which I had once feared to lose and was now glad to reject! You drove them from me, you who are the true, the sovereign joy. You drove them from me, and took their place, you who are sweeter than all pleasure . . . O Lord my God, my Light, my Wealth, and my Salvation.[27]

The taste of transcendent joy in Christ liberated Augustine from his sexual addiction and transformed his life forever.[28] All of these examples demonstrate how God's promises are designed to help us fight sin. John Piper is right:

Sin is what you do when your heart is not satisfied with God. No one sins out of duty. We sin because it holds out some promise of happiness. That promise enslaves us until we believe that God is more to be desired than life itself (Ps. 63:3). *Which means that the power of sin's promise is broken by the power of God's.* All that God promises to be for us in Jesus stands over against what sin promises to be for us without him.[29]

A Sweeter Song

Satisfaction in God is the only power that will sever the stranglehold of sin from our lives. We desperately need to be captivated with the delights of our rich and glorious inheritance in Christ. The more ravished we are by his beauty and joy, the more we will experience freedom from the monotony of powerless religion, the sterility of loveless priorities, and the tyranny of joyless pleasures. The battle for holiness is the battle to keep our hearts satisfied in God. It is the fight for joy.

In his book, *One Thing,* Sam Storms (another Christian Hedonist whose books and preaching I love) tells the story of two men who encountered the same temptations, yet fared very differently. The story comes from ancient Greek mythology and concerns Ulysses and Jason and their encounter with the seductive Sirens, beautiful women of the sea whose mesmerizing songs lured sailors to their destruction.

Countless were the unwitting sailors who, on passing by their island, succumbed to the outward beauty of the Sirens and their seductively irresistible songs. Once lured close to the shore, their boats crashed on the hidden rocks lurking beneath the surface of the sea. These demonic cannibals whose alluring disguise and mesmerizing melodies had drawn them close wasted no little time in savagely consuming their flesh.

Ulysses had been repeatedly warned about the Sirens and their lethal hypocrisy. Upon reaching their island, he ordered his crew to put wax in their ears lest they be lured to their ultimate demise. He commanded them to look neither to the left nor right but to row for their lives. Ulysses had other plans for himself. He instructed his men to strap him to the mast of the ship, leaving his ears unplugged. "I want to hear their song. No matter what I say or do, don't untie me until we are safely at a distance from the island."

The songs of the Sirens were more than Ulysses' otherwise strong will could resist. He was utterly seduced by their sound and mesmerized by the promise of immediate gratification. One Siren even took on the form of Penelope, Ulysses' wife, seeking to lure him closer on the delusion that he had finally arrived home. Were it not for the ropes that held him tightly to the mast, Ulysses would have succumbed to their invitation. Although his hands were restrained, his heart was captivated by their beauty. Although his soul said, "Yes," the ropes prevented his indulgence. *His "no" was not the fruit of a spontaneous revulsion but the product of an external shackle.*

Ulysses' encounter with the Sirens, together with his strategy for resisting their appeal, is all too similar to the way many Christians try to live as followers of Jesus Christ. Like him, their hearts pant for the passing pleasures of sin. Their wills are no match for the magnetic power of sensual indulgence. Although they understand what is at stake, they struggle through life saying no to sin, not because their souls are ill-disposed to evil but because their hands have been shackled by the laws and rules imposed by an oppressive religious atmosphere.

Jason, like Ulysses, was himself a character of ancient mythology, perhaps best known for his pursuit of the famous Golden Fleece. Again, like Ulysses, he faced the temptation posed by the sonorous tones of the Sirens. But his solution was of a different sort. Jason brought with him on the treacherous journey a man named Orpheus, the son of Oeager. Orpheus was a musician of incomparable talent, especially on the lyre and flute. When his music filled the air it had an enchanting effect on all who heard. There was not a lovelier or more melodious sound in all the ancient world.

When it came time, Jason declined to plug the ears of his crew. Neither did he strap himself to the mast to restrain his otherwise lustful yearning for whatever pleasures the Sirens might offer. But this was not the reckless decision of an arrogant heart. Jason had no illusions about the strength of his will or his capacity to be deceived. He was no less determined than Ulysses to resist the temptations of the Sirens. But he chose a different strategy.

He ordered Orpheus to play his most beautiful and alluring songs. The Sirens didn't stand a chance! Notwithstanding their collective al-lure, Jason and his men paid no heed to the Sirens. They were not in the least inclined to succumb. Why? Was it that the Sirens had ceased to sing? Was it that they had lost their capacity to entice the human heart? Not at all. Jason and his men said "No" because *they were captivated by a transcendent sound.* The music of Orpheus was altogether different and exalted in nature. Jason and his men said "No" to the sounds of the Sirens because they had heard something far more sublime. They had tasted something far sweeter. . . . Ulysses may have *survived* the sounds of the sirens. But only Jason *triumphed* over them.[30]

The only way to triumph over the tyranny of the seductive and de-structive siren-song of sin is to hear the more beautiful sound of a sweeter song, to taste the sweeter fruits of a heavenly country. As Storms writes:

There are, I believe, only two kinds of Christians: those *driven* by fear and uncertainty, on the one hand, and those *drawn* by fascination and joy on the other. The former motivate themselves to "obey" with the constant reminder of the dreadful consequences of failure or the shameful humiliation of "getting caught" . . . But [the others'] hearts are energized by the incomparable attraction of divine beauty.[31]

Which kind of Christian are you? Are you driven by fear or drawn by joy? Are you like Ulysses, seduced by the alluring songs of sin, but lashed to the mast of the church by the ropes of rules and regulations? Or are you like Jason, fighting the deceitful promises of satisfaction in sin, through the expulsive power of a sweeter song?

PART THREE

THE MEANS
OF PERSONAL CHANGE

We do not live the Christian life in an ivory tower contemplating the intricacies of theology, but in the hustle and bustle of the workaday world. The stress of work, the strain of relationships, the tedium of daily routines, the toll of suffering and trial—this is the stuff that makes up our lives. The truths we learn in books, seminars, and sermons can help us understand our lives better. But the majority of believers spend their waking hours navigating the turbulence of life's storms.

This apparent disconnect between the doctrines we believe and practicalities of daily life could lead you into either of two errors. On one hand, you might just write theology off as impractical or irrelevant. After all, how is the knowledge that you are justified by faith going to help you weather conflict with your spouse or face cancer? On the other hand, you might come to resent the stuff that fills your days, wishing you could retreat into a monastery and contemplate Christ instead!

Both ways of thinking are wrong, for, contrary to the first error, there *is* a vital connection to what we believe and how we live. Our deepest held beliefs determine our perspectives and shape our attitudes. If you are gripped with the unfailing acceptance of your Father (justification) and his unstoppable purpose to make you more like Jesus (sanctification), it *will* affect how you handle conflicts and face suffering.

And, in answer to the second error, when you realize that all the routines, trials, and relationships that fill your daily life can be used by God as means for carrying on his work in your heart, you will not resent them as unwelcome intrusions, but receive them as God's chosen tools for transforming you. Part Three of this book is about these tools and how God uses them to change us.

As I've already implied, these tools fit into three broad categories: the routines of spiritual disciplines, the difficulties of suffering and trial, and the challenges of personal relationships.

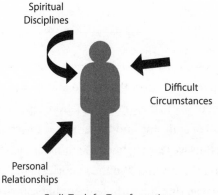

God's Tools for Transformation

First, God uses spiritual disciplines to help us change. These habits of holiness are practices that have been observed by followers of Christ for centuries. The disciplines are the most direct means for spiritual growth available to us because we have the ability to choose how and when to use them. This is the focus of chapter 10.

Second, like a refiner's fire, God uses suffering to test our faith and purify our hearts. Of these tools, we have the least amount of control over our trials and afflictions. But as we'll learn in chapter 11, God will use suffering in extraordinary ways in our lives, when we respond to it with humble faith.

Third, the Lord uses our relationships with others to further our transformation. Though we have somewhat less control over relationships than the disciplines, these relationships are also a crucial means of grace. But, again, we must cooperate with the Lord's work by embracing these relationships, which is the purpose of chapter 12.

10

Training in the Spirit

Disciplines

To stand in the presence of God is, as it was with Moses' shining face, to reflect his glory. Not only that, but it is to absorb his glory, to be transformed into his likeness. Like film in a camera, when the shutter opens to the light, we bear the likeness of the One who shines the light on us when we pray.

—Ben Patterson

From his home, the man had an unobstructed view of the new construction site. It appeared to be a commercial building of some kind. And though the work had begun normally enough, the man's curiosity was soon aroused by something odd. With the help of a crane, a silver box was maneuvered into the center of the slab. It was the size of a large living room, and taller than any of the men. In the days that followed, as the crew began to frame the building and add drywall, the huge, glistening box was gradually hidden from view. Still curious, the man decided to walk over and ask what it was.

He learned that the building was to be a bank, and the silver box was its vault. The vault was not only large in size, it was central to everything the bank stood for. The building was therefore being constructed around it. The vault lay at the heart of the bank, defining its purpose, giving it value, and making it distinct from every other building in the area.

Discipleship is about building our lives around Jesus. He is our treasure and great reward. And like the construction of a bank around its vault, all the various parts of our lives should be built around Christ and the certain hope of eternal, unfading riches that are ours in him.

Why is it, then, that we who claim to follow Jesus so often fail to organize our lives around him? If he really holds the center of gravity in our souls, then our thoughts, habits, schedules, and routines should orbit around him. The spiritual disciplines enable us to center our lives on Jesus, becoming like him in his self-giving love. The disciplines are not the end themselves. They are practices that help us remember the gospel and apply it to our lives as we develop our relationship with God. They are also our focus in this chapter.

A Rocky Wannabe

As a boy, I had a powerful attachment to the *Rocky* movies. Sylvester Stallone's character may have been an unlikely role model for a scrawny twelve-year-old kid living on a dusty farm in West Texas, but that didn't stop me from making him an idol. I owned a scratchy tape recording of the first *Rocky* soundtrack, and I listened to it for inspiration as I did push-ups, strained through sit-ups, and sweated through jumping rope and lifting weights.

Why in the world was I doing this? Being twelve, I never got far enough in my thinking to have a clearly defined goal. If you had asked, I probably would have said, "I want to look like Rocky," or, "I want to be the heavyweight champion of the world." Needless to say, I never achieved either. Why? Probably lots of good reasons. But for our immediate purposes, I want to focus on just one: Apparently, two weeks isn't long enough to transform a skinny weakling into a stallion, and that's about as long as I stuck to my vague plan. I never became Rocky because I didn't keep up the exercise routine.

Too often the same could be said of our spiritual lives. You hear a sermon, attend a conference, are inspired by a missionary, or read a stirring book. An image forms in your mind of who you could become. You envision yourself as a genuinely Christlike person, a spiritual giant, marked by the depth of your love, the maturity of your faith, and your unruffled joy and peace. As the music rises in your soul, you resolve to get disciplined: read through the Bible in a year, memorize a verse of Scripture each day, pray thirty minutes every morning, fast every Thursday, increase your giving by 10 percent.

But before long, like a twelve-year-old briefly obsessed with body-building, you quickly lose steam and your new routines sputter to a halt. Consequently, you never become the spiritual giant you envisioned. Sound familiar?

If talk about spiritual disciplines is more intimidating than inviting, I understand.

Yet there is also something inside me that finds discipline attractive. I respect disciplined people who eat nutritious meals and exercise regularly. I also admire people who practice calisthenics for the soul called spiritual disciplines—and I've slowly discovered how important these practices are to my ongoing spiritual transformation.

Training versus Trying

Suppose you were to ask me to run with you in a marathon next week. I could say yes, and have every intention of doing so. But I would never make the finish line. My good intentions couldn't possibly compensate for the lack of training. Now if you asked to me to run a marathon that is ten months away, I could do it—if I spent adequate time in training. But trying harder simply wouldn't work because, as John Ortberg observes, "There is an immense difference between training to do something and trying to do something."[1]

Respecting the distinction between training and merely trying is the key to transformation in every aspect of life. People sometimes think that learning how to play Bach at the keyboard by spending years practicing scales and chord progressions is the "hard" way. The truth is the other way around. Spending years practicing scales is the easy way to learn to play Bach. Imagine sitting down at a grand piano in front of a packed concert hall and having never practiced a moment in your life. That's the hard way.[2]

Living the Christian life is about training, not trying. But we often forget this. We try to be patient with our children, to show love to people who irritate us, to refrain from lust when confronted with sensuality, and to not feel anxious about difficult circumstances. But try as we will, we won't succeed if we haven't strengthened and shaped our souls through spiritual training.

Listen. You'll never become like Christ by simply exerting more effort in trying harder to be a better person. You have to develop new capacities in your character. And that requires the power of the Spirit in forming your soul through disciplines. Spiritual disciplines, "those personal and corporate disciplines that promote spiritual growth,"[3] are the means God has given us for training to live as Jesus lived. These practices are called *disciplines* because they involve our deliberate participation in training for the purpose of godliness. They are called *spiritual* disciplines because their effectiveness depends on the gracious work of the Spirit of God.

So, the key word is *train*. As Paul says to Timothy, "*Discipline* yourself for the purpose of godliness" (1 Tim. 4:7, NASB). The Greek word for "discipline" is *gumnazo* (our words gymnastics and gymnasium derive from its root). Translated "train" (ESV, NIV), "exercise" (KJV), and "discipline" (NASB), *gumnazo* was used to describe the intense discipline of athletes in first-century Greco-Roman culture. Competitors in the Olympic or Isthmian games were so relentless in pursuit of a champion's wreath that they trained in the nude, part of a strict environment that eliminated all non-essentials.

The New Testament urges us to adopt a similarly radical regimen in the spiritual life. We are called to discipline our bodies, keeping them under control as we pursue an imperishable crown (1 Cor. 9:24–27). We must strip off "every weight" and the "sin which clings so closely" and run the race set before us (Heb. 12:1). We should forget what is behind and strain forward to what lies ahead as we "press toward the goal for the prize of the upward call of God in Christ Jesus" (Phil. 3:13–14). As we have learned, God's ultimate goal is to glorify himself through transformed human beings. We further that goal as we deliberately engage in practices that train us for godliness. If we're serious about this pursuit we will train with intensity, like an Olympic athlete.

No Shortcuts

There are no shortcuts to spiritual growth. Oak trees do not grow overnight, but over decades. The formation of the character of Christ within us is a lifelong process, and the spiritual disciplines are means for helping us in that process. They are of such central importance that even Jesus practiced them.

The Gospels frequently record Jesus' retreats for times of solitude and prayer. His teaching reveals how deeply he drank from the wells of Scripture. His entire life was one of love and service to others. If Jesus' communion with God was maintained through the practice of spiritual disciplines, we shouldn't assume there is a quicker route for us. As Sinclair Ferguson writes, "Jesus did not possess any special means of spiritual growth which are not available to us. It is essential to realize this if we are to understand Jesus, if we are to become like him."[4]

Just what are these spiritual disciplines? Teachers and authors have compiled numerous lists of disciplines, showing significant variety and diversity. In this chapter, I want to highlight the two most foundational spiritual disciplines: meditation on Scripture, and prayer. Then I will suggest several principles to guide our use of all the disciplines as we pursue spiritual growth.

Remember, the disciplines are about being with God, about cultivating a relationship with him. Like any other relationship, the only way to grow close to God is by spending time with him: listening to him and talking to him.

Listening to God: Meditation on Scripture

God speaks to us through his Word. Meditation on Scripture is therefore the only fully reliable means by which we can listen to God. Scriptural meditation is a foundational discipline in any healthy Christian life.

A mind filled with God's Word will result in a fruitful life. As the first psalm says:

> Blessed is the man who walks not in the counsel of the wicked,
> nor stands in the way of sinners,
> nor sits in the seat of scoffers;
> but his delight is in the law of the Lord,
> and on his law he meditates day and night.
> He is like a tree
> planted by streams of water
> that yields its fruit in its season,
> and its leaf does not wither.
> In all that he does, he prospers.
>
> —Psalm 1:1–3

What a portrait! Here is someone who is *sanctified*—who doesn't walk in the counsel of the wicked, stand in the way of sinners, or sit in the seat of scoffers. This person is also *satisfied*—"blessed" or happy, and delighting in the law of the Lord. More than that, this person, like a fruitful tree with leaves that do not wither, is *sustained.* This is a picture of consummate spiritual health. Where does it come from? Meditation: "his delight is in the law of the Lord, and on his law he meditates day and night."

What Is Meditation?

What is meditation? Let me first say what meditation is not.

Meditation is not mental passivity. When some people think of meditation they think about some Asian guru sitting cross-legged with palms up, contemplating nothingness. That is not what the Bible means by meditation. Richard Foster said: "Eastern meditation is an attempt to empty the mind; Christian meditation is an attempt to fill the mind."[5] Meditation is the practice of filling your mind with the truth of God's Word. The objects of meditation include the Word of God, the character and worth of God, the works of God, and the wonder of the gospel. All genuine meditation is rooted in God's revelation of himself, his character, his deeds, and his saving plan as seen in Scripture.

Meditation is not reading, hearing, or memorizing. It is possible to engage in all of these helpful disciplines and yet not meditate. When you *read* you allow the Word to pass through the mind, but when you meditate you cause the Word to *stay* on the mind. When you *hear* the Word preached your heart is like a plot of ground on which seed is sown. Whether the seed will germinate, take root, and bear fruit depends on the condition of the soil in your heart when you read, and whether you fertilize and water the seed after it is planted. And that takes meditation.

Meditation is not study. There are similarities between meditation and study, but meditation goes deeper and further. When we study we gather and synthesize new information. But in meditation we apply the Word to our hearts and lives. As Charles Bridges said, meditation "is the digestive faculty of the soul, which converts the word into real and proper nourishment."[6]

So, what is meditation? The word "meditate" (Hebrew, *hagaw*) literally means "to mutter." So the idea is that of a person who mutters the Word to himself or herself continually, day and night. But this cannot be done unless the Word is in the mind, which implies regular intake of Scripture through hearing, reading, or memorization. Don Whitney defines meditation as "deep thinking on the truths and spiritual realities revealed in Scripture for the purposes of understanding, application, and prayer."[7] Here is my definition: *Meditation is listening to God speak to us through his Word for the purpose of transformation.*

The Value of Meditation

One of the best ways to understand the value of meditation is to consider it as a bridge. Just as a bridge connects two masses of land, meditation bridges some of the gaps in our spiritual lives.

A Bridge Between Reading and Praying

Meditation and prayer are often closely joined in Scripture (Ps. 5:1–3; 19:14), and for good reason. It is difficult to pray when we've neglected to reflect on God's Word. "Prayer is the child of meditation."[8]

To drive a car with a standard transmission you begin in first gear and manually shift to higher gears as your speed increases. If you've ever tried to shift directly from first gear to the highest gear, you know it doesn't work. The engine will lurch and cut off. Meditation is like a middle gear between reading the Word and prayer. Our neglect of meditation is one reason we often struggle to pray. Thomas Manton said:

> Meditation is a middle sort of duty between the word and prayer, and hath respect to both. The word feedeth meditation, meditation feedeth prayer. These duties must always go hand in hand. . . . It is rashness to pray and not to meditate. What we take in by the word we digest by meditation and let out by prayer. These three duties must be ordered that one may not jostle out the other. Men are barren, dry, and sapless in their prayers for want of exercising themselves in holy thoughts.[9]

God desires for our prayers to be informed by Scripture. But he did not save us that we might be like trained parrots, spouting phrases automatically. Meditation moves us from careful reading to biblical praying.

A Bridge Between Mind and Heart

At another level, it is one thing to know a truth from Scripture intellectually, but something else altogether to feel its power. Are we deeply touched in our souls by the gospel? Meditation bridges the gap between mind and heart. The Puritan, Thomas Watson said, "Without meditation the truths which we know will never affect our hearts . . . As a hammer drives a nail to the head; so meditation drives a truth to the heart."[10]

This is also evident in Psalm 1: "his *delight* is in the law of the Lord." There is not only intellectual engagement, but emotional engagement.

Meditation kindles the fires of love for God in our cold hearts. During a time of personal distress, David wrote, "My heart became hot within me. As I mused, the fire burned; then I spoke with my tongue: 'O Lord, make me know my end and what is the measure of my days; let me know how fleeting I am!' " (Ps. 39:3–4). When David mused, a fire burned in his soul. If your heart is cold, your passion for God lifeless, your desire for eternal things dormant, it probably reflects too little meditation. Watson said, "We light affection at this fire of meditation ... the reason our affections are so chill and cold in spiritual things, is because we do not warm ourselves more at the fire of meditation."[11]

God is infinitely passionate about his people, his kingdom, and his glory. He desires for us to feel his truths deeply, as he does. And these desires, through the grace of the Spirit, are possible for us! But we must learn, as Jonathan Edwards said, to "promote spiritual appetites by laying [ourselves] in the way of allurement."[12] One way we do this is through meditation. Meditation moves us from mental assent to joyful passion for God.

A Bridge Between Hearing and Doing

It is not enough for us to take in truth through eye or ear. We must also apply this truth to our lives and put it into practice. James writes,

> Be doers of the word, and not hearers only, deceiving yourselves. For if anyone is a hearer of the word and not a doer, he is like a man who looks intently at his natural face in a mirror. For he looks at himself and goes away and at once forgets what he was like. But the one who looks into the perfect law, the law of liberty, and perseveres, being no hearer who forgets but a doer who acts, he will be blessed in his doing.
>
> —James 1:22–25

When you hear the Word but fail to obey, it's like failing to wash up after gazing at your dirty face in the bathroom mirror. Meditation helps us obey by pressing our hearts toward application. Praying is vital. Understanding the Word of God is essential. But until we act on what we see in Scripture, all this remains theoretical. Ultimately, God is interested in our obedience. It is to be informed, heartfelt obedience, but obedience just the same. Without meditation, we cannot genuinely move from hearing to doing.

Talking to God: Prayer

The other foundational discipline is prayer (which, as we just read, is closely tied to meditation). God speaks to us in his Word, and we speak to him through prayer informed by his Word. In prayer we tell God about ourselves, our circumstances, and the circumstances of others. We express to him our affection, ask for his help and grace, and enjoy his transforming presence. By spending time with God, we become more like him. As Ben Patterson writes in his fine book on prayer:

> To stand in the presence of God is, as it was with Moses' shining face, to reflect his glory. Not only that, but it is to absorb his glory, to be transformed into his likeness. Like film in a camera, when the shutter opens to the light, we bear the likeness of the One who shines the light on us when we pray.[13]

The goal of prayer, then—as it relates to spiritual formation—is the increasing transformation of the soul into the likeness, the image, the character of Christ. As the eighteenth-century pioneer missionary William Carey said, "Prayer—secret, fervent, believing prayer—lies at the root of all personal godliness."[14]

Obstacles to Prayer

But let's face it—when we think about the "discipline of prayer," our initial emotional reaction is one of guilt, not delight. Like many other believers, I know that I *should* pray more than I do, and often feel guilty that I don't. I hear (and sometimes even preach!) sermons, read books, and attend seminars on prayer. But when I try to cultivate a vibrant prayer life of my own, I find myself faced with numerous obstacles.

Legalism: Sometimes I'm more motivated by a sense of obligation than privilege, and begin to think of prayer in terms of law rather than grace. After all, I'm a pastor. I'm supposed to be a mature Christian! Why then is prayer so difficult? As Paul Miller rightly says, "Private, personal prayer is one of the last great bastions of legalism."[15]

Self-sufficiency: Often, I'm too self-sufficient to pray. I either let busyness crowd out time with God, or, when I actually start praying, I try to fix myself up to sound or feel more "spiritual" than I really am.

But what's missing in both cases is a clear sense of my helplessness—my need for God.[16]

Unbelief: And sometimes the obstacle is a simple lack of faith. It's not that I stop believing in God altogether, but that I forget his character. When I imagine him looking at me, I see an angry judge or a disappointed authority figure, rather than the kindness and love of a father.

These attitudes cling to me like barnacles to a ship and poison my relationship with God, rendering prayer almost impossible. When faced with these obstacles, I don't need new strategies or methods for prayer, as helpful as these can be in other situations. The only thing that will counteract these toxic thought patterns is the antidote of the gospel applied to prayer.

Prayer and the Gospel

Praying in Jesus' Name: The Antidote to Legalism

The antidote to legalism is remembering that our access to God in prayer comes only through Christ. This is why we pray "in Jesus' name." I know—we often just attach this phrase to the end of our prayers with little thought. But the truth is that we can come to God through Jesus, and in no other way.[17]

This hit home with me a couple of years ago. On one of my days off, I went to Starbucks to do some devotional reading. I was reading a book on spiritual formation that focused on how to cultivate the presence of God. The author talked about God being nearer to us than we realize, and how some people have a God-radar that can detect his presence in a situation, and how there are many different pathways for connecting to God—intellectual, aesthetic, contemplative, through service, and so on.

Of course, there were lots of helpful things in this book and I'm sure the author is theologically orthodox. But as I was reading, I began to notice a glaring absence: Jesus Christ, crucified and risen. I was especially struck with the difference between this book's emphasis and the emphasis in the letter to the Hebrews, where I was reading devotionally that day.

> Since then we have a great high priest who has passed through the heavens, Jesus, the Son of God, let us hold fast our confession. For we do not have a high priest who is unable to sympathize with our weaknesses, but one who in every respect has been tempted as we are, yet without sin. Let us then with confidence draw near to the throne of grace, that we may receive mercy and find grace to help in time of need.
>
> —Hebrews 4:14–16

Jesus is our great high priest—the imagery literally dominates Hebrews. And it struck me that the New Testament is surging with language of atonement and sacrifice and cross and resurrection.

The author of the book I was reading probably assumed his readers understood that Christ is the way to the Father. But in Scripture this is not an assumption. It is an explicit declaration, a stunning and startling spiritual reality that is celebrated on virtually every page of the New Testament letters and epistles. Paul says that it is *"through him* we both have access in one Spirit to the Father" (Eph. 2:18). Peter says that we "offer spiritual sacrifices acceptable to God *through Jesus Christ"* (1 Peter 2:4–5). In Romans we read that "since we have been justified by faith, we have peace with God *through our Lord Jesus Christ. Through him we have also obtained access* by faith into this grace in which we stand, and we rejoice in hope of the glory of God" (Rom. 5:1–2). And Jesus himself said, "I am the way, and the truth, and the life. No one comes to the Father except *through me"* (John 14:6).

Later that week I was freshly moved by the words of an old hymn written by Horatius Bonar.

> *Not what my hands have done can save my guilty soul;*
> *Not what my toiling flesh has borne can make my spirit whole.*
> *Not what I feel or do can give me peace with God;*
> *Not all my prayers and sighs and tears can bear my awful load.*
>
> *Your voice alone, O Lord, can speak to me of grace;*
> *Your power alone, O Son of God, can all my sin erase.*
> *No other work but Yours, no other blood will do;*
> *No strength but that which is divine can bear me safely through.*[18]

When we thoughtfully and intentionally pray in Jesus' name, we undercut the legalism that so often drives prayer. We're not praying in order to get God to accept us. We're coming because we are already accepted in Christ!

Praying Like a Little Child: The Antidote to Self-Sufficiency

The antidote to self-sufficiency is remembering our helplessness and learning to come to the Father as little children. Over and over in the Gospels, Jesus teaches us that we must be like children (see Mark 10:14–15; Matt. 18:3; Luke 10:21). I've always thought this meant we needed to be humble. But Paul Miller, in his immensely helpful book, *A Praying Life,* enabled me to see that this also means we need to come messy and without pretense. To come as we are.

> Jesus wants us to be without pretense when we come to him in prayer. Instead, we often try to be something we aren't. We begin by concentrating on God, but almost immediately our minds wander off in a dozen different directions. The problems of the day push out our well-intentioned resolve to be spiritual. We give ourselves a spiritual kick in the pants and try again, but life crowds out prayer. We know that prayer isn't supposed to be like this, so we give up in despair. We might as well get something done.
>
> What's the problem? We're trying to be spiritual, to get it right. We know we don't need to clean up our act in order to become a Christian, but when it comes to praying, we forget that. We, like adults, try to fix ourselves up. In contrast, Jesus wants us to come to him like little children, just as we are.
>
> The difficulty of coming just as we are is that we are messy. And prayer makes it worse. When we slow down to pray, we are immediately confronted with how unspiritual we are, with how difficult it is to concentrate on God. We don't know how bad we are until we try to be good. Nothing exposes our selfishness and spiritual powerlessness like prayer.[19]

Miller then describes what all parents know. Children are very unpretentious. They don't try to fix themselves up and appear less selfish than they really are when they have a need. They simply cry out and expect their parents to help! When my four-year-old son has hurt his knee, or is hungry, or can't get a toy to work correctly, he simply comes to me or his mom expecting us to meet his need. As Miller says, "Little children never get frozen by their selfishness . . . they come just as they are, totally self-absorbed."[20] And loving parents are usually delighted to meet the needs of their children.

> This isn't just a random observation about how parents respond to little children. This is the gospel, the welcoming heart of God. God also cheers when we come to him with our wobbling, unsteady prayers. Jesus does not say, "Come to me, all you who have learned how to concentrate in prayer, whose minds no longer wander, and I will give you rest." No, Jesus opens his arms to his needy children and says, "Come to Me, all who are weary and heavy-laden, and I will give you rest" (Matthew 11:28, NASB). The criteria for coming to Jesus is weariness. Come overwhelmed with life. Come with your wandering mind. Come messy.[21]

Unfortunately, many of us have been taught to pray in very *un*-child-like ways. We change our tone. We use spiritual sounding words. We attempt to do "adoration" prior to "supplication." Consequently, we veil our hearts and pretend to be something we're not. We try to act all grown up and in the process lose our sense of helplessness. But as Miller says, "Don't try to get the prayer right; just tell God where you are and what's on your mind. That's what little children do. They come as they are, runny noses and all."[22]

Praying to the Father: The Antidote to Unbelief

Self-sufficiency is closely related to unbelief. When we forget to come to God as children, we're also forgetting that we come to *him* as our Father. And thus we distrust his heart. The antidote is to remember his character as our kind and loving heavenly Father. Jesus taught us that God is our Father, who knows what we need before we ask (Matt. 6:8). He graciously clothes the grass of the field with beautiful flowers (Matt. 6:26–28). It is only our "little faith" that keeps us from believing that he will also take care of us.

I remember an occasion, early in our marriage, when Holly and I found ourselves in a financial strait. I don't remember the details of the circumstances now, but I remember that things were very tight and we were slipping behind. In a desperate moment, I decided to talk to the most generous person I knew—my grandfather. So I went to see him and rather reluctantly admitted that we needed some help. He asked how much we needed. I told him the amount. And do you know what he did? He gave me a check for three times what I asked! He not only gave me all that I had asked, he gave more than I had asked or imagined!

Scripture teaches us that God is like this. Paul says that God "is able to do far more abundantly than all that we ask or think" (Eph. 3:20). Commenting on this verse, F. F. Bruce said that God's "capacity for giving far exceeds [our] capacity for asking."[23]

A story is told about a philosopher in the court of Alexander the Great who had outstanding ability but little money. He asked Alexander for financial help and was told to draw whatever he needed from the imperial treasury. But when the man requested an amount equal to $50,000, he was refused. The treasurer wanted to verify that such a large sum was authorized. When he asked Alexander, the ruler replied, "Pay the money at once. The philosopher has done me a singular honor. By the largeness of his request he shows that he has understood both my wealth and generosity."[24]

The great English hymn-writer, John Newton, wrote:

> *Thou art coming to a King,*
> *Large petitions with thee bring;*
> *For His grace and pow'r are such*
> *None can ever ask too much.*[25]

A Palette of Practices

There are, of course, many other important and helpful spiritual disciplines. But all of them really just serve to cultivate and enhance our relationship with God, which is centered in meditation and prayer. Rather than viewing the disciplines as an ever-lengthening list of religious things to do, think of them as a palette of practices from which you can develop your own particular plan for spiritual growth. An artist does not color by number, but skillfully combines the varied colors of the palette in her unique painting. Believers enjoy a similar flexibility in their use of the disciplines.

For a thorough, but by no means exhaustive, list of disciplines see the table below, where the disciplines are categorized as inward disciplines (to cultivate the heart and mind), outward disciplines (to embody the virtues of Christ in personal practice), and corporate disciplines (to practice with other believers).[26]

Inward Disciplines	Outward Disciplines	Corporate Disciplines
Read Scripture	Solitude	Celebration
Memorization	Simplicity	Family & Corporate Worship
Meditation	Generosity	Listening to Preaching
Prayer	Chastity	Witness
Private Worship	Submission	Serving
Fasting	Serving	Fellowship
Slowing	Secrecy	Giving
Silence	Friendship	Baptism
Study	Enjoying Creation	Observing the Lord's Table
Learning	Genuine Recreation	
Journaling	Work	

Diagram 10.1: List of Spiritual Disciplines

But don't feel overwhelmed by the sheer number of disciplines! Rather, be encouraged, for as my friend Del Fehsenfeld writes, "The spiritual disciplines are varied and practical enough that all of daily life can be lived within their basic structure."[27]

The wide variety of these practices reminds us that God not only uses prayer and meditation on Scripture to help us grow, but also for serving in our church or community, celebrating life with family and friends, and so much more. The disciplines help us pay attention to God's presence in daily life. Through these practices we remind ourselves of God's *saving* grace given to us in Christ and revealed to us by the Spirit through God's Word. And we also cherish God's *common* grace in the blessings of friendship, rest, and community.

We should remember that no two people's practice of the disciplines will be identical. Your disciplines should not and will not look precisely like mine, or mine like yours. The disciplines of a plumber will be different, though no less important, than those of a pastor. A mother of preschoolers will not have the same rhythms and routines as a single woman. Resist comparing your practices with others or trying to measure up to what someone else is doing. Instead, recognize both your needs and your limitations and prayerfully develop a plan suited to your circumstances and season of life.

We will be most effective when we are intentional in the practice of daily disciplines and recognize the need for occasionally devoting more prolonged periods of time to nurturing our spiritual lives. A helpful adage says, "Divert daily, withdraw weekly, abandon annually."[28] This advice reflects both realism and wisdom. Most people will find it difficult to sustain a commitment to pray or meditate for several hours each day. But committing a few *minutes* a day, a few *hours* a week, and a few *days* a year is doable for most people. We must recognize and live within the limitations of our unique circumstances and individual responsibilities. But we must also be intentional in doing what we can.

Different individuals will choose their own unique mix from this palette of disciplines, but meditation and prayer, like primary colors, will be present in any healthy plan for spiritual growth.

The Right Use of Disciplines

More detailed descriptions of these many disciplines is beyond the scope of this book, so in the rest of this chapter I just want to suggest some guidelines in how to use any of them in ways that will help, not hinder, spiritual growth.[29]

Receiving versus Achieving

First, remember that the disciplines are about receiving, not achieving. Using the disciplines wisely does not mean checking things off a religious to-do list. The Pharisee in Luke 18 did that, boasting in his prayers, "I fast twice a week; I give tithes of all that I get." He had two disciplines nailed down, fasting and giving. He thought he had achieved much. But Jesus contrasted this man with a humble and broken tax collector, who wouldn't even lift his eyes to heaven, but pleaded, "God, be merciful to me a sinner!" The tax collector's focus was not on his achievements, but on his deep need for mercy (Luke 18:12–13). Beware of using spiritual disciplines to achieve something with God! The disciplines are not about achieving, but receiving.

As Bryan Chapell writes, we should view:

the Christian disciplines as means of opening our mouths to breathe in all the loving resources God has already provided. Opening my mouth in prayer and praise does not manufacture more of God's love for me, any more than opening my mouth makes more air. The means of grace simply allow me to experience the fullness of the love that God has already fully and completely provided.[30]

Do not approach the disciplines as if you are benefiting God or meriting his favor. You are not. When you read or meditate on Scripture, seek the Lord in prayer, worship with the Lord's people, or give yourself to serving others, you come to an overflowing fountain of divine grace. When you come to this fountain, do not bring a cup full of self-sufficiency, thinking you can add something to God's infinite mercy. Come instead with an empty cup of need for God to fill.

Communion with God versus Compartmentalizing

Second, learn to integrate the disciplines into the whole of life as you cultivate your relationship with God. One reason our resolves do not last is because we compartmentalize our lives, dividing the sacred from the secular. We treat Bible reading and prayer as sacred duties, but then live daily life with little thought of God. This reflects a misunderstanding of how the disciplines should serve us. The disciplines are given to help us cultivate ongoing communion with God. I have a friend who sometimes programs his phone to go off periodically throughout the day as a reminder to pause and give attention to God. Do you regulate God to fifteen minutes of devotional time, but quickly forget him when at work or play? If your "quiet times" aren't raising your awareness of God's presence in the other ordinary moments of the day, you may need to rethink your strategy. The goal is not merely to meet with God in a sacred place, but to walk with him throughout the day.

Measured Regularity versus Short Bursts

Third, consider the benefits of measured regularity. Sometimes we go hard after God with short bursts of energy that quickly fizzle and fade. New Year's resolutions are notoriously short-lived. New commitments to spend hours in prayer or reading Scripture are difficult to sustain.

The disciplines benefit us most when we practice them with measured regularity. Along with many others, I have been helped and inspired by the example of Robert Murray M'Cheyne, a nineteenth-century Scottish pastor. M'Cheyne's biographer wrote:

> His incessant labors left him little time, except what he scrupulously spent in the direct exercises of devotion. But what we have seen of his manner of study and self-examination at Larbert, is sufficient to show in what a constant state of cultivation his soul was kept; and his habits in these respects continued with him to the last. Jeremy Taylor recommends: "If thou meanest to enlarge thy religion, do it rather by enlarging thine ordinary devotions than thy extraordinary." This advice describes very accurately the plan of spiritual life on which Mr. M'Cheyne acted. He did occasionally set apart seasons for special prayer and fasting, occupying the time so set apart exclusively in devotion. But the real secret of his soul's prosperity lay in the daily engagement of his heart in fellowship with his God.[31]

To keep your soul in constant cultivation requires the daily engagement of your heart in fellowship with God. Only by regular and sustained exposure to the light of his presence, as you walk with him throughout the day, will the image of Christ be formed in you.

The Key to Transformation

In all our consideration and all our practice of the spiritual disciplines, we must remember that only the gospel can change us. Religious practices alone will not. Never be content with the mere forms of piety. Always be feeding your soul at the banqueting table of God's love in Christ! John Owen wrote:

> Let us live in the constant contemplation of the glory of Christ, and virtue will proceed from him to repair all our decays, to renew a right spirit within us, and to cause us to abound in all duties of obedience ... The most of our spiritual decays and barrenness arise from an inordinate admission of other things into our minds; for these are they that weaken grace in all its operations. But when the mind is filled with thoughts of Christ and his glory, when the soul thereon cleaves unto him with

intense affections, they will cast out, or not give admittance unto, those causes of spiritual weakness and indisposition.[32]

The spiritual disciplines are really all about keeping your heart in the constant contemplation of Christ. Fill your mind with the gospel and cleave to Christ with all your heart. Think of Christ often. Marvel at his incarnation—the Word was made flesh! Meditate on the achievements of the cross and the dying love of Jesus. Celebrate in your soul the resurrection of Christ. Death is defeated once and for all. Stand in awe at the ascension and enthronement of the God-Man, Jesus Christ. God's plan for his image-bearing human beings is restored in Christ. The second Adam reigns! As you soak your mind with the gospel and deeply absorb its truths in your soul, you will be changed.

The Purpose of Spiritual Disciplines

Finally, remember that the purpose of spiritual disciplines is to form you more and more into the image of Christ so that you will reflect his worth and glory to others through a life of love. We stray in our thinking about spiritual disciplines when we forget their purpose. The disciplines are not rungs to be climbed on a ladder of meritorious works that secure favor with God. Neither are they divinely prescribed yardsticks for measuring spiritual growth. You cannot determine your status with God or discern your level of maturity by the number of chapters you read in the Bible each day or the length of your prayers. Nor do the disciplines themselves change us. Jesus changes us through the application of the gospel by the power of the Spirit. The goal of the disciplines is to help us keep Christ central.

This means we should be wary of monasticism in our practice of the disciplines. Monasticism wrongly supposes that the highest forms of devotion to God will lead a person away from interaction with people and engagement with the world. But the goal of the disciplines is not to isolate us from others, but to equip us in carrying the good news of God's saving work in Christ to the world. The disciplines are meant to turn us into missionaries, not monks. As G. C. Berkouwer said, "the imitation of Christ can . . . never consist in the seclusion of prayer and meditation; instead it takes us into the broad daylight of commonplace affairs."[33]

Consider Eugene Peterson's reflections on how the Scriptures serve the outward goal of mission:

> Christians feed on Scripture. Holy Scripture nurtures the holy community as food nurtures the human body. Christians don't simply learn or study or use Scripture; we assimilate it, take it into our lives in such a way that it gets metabolized into acts of love, cups of cold water, missions into all the world, healing and evangelism and justice in Jesus' name, hands raised in adoration of the Father, feet washed in company with the Son.[34]

The disciplines are not simply about learning, but about being and becoming. The disciplines start in the closet, but end in the street.[35] If you stay in the closet, you have missed the whole point. True Christlikeness is measured not by the breadth of your knowledge or the length of your prayers, but the depth of your love for others.

11

The Refiner's Fire

Suffering

God's rod is a pencil to draw Christ's image more lively on us.

—Thomas Watson

When I was a teenager, my mother lost two children through miscarriages. When we learned that my yet unborn sister, Hannah Grace, had died, my godly parents gathered my siblings and me into the living room to read the words of Job, "Naked came I out of my mother's womb, and naked shall I return thither: the LORD gave, and the LORD hath taken away; blessed be the name of the LORD" (Job 1:21, KJV). Then we sang a hymn written by William Cowper,

> *God moves in a mysterious way*
> *His wonders to perform;*
> *He plants His footsteps in the sea*
> *And rides upon the storm.*

Deep in unfathomable mines
Of never failing skill
He treasures up His bright designs
And works His sovereign will.

Ye fearful saints, fresh courage take;
The clouds ye so much dread
Are big with mercy and shall break
In blessings on your head.

Judge not the Lord by feeble sense,
But trust Him for His grace;
Behind a frowning providence
He hides a smiling face.

His purposes will ripen fast,
Unfolding every hour;
The bud may have a bitter taste,
But sweet will be the flower.

Blind unbelief is sure to err
And scan His work in vain;
God is His own interpreter,
And He will make it plain.[1]

The depth of my parents' trust in God's sovereign goodness in this and other trials had a profound and formative influence on me. The hymn we sang that night has brought me comfort many times since.

Everything Is Broken

The pathways of our lives are far more often paved with adversity than strewn with flowers. The older I get, the clearer this becomes. Though I have so far been spared much physical suffering, I have felt the dull ache of disappointment, the sharp sting of criticism and betrayal, and the relentless weight of burdensome circumstances. As a pastor, I have often had a front-row seat to suffering; couples looking for a shred of hope in a failing marriage, parents anxious about the choices of wayward children, saints grieving the loss of loved ones through death.

I've now been in the ministry long enough to have buried quite a few people, sometimes after watching their bodies waste away over weeks or months.

From near and far, we have all seen people endure trials of every sort:

- Financial (poverty, debt, bankruptcy)
- Vocational (unemployment, unremitting stress, business-related lawsuits)
- Relational (strained friendships, communication struggles, recurring conflict, wayward children, infidelity, divorce)
- Emotional (guilt, fear, disillusionment, discouragement, depression)
- Physical (chronic pain, terminal disease, suicide, death)

In most lives, of course, suffering is not so neatly compartmentalized. Financial pressures may be due to unemployment and can easily bleed over into emotional distress, marital conflict, and health problems. Emotional suffering is almost always tied to other situations in life, as either cause or effect. Marriage difficulties take a huge emotional toll and always affect other relationships. Persecution can happen in any or all of these ways.

But none of us are mere observers. We are all participants in pain. Even as I write this, there are three situations in my life I would change in a minute if given the option. Life is hard. For everyone.

All this adversity, affliction, pain, and death stems from one basic cause: the world is fallen. Since the moment of man's initial rebellion against God we have lived under a curse (Gen. 2:17; 3:16–19). Though unwillingly subjected to futility, even the material creation groans as it awaits eventual rebirth (Rom. 8:20–22). But for the present, as Bob Dylan's ballad captures well, "Everything is Broken."[2]

Yet there is good news in the middle of this mess. God's answer to the brokenness of our world was not to abandon and give up on it, but to redeem it. By sending his Son to bear the dreadful curse of our sin (Gal. 3:13), and then raising him from the dead, God has inaugurated the new creation (1 Cor. 15:20–28).

Our God Is a Suffering God

Any discussion of human suffering rightly begins with a two-part recognition. First, suffering is an alien invasion into God's good creation that results from human rebellion and sin. Second, suffering is addressed by our saving God in the cross and empty tomb of Jesus. This second reality asserts something remarkable: When God allowed sin to enter this world, even he was affected. It is not only humanity that has suffered as a result of sin. God himself chose to suffer both with us and for us in order to rescue and redeem the good world he created. As D. A. Carson thoughtfully writes:

> When Christians think seriously about evil and suffering, one of the paramount reasons we are so sure that God is to be trusted is because he sent his Son to suffer cruelly on our behalf. Jesus Christ, the Son who is to be worshiped as God, God's own agent in creation (John 1:2–3), suffered an excruciatingly odious and ignominious death. The God on whom we rely knows what suffering is all about, not merely in the way that God knows everything, but by experience.[3]

The ultimate answer to human suffering, then, is in the suffering of God himself through the cross. The letter of Hebrews says that Jesus was "crowned with glory and honor because of the suffering of death, so that by the grace of God he might taste death for everyone." God, the eternal One, the source of all life, suffered the taste of death; his plan for bringing many sons to glory was only accomplished by making "the founder of [our] salvation perfect through suffering." This means Jesus is a high priest who sympathizes with our weaknesses, since "in every respect [he] has been tempted as we are, yet without sin" (Heb. 2:9–10, 18; 4:15; 5:10). Jesus knows our pain.

Our God, revealed in Jesus Christ, is unique among the religions of the world. He alone has entered into the reality of our suffering. "Jesus of the Scars," a poem written by Edward Shillito in the wake of World War I, beautifully captures this:

> *If we have never sought, we seek Thee now;*
> *Thine eyes burn through the dark, our only stars;*
> *We must have sight of thorn-pricks on Thy brow;*
> *We must have Thee, O Jesus of the Scars.*

The heavens frighten us; they are too calm;
In all the universe we have no place.
Our wounds are hurting us; where is the balm?
Lord Jesus, by Thy Scars, we claim Thy grace.

If, when the doors are shut, Thou drawest near,
Only reveal those hands, that side of Thine;
We know to-day what wounds are, have no fear,
Show us Thy Scars, we know the countersign.

The other gods were strong; but Thou wast weak;
They rode, but Thou didst stumble to a throne;
But to our wounds only God's wounds can speak,
And not a god has wounds, but Thou alone.[4]

The purpose of this chapter is not to exhaustively treat the problem of suffering; that would require an entire book.[5] Instead, I want to highlight how God uses suffering as part of his plan to restore his image within us. While this isn't the only (or even the most important) thing to be said about suffering, it is still true that God uses difficult circumstances of all sorts for our ultimate good.

You and I may have very little control over how much we suffer. What we *can* do, however, is choose to cooperate with the Lord's perfecting process by responding to suffering in faith. That's what this chapter is about.

God's Ultimate Purpose Through Suffering

The writers of Scripture felt the reality of suffering keenly and addressed it often. One of the most profound passages addressing suffering is found in Romans 8. Paul's words offer an insight that should radically transform our perspective on suffering. Here is one of the keys to understanding how and why God works out his purposes in our lives. In this passage we see that God uses suffering—all suffering, without exception—to accomplish his ultimate purpose and our everlasting good. God uses suffering to conform us to the image of Christ.

And we know that for those who love God all things work together for good, for those who are called according to his purpose. For those whom he foreknew he also predestined to be conformed to the image of his Son, in order that he might be the firstborn among many brothers.

—Romans 8:28–29

Notice that Paul doesn't say suffering itself is good. He says all things (including suffering) *work together for* the good of Christians. The context of this passage makes it especially clear that Paul has suffering in mind, for he refers to "the sufferings of this present time," the created world's "bondage to decay," our "groaning" for the future redemption of the body, and the reality of suffering and persecution for the name of Christ (vv. 17–23, 35–36).

So suffering is not good, but God uses it for good. I find the distinctions made by C. S. Lewis wise and helpful:

Suffering is not good in itself . . . In the fallen and partially redeemed universe we may distinguish between (1) the simple good descending from God, (2) the simple evil produced by rebellious creatures, and (3) the exploitation of that evil by God for His redemptive purpose, which produces (4) the complex good to which accepted suffering and repented sin contribute.[6]

The good promised in Romans 8:28–29 is a "complex good" in which the dark threads of evil and suffering, culminating in the cross, are woven together by God to accomplish his ultimate purpose. He aims to produce a new race of human beings, restored in his divine image, who will live in a new world.

The New Race: Transformed Human Beings

On the personal level, Scripture promises the final and consummate transformation of our bodies. That's why Paul says that "our citizenship is in heaven, and from it we await a Savior, the Lord Jesus Christ, who will transform our lowly body to be like his glorious body, by the power that enables him even to subject all things to himself" (Phil. 3:20–21).

Paul describes this with breathtaking detail in 1 Corinthians 15. He tells us that though our perishable bodies will be sown (buried like a seed in the earth) in dishonor, they will be raised in imperishable glory. Though sown in weakness, they will be raised in glory. Reminding us again that Christ is the new Adam, Paul says that "just as we have borne the image of the man of dust [Adam], we shall also bear the image of the man of heaven [Christ]" (v. 42–43, 49).

Can you imagine it? Your body will be transformed and made like Christ's glorious, resurrected body. You will never be weary or ill again. Suffering will be no more. The last vestiges of indwelling sin will be laid aside once and for all. There will no longer be pride, greed, or jostling for power. Fear, anger, and lust will all be irreversibly eradicated from our hearts. We will be fully human—more fully human than we've ever been, in fact—gloriously transformed in both soul and body, made like our glorified Lord, in both physical and moral perfection. This is the goal towards which we reach. We make advances in sanctification now that are both lasting and important. But we are still waiting for the full consummation of God's redeeming work.

The New World: Transformed Creation

The hope of the glory of God also has a cosmic dimension. The Old Testament prophets declared with confident hope that "the earth will be filled with the knowledge of the glory of the Lord as the waters cover the sea" and that God would create a new heavens and new earth (Hab. 2:14; Is. 65:17; 66:22).

The realization of this hope through the Christ, the conquering king and triumphant lamb, is captured in Revelation 21:1–5, where John sees a "new heaven and a new earth" and the "holy city, the new Jerusalem, coming down out of heaven from God, prepared as a bride adorned for her husband." When the city arrives, a voice cries out from the throne, "Behold, the dwelling place of God is with man. He will dwell with them, and they will be his people, and God himself will be with them as their God." And then the promise: "He will wipe away every tear from their eyes, and death shall be no more, neither shall there be mourning nor crying nor pain anymore, for the former things have passed away." Then, the enthroned king says, "Behold, I am making all things new."

The cosmic proportions of this renewal of the earth are also evident in Romans 8, where Paul says:

> For the creation waits with eager longing for the revealing of the sons of God. For the creation was subjected to futility, not willingly, but because of him who subjected it, in hope that the creation itself will be set free from its bondage to decay and obtain the freedom of the glory of the children of God. For we know that the whole creation has been groaning together in the pains of childbirth until now. And not only the creation, but we ourselves, who have the firstfruits of the Spirit, groan inwardly as we wait eagerly for adoption as sons, the redemption of our bodies.
>
> —Romans 8:19–23

We are hoping for nothing less than a resurrected earth—the renewal of the fallen created order itself. As David Peterson writes, "Paul indicates that the Old Testament hope of a renewed creation, set free from suffering, corruption and death (e.g. Isa. 11:6–9; 65:17–25; 66:22) will be fulfilled when Christians are resurrected and experience the redemption of their bodies. Creation itself must be redeemed so that humanity may have a fitting environment in which to live."[7]

Passages about this hope for cosmic renewal remind us that the best is yet to come! God's grace has already dawned in the coming, living, dying, and rising of Jesus Christ. Through faith we have access into that grace now. But the consummation of that grace has not yet arrived. We wait for it eagerly.

But we must also face the hard truth that the promise of Romans 8:28–29 is not for all people. It is for those "who love God" and "are called according to his purpose." Only those who are called by God and love him, those who "have the firstfruits of the Spirit," truly share this hope (vv. 23–25). Scripture never holds out hope of a utopia for all of humanity.

Nor does this passage even begin to suggest that in this life all our problems will be solved, the whole of our sufferings will end, or each of our difficulties will turn out okay. These hopes will not be fulfilled in our fallen world, but await realization following the return of Christ.

But the promise of Romans 8 is that *God is working even now*. He is exploiting suffering to accomplish his ultimate saving purpose of making us more like his Son, Jesus Christ.

Trusting the Father When We Suffer

The promises of Romans 8 assure us that God's divine purpose is working through events that might otherwise seem random and pointless. Yet, while we may acknowledge the truth of this promise in theory, it is far more difficult to trust God's sovereign goodness and wisdom when we're actually in the midst of trials. It's always easier to trust God in theory, when things are going well, than it is to trust him in practice, when we are suffering.

This is why Jesus taught us to trust our Father. When preparing his disciples for the inevitability of persecution, he assured them of God's fatherly care. "Are not two sparrows sold for a penny? And not one of them will fall to the ground apart from your Father. But even the hairs of your head are all numbered. Fear not, therefore; you are of more value than many sparrows" (Matt. 10:29–31).

The Providence of God

Jesus' teaching assures us that our lives are governed not by blind fate, or random chance, but by the wisdom and goodness of our all-knowing Father. This is what theologians call the providence of God. The *Heidelberg Catechism* beautifully defines the providence of God as:

> The almighty and everywhere present power of God; whereby, as it were by his hand, he upholds and governs heaven, earth, and all creatures; so that herbs and grass, rain and drought, fruitful and barren years, meat and drink, health and sickness, riches and poverty, yea, and all things come, not by chance, but by his fatherly hand.[8]

The next question in the catechism asks, "What advantage is it to us to know that God has created, and by his providence does still uphold all things?" The answer, once again, is very helpful:

That we may be patient in adversity; thankful in prosperity; and that in all things, which may hereafter befall us, we place our firm trust in our faithful God and Father, that nothing shall separate us from his love; since all creatures are so in his hand, that without his will they cannot so much as move.[9]

Observe the wisdom of this perspective. The catechism teaches us to view adversity and prosperity, blessing and trial, as coming to us by the will of our almighty, everywhere present, loving, and faithful God, who is our heavenly Father. This is a clear echo of Scripture itself, which says, "Consider the work of God: who can make straight what he has made crooked? In the day of prosperity be joyful, and in the day of adversity consider: God has made the one as well as the other, so that man may not find out anything that will be after him" (Eccl. 7:13–14).

Tailor-made Trials

The problem is that suffering usually seems so random. It appears to be without purpose. It feels harmful to us, not helpful. While we want to thank God for the good things, we sometimes forget that his providence embraces bad things, too.[10] We often talk about how God's timing is perfect with respect to blessings, but somehow we don't see our trials that way. But it's really all one package, one purpose, with all things pointing in one direction: God is at work to conform us to the image of his Son.

Of course, discerning the loving purposes of God in the afflictions of someone else often seems easy! (Although we are as often wrong as we are right in our diagnosis—remember Job's friends?) But it is not so easy to trust the Lord when the heat is on in our own lives. Our own trials always seem unusually difficult. Why is this?

Because God tailor-makes our sufferings. Gene Edwards writes:

What kind of person can best endure suffering? Quite frankly, once suffering takes up residence, it seems none of us are qualified. Why? Suffering that comes from the hand of God seems to be so selected, so tailored for the one to whom it is sent. The thing you might shoulder the easiest may never come to you; but that one weakness you were never prepared for, that one hidden portion of your life you probably didn't even know about—*there* is where the blow will fall . . . What kind of Christian can best endure suffering? He doesn't exist. I could handle your problems easily. You could handle mine with a yawn. But it didn't happen that way. I got the ones *I* couldn't handle; so did you.[11]

I find this helpful. It reminds me that the tough stuff in my life *doesn't* just happen. No, my circumstances are sifted through the fingers of a wise and loving Father. As a master artisan who designs to restore his image within me, he knows which tools to use in my life, precisely where to use them, and exactly how much pressure to apply. As someone once said, "God is too good to be unkind. He is too wise to be confused. If I cannot trace His hand, I can always trust His heart."[12]

A Gospel-Shaped Perspective on Trials

But how do we know we can trust God's heart? Because of the gospel. The promise of Romans 8:28–29 isn't built on sand, but on the rock who is Christ. The cross and empty tomb of Jesus are the ultimate unveiling of God's love for us. God has shown his love in giving us his Son, and he has shown his infinite power in raising Jesus from the dead. That is why we can rest with confidence in God's goodwill toward us.

The language immediately following Romans 8:28–29 is lavishly embedded with promises that are ours in the gospel. Consider these:

- God has not only predestined us to become like Jesus, he has called, justified, and glorified us (v. 30).
- God is *for us* (v. 31). He is in our side!
- God has demonstrated his love for us by not sparing his Son, but giving him up for us. Since he has already given his greatest gift, we know he will graciously give us everything else we need (v. 32).
- No charge can be brought against us, for we are justified. The verdict of the judge is in. We are declared not guilty (v. 33)
- No one can condemn us, for Christ has died and was raised on our behalf (v. 34a).
- More than that, he is our advocate at God's right hand, pleading our case (v. 34b).

- Therefore adversity should never threaten us, for nothing can separate us from the love of God revealed in Christ (vv. 35–39).

We cannot always readily perceive the love and goodness of God in our circumstances. But the gospel invites us to look beyond our situation to the sacrificial love of our saving Lord. As one author discovered:

> More than anything else I could ever do, the gospel enables me to embrace my tribulations and thereby position myself to gain full benefit from them. For the gospel is the one great permanent circumstance in which I live and move; and every hardship in my life is allowed by God only because it serves His gospel purposes in me. When I view my circumstances in this light, I realize that the gospel is not just one piece of good news that fits into my life somewhere among all the bad. I realize instead that the gospel makes genuinely good news out of every other aspect of my life, including my severest trials. The good news about my trials is that God is forcing them to bow to His gospel purposes and do good unto me by improving my character and making me conformed to the image of Christ.[13]

How God Uses Suffering

So the cross and resurrection are the ultimate answer to suffering. And we really can trust the good purposes of God in using suffering to make us more like Jesus. But it is still helpful to inquire further into the specific ways God uses trials in our lives. Understanding God's various purposes will help us better cooperate with him in our responses.

Let's explore Scripture to discover six ways God utilizes suffering in our lives, understanding that each of these uses serve God's ultimate purpose of glorifying himself by restoring his image within us.

1. God Uses Suffering to Teach Us His Word

God uses suffering to make our hearts more receptive to his transforming Word. As Richard Baxter said, "Though the word and Spirit do the main work, yet suffering so unbolts the door of the heart, that the word hath easier entrance."[14] Thomas Watson called affliction our "preacher and tutor," and said: "A sick-bed often teaches more than a sermon."[15]

Several verses from Psalm 119 view affliction from this perspective.

Before I was afflicted I went astray, but now I keep your word (Ps. 119:67).

It is good for me that I was afflicted, that I might learn your statutes (Ps. 119:71).

I know, O Lord, that your rules are righteous, and that in faithfulness you have afflicted me (Ps. 119:75).

Martin Luther's comments on these verses are perceptive. He viewed affliction, along with prayer and meditation, as one of God's regular teaching methods.

I want you to know how to study theology in the right way. I have practiced this method myself . . . The method of which I am speaking is the one which the holy king David teaches in Psalm 119 . . . Here you will find three rules. They are frequently proposed throughout the psalm and run thus: *oratio, meditatio, tentatio* [prayer, meditation, trial.][16]

2. God Uses Suffering to Wean Us from Idols

How, then, do trials help us learn truth? The Lord does not give us new revelation of truth when we suffer. He uses trials to wean our hearts from idols, our other sources of hope, so we might set our hearts on him and his Word.

The weaning process often begins as God uses suffering to unveil sinful dependencies and desires we didn't even know we had. As Tim Chester observes, "Sinful desires can lurk in our hearts unnoticed because those desires are neither threatened nor thwarted. But suffering stirs the calm waters of latent sinful desires. It reveals the true state of our hearts. It's God's diagnostic tool, preparing the way of the medicine of gospel truth."[17]

But when our hearts loosen their grasp of idolatrous desires, we will discover afresh the sweetness of the gospel and God himself. This was the insight of David Brainerd, who ministered to Native Americans in Colonial North America amidst severe conditions. When dying of tuberculosis, he wrote that, "Such fatigues and hardship as these serve to wean more from the earth: and, I trust, will make heaven the sweeter."[18] As Luther said, affliction "teaches you not only to know and understand, but also to experience how right, how true, how sweet, how lovely, how mighty, how comforting God's Word is."[19] Psalm 119, again, bears this out:

> This is my comfort in my affliction, that your promise gives me life (Ps. 119:50).

> If your law had not been my delight, I would have perished in my affliction (Ps. 119:92).

> I am severely afflicted; give me life, O Lord, according to your word! (Ps. 119:107).

> Look on my affliction and deliver me, for I do not forget your law (Ps. 119:153).

This also seems to be the point of Ecclesiastes 7:13–14, which says, "Consider the work of God: who can make straight what he has made crooked? In the day of prosperity be joyful, and in the day of adversity consider: God has made the one as well as the other, so that man may not find out anything that will be after him."

Without suffering, our hearts are easily divided between God and the world, like a needle being pulled by two magnets. God sometimes removes the magnet of earthly comforts, so that our whole heart may be drawn to him.

3. God Uses Suffering to Discipline Us

The writer to the Hebrews teaches us to view affliction as our Father's loving discipline.

> And have you forgotten the exhortation that addresses you as sons? "My son, do not regard lightly the discipline of the Lord, nor be weary when reproved by him. For the Lord disciplines the one he loves, and chastises every son whom he receives." It is for discipline that you have to endure. God is treating you as sons. For what son is there whom his

father does not discipline? If you are left without discipline, in which all have participated, then you are illegitimate children and not sons. Besides this, we have had earthly fathers who disciplined us and we respected them. Shall we not much more be subject to the Father of spirits and live? For they disciplined us for a short time as it seemed best to them, but he disciplines us for our good, that we may share his holiness. For the moment all discipline seems painful rather than pleasant, but later it yields the peaceful fruit of righteousness to those who have been trained by it.

—Hebrews 12:5–11

Observe both the honest realism and the hopeful outlook of this passage. The author acknowledges that "all discipline seems painful rather than pleasant." This is no pious sugarcoating of suffering, no denial of the distress it brings into our lives. Suffering hurts. Yet, even while granting the pain of present affliction, Scripture teaches us to look upward to our Father's tender care. We should not grow weary with God's discipline, but view it as a badge of sonship, "For the Lord disciplines the one he loves and chastises every son whom he receives."

It is important to see that this passage doesn't draw a one-to-one analogy between the discipline of an earthly father and the reproof of the Lord. Earthly parents are imperfect and sinful. Children are often disciplined according to the whims of their parents, sometimes even to the point of abuse. "They disciplined us for a short time as it seemed best to them." But God is not capricious in his discipline. His discipline is purposeful and good, because "he disciplines us for our good, that we may share his holiness."

We should also draw a distinction between God's fatherly discipline and punishment for guilt. There is a difference. When we suffer as Christians, God is not punishing us for our sins. As Psalm 103:10–13 says:

He does not deal with us according to our sins,
    nor repay us according to our iniquities.
For as high as the heavens are above the earth,
    so great is his steadfast love toward those who fear him;
As far as the east is from the west,
    so far does he remove our transgressions from us.

> As a father shows compassion to his children,
> so the Lord shows compassion to those who fear him.

When we suffer as his children, God reproves and corrects us, but he is not punishing us. He is not giving us what we deserve. He relates to us not as Lawgiver and Judge, but as Father and Redeemer. The suffering is, in fact, a part of our *training.* "For the moment all discipline seems painful rather than pleasant, but later it yields the peaceful fruit of righteousness to those who have been trained by it" (Heb. 12:11). As Thomas Watson said, "God's rod is a pencil to draw Christ's image more lively on us."[20]

One of the stunning implications of this passage is that we shouldn't wish away our sufferings, for to be without God's discipline is to be without a Father. He disciplines us for our good, and his rod of correction is a proof not of his anger, but his love. As William Cowper wrote:

> *Did I meet no trials here,*
> *No chastisement by the way,*
> *Might I not with reason fear*
> *I should prove a castaway?*
> *Bastards may escape the rod,*
> *Sunk in earthly vain delight;*
> *But the true-born child of God*
> *Must not—would not, if he might.*[21]

4. God Uses Suffering to Test and Purify Our Faith

Another way God uses suffering is to test and purify our faith. Through suffering, he reveals the genuineness of faith—or the lack thereof. Peter writes:

Blessed be the God and Father of our Lord Jesus Christ! According to his great mercy, he has caused us to be born again to a living hope through the resurrection of Jesus Christ from the dead, to an inheritance that is imperishable, undefiled, and unfading, kept in heaven for you, who by God's power are being guarded through faith for a salvation ready to be revealed in the last time. In this you rejoice, though now for a little while, as was necessary, you have been grieved by various trials, so that the tested genuineness of your faith—more precious than gold that perishes though it is tested by fire—may be found to result in praise and glory and honor at the revelation of Jesus Christ.

—1 Peter 1:3–7

The reality of our faith is revealed when we rejoice in our imperishable, undefiled, and unfading future inheritance, even though we are grieved with various trials. The result of a tested faith is "praise and glory and honor" when Jesus Christ is revealed in his future return. Rejoicing in trials reveals the genuineness of our faith.

On the other hand, Jesus taught that those who desert him because of tribulation and persecution show that the seed of the gospel has not penetrated deeply enough into their lives (Mark 4:17). Endurance is essential, not optional. "The one who endures to the end will be saved" (Matt. 10:20). But *endurance will never develop apart from suffering.* This is why Paul said, "We rejoice in our sufferings, knowing that suffering produces endurance, and endurance produces character, and character produces hope, and hope does not put us to shame, because God's love has been poured into our hearts through the Holy Spirit who has been given to us" (Rom. 5:3–5).

Consider also the exhortation James sent to early Christians who had been scattered by persecution, "Count it all joy, my brothers, when you meet trials of various kinds, for you know that the testing of your faith produces steadfastness. And let steadfastness have its full effect, that you may be perfect and complete, lacking in nothing" (James 1:2–4).

James uses the word "testing," (from the phrase "testing of your faith") twice, the only appearances of the word in the New Testament. But the word also shows up in two Old Testament contexts[22] (Ps. 12:6; Prov. 27:21), each of which refers to a crucible or refiner's fire. As Douglas Moo notes:

> The two OT occurrences both denote the process of refining silver or gold, and this is the way James uses the word. The difficulties of life are intended by God to refine our faith: heating it in the crucible of suffering so that impurities might be refined away and so that it might become pure and valuable before the Lord.[23]

We see this at work in the story of Job. After losing everything—wealth, children, and health—the quality of Job's faith was evident. Though he didn't understand God's purposes and couldn't perceive God's presence, he confessed, "But he knows the way that I take; when he has tried me, I shall come out as gold" (Job 1:13–19; 2:7–8; 23:1–10).

Charles Spurgeon used a great illustration about an ancient warrior who said, "I cannot use in battle a sword that has not been ofttimes annealed;[24] but give me a Damascus blade that has been so prepared, and I will cut through a coat of mail, or split a man from head to foot at a single stroke. It gets its temper and keenness of edge from having *slept with the flames again and again.*"[25] Like a Damascus blade, a believer is strengthened only by sleeping in the flames.

Suffering, then, is the crucible that makes endurance possible and, as we endure, affirms and purifies our faith. Adversity is a fiery test that reveals the quality of our trust in Christ and results in our greater steadfastness and maturity, and Christ's greater praise (James 1:4; 1 Peter 1:6–7). Of course, "the benefits of testing come only to believers who respond to them in the right way."[26] That is why both James and Peter teach us to rejoice, keeping in view the good purposes of God.

5. God Uses Suffering to Increase Our Usefulness

The Puritan, John Flavel wrote, "Let a Christian . . . be but two or three years without an affliction, and he is almost good for nothing."[27] And it was A. W. Tozer who said, "It is doubtful whether God can bless a man greatly until He has hurt him deeply."[28] Each of these men perceived another purpose for which God designs suffering: to increase our effectiveness in ministry to others. He does this in a couple of different ways.

Sometimes he uses suffering to work on our character, so that we'll become more dependent on Christ, and as a result, more useful to others. Jesus teaches this in John 15:1–2, using the powerful image of a vine and its branches. "I am the true vine, and my Father is the vinedresser. Every branch in me that does not bear fruit he takes away, and every branch that does bear fruit he prunes, that it may bear more fruit." Just as a vinedresser cuts away excess foliage from the branches of a vine in order to make them more fruitful, so the Father uses the pruning knife of afflictions to cut away the things in our lives that keep us from being more fruitful.

Sometimes, God positions us in difficult circumstances that paradoxically make us more effective. These circumstances, from a human perspective, place unwelcome limitations on our lives. But we don't see what God sees. The perfect example is Paul in Philippians 1 where, though he writes from prison, he rejoices because his imprisonment has "served to advance the gospel," as his suffering for Christ had become known throughout the imperial guard. And as others saw Paul suffer courageously, they became more confident in fearlessly preaching Christ (Phil. 1:12–14). From the distance of nearly two thousand years, we discern a further benefit from Paul's suffering: in the letters he wrote to churches now preserved for us in Scripture.

We also see this in 2 Corinthians, the most heart-baring of all Paul's letters. In the first chapter, he blesses God as the Father of mercies and God of all comfort for comforting him in his affliction, thus equipping him to comfort others with the same comfort he had received (2 Cor. 1:3–7). In the fourth chapter, he says:

> But we have this treasure in jars of clay, to show that the surpassing power belongs to God and not to us. We are afflicted in every way, but not crushed; perplexed, but not driven to despair; persecuted, but not forsaken; struck down, but not destroyed; always carrying in the body the death of Jesus, so that the life of Jesus may also be manifested in our bodies. For we who live are always being given over to death for Jesus' sake, so that the life of Jesus also may be manifested in our mortal flesh. So death is at work in us, but life in you.
>
> —2 Corinthians 4:7–12

For much of his ministry, Paul lived in constant danger of persecution and death. But far from being discouraged, he viewed his weakness and frailty as a jar of clay—a lowly vessel perfectly suited for carrying the valuable treasure of the gospel. Though afflicted, struck down, persecuted and perplexed, he was not forsaken, crushed, destroyed, or given to despair. He understood that the pattern of the death and resurrection of Jesus himself was being manifested through his mortal body for the sake of others. Death was at work in him, but this brought life to those he served. This is the paradox of the cross in our personal lives. God brings blessing to others through our weakness. The gospel achieves victory through our apparent defeat.

While you and I may never be imprisoned for our forthright expressions of faith, or live with a persistent physical challenge, we are still likely to suffer limitations as we seek to bring the name of Jesus to a world that is hostile to the gospel. We can trust God to use these limitations for good.

An anonymous author vividly captured this truth with the following poem.

When God wants to drill a man,
and thrill a man, and skill a man,
When God wants to mold a man
to play the noblest part,
When He yearns with all His heart
to create so great and bold a man,
That all the world shall be amazed,
Watch His methods! Watch His ways!
How He ruthlessly perfects
whom He royally elects
How He hammers him and hurts him,
And with mighty blows converts him
into trial shapes of clay,
which only God understands
While his tortured heart is crying and he lifts beseeching hands.
How He bends but never breaks
When His good He undertakes,
How He uses whom He chooses
and by every purpose fuses him,
by every act induces him
to try his splendor out
God knows what He's about.

6. God Uses Suffering to Prepare Us for Glory

Paul's reflections on suffering offer a final insight into their purpose: present afflictions actually work for our *future glory*. "For I consider that the sufferings of this present time are not worth comparing with the glory that is to be revealed to us" (Rom. 8:18). Paul's point is that future glory will far outweigh and compensate for present suffering. But in 2 Corinthians he says even more:

> So we do not lose heart. Though our outer self is wasting away, our inner self is being renewed day by day. For this light momentary affliction is preparing for us an eternal weight of glory beyond all comparison, as we look not to the things that are seen but to the things that are unseen. For the things that are seen are transient, but the things that are unseen are eternal.
>
> —2 Corinthians 4:16–18

Paul has a confidence that holds him steady through trials. He doesn't lose heart, because he knows God will raise him from the dead, as he did Jesus. He further knows that his afflictions are being used to extend grace to others and thus increase the thanksgiving and glory God will receive. This is why he is not discouraged. Though his body wastes away with affliction, persecution, and probably death, his inner nature is being renewed (vv. 8–16).

Then in verse 17, Paul says something stunning: "This light momentary affliction is preparing for us an eternal weight of glory beyond all comparison." The afflictions will not only be more-than-compensated-for by glory, they are actually *preparing* glory. "Preparing" is a common word in the New Testament that means to produce something. James uses this word when he says "the testing of your faith *produces* steadfastness" (James 1:3). Paul's meaning is unmistakable—there is something about suffering now that results in glory in eternity. As C. S. Lewis said, "They say of some temporal suffering, 'No future bliss can make up for it,' not knowing that Heaven, once attained, will work backwards and turn even that agony into a glory."[29]

This truth teaches us to view our trials as seeds of eternal glory planted in the soil of our present lives. Thinking of difficult circumstances like this doesn't come naturally to us short-sighted, time-bound mortals. It's difficult to see past the immediacy of poverty, divorce, cancer, or persecution. But faith in Christ enables us to "look not to the things that are seen but to the things that are unseen" (v. 18).

One of the most helpful word-pictures for this comes, once again, from C. S. Lewis:

Imagine yourself as a living house. God comes in to rebuild that house. At first, perhaps, you can understand what He is doing. He is getting the drains right and stopping the leaks in the roof and so on: you knew that those jobs needed doing and so you are not surprised. But presently he starts knocking the house about in a way that hurts abominably and does not seem to make sense. What on earth is He up to? The explanation is that He is building quite a different house from the one you thought of—throwing out a new wing here, putting on an extra floor there, running up towers, making courtyards. You thought you were going to be made into a decent little cottage: but He is building a palace. He intends to come and live in it Himself.[30]

When we view our afflictions from this perspective, we realize that God is using them to make us into better, more beautiful creatures than we could ever otherwise become. The refiner's fire is hot—but the fire burns away dross and tempers the metal of our faith, making it stronger. God's fatherly discipline does not bring immediate joy—but his rod helps us share his holiness. The palace will not be built as long as the remnants of the cottage stand. The demolition is painful—but this is the price God is willing to pay in preparing us for glory. Faith permits us to see difficult circumstances from God's perspective and confess with John Flavel:

Oh what owe I to the file, and to the hammer, and to the furnace of my Lord Jesus! who has now let me see how good the wheat of Christ is, that goes through his mill, and his oven, to be made bread for his own table. Grace tried is better than grace, and more than grace. It is glory in its infancy.[31]

So, suffering:

• teaches us God's Word
• weans us from our idols
• disciplines us as God's children

- tests and purifies our faith
- increases our usefulness
- and prepares us for future glory.

Suffering is not good in itself. It is the result of sin and brokenness in our world. Yet God promises to weave the dark threads of affliction and trial into the tapestry of his ultimate saving plan. He is a sovereign God, but his ways involve suffering. With wisdom, love, and goodness, he designs our difficulties and assigns our afflictions to conform us to the character of Christ.

Suffering Ways of a Sovereign God

I began this chapter with a story about my parents' faith in God's sovereign goodness when I was a teenager. Though Mom lost two children through miscarriages, God later blessed her with another child when my sister, Anna, was born. But an even more difficult trial came later.

In the course of the past several years, Mom, only in her late fifties, began to suffer the limitations of rapidly progressive dementia. Nothing has caused me more personal sadness than the effects of this degenerative illness on Mom. She had to stop cooking and driving several years ago. Now she can no longer recognize me as her son or readily recall my name. The pain of this suffering for our family is ongoing. As anyone who has walked through dementia with a close relative would know, the stress on Dad has been incalculable.

A couple of years ago, while already facing the mounting pressure of caring for Mom, one of Dad's close friends tragically and unexpectedly died. Dad was also in the middle of a very stressful trial related to his business. Wanting to express as much empathy to him as possible, I said, "I can't imagine what you're feeling right now. You must feel stretched to the breaking point." His voice broke. Through tears he agreed. And then he quoted from the book of Job: "He knoweth the way that I take: when he hath tried me, I shall come forth as gold" (Job 23:10, KJV). Despite the unrelenting intensity of these trials, he continued to trust in God's good and sovereign purpose to refine him through affliction.

My father's example, along with the examples of many others who have faced suffering with faith, has strengthened my trust in the suffering ways of our sovereign God. I certainly do not fully understand the ways of God with suffering. Trials are always difficult to endure when I face them in my own life or the lives of those I love. I cannot always perceive immediate benefits from afflictions in my life. I often just want them to end.

But I am slowly learning to trust the heart of God and embrace suffering as one of his tools for transforming me into a more Christlike person. My greatest comfort comes from knowing that, because of the suffering, death, and resurrection of Jesus; the suffering will someday cease once and for all, and that God's ultimate purpose to glorify himself in bringing many sons and daughters to glory will be fulfilled.

12

Life Together

Community

You cannot talk about human beings made in God's image without talking about relationships. Yet it is often the first thing we overlook. Only when human beings live in community do we fully reflect the likeness of God.

—Tim Lane & Paul Tripp

Lots of things were on my mind that morning in the café. The last thing I wanted was some cheerful stranger invading my privacy.

Along with several men from our church, I was out of town attending a conference. I had gotten up early and slipped away to a pleasant café to read Scripture, eat breakfast, and catch up with e-mail. The whirlwind of the conference would resume shortly. Then there would be the long drive home and my return to a life wonderfully blessed by God, yet busier than I had once imagined adulthood could be. Looming especially large was the sermon I was set to give on Sunday, a message focusing on community, relationships, and the importance of small groups.

So, when a man strolled up to my table and asked if he could join me—taking a seat before the words were even out of his mouth—honestly, I was a bit annoyed. I faked a smile and tried to be friendly. We exchanged names (his was Kevin) and began talking. He learned that I was a pastor and I discovered that he was a Christian, a businessman, a poet, and close friends with an author whose work had significantly affected me several years before. But while it turned out to be an interesting conversation, I was still irked by the loss of solitude. After all, I was trying to do my devotions! I really didn't have time for interruptions.

That's when God sent me a message through this brother in Christ. As I was describing our church, I mentioned that we put a high value on community. Then Kevin, who knew nothing about the sermon incubating in my mind, looked at me and said, "The next time you are standing before your congregation, remember that people are hungry to be less selfish than they are, to be more connected to others than they are, to have deeper relationships than they have, and to feel less isolated than they feel—*and they're not going to get any of it if they are looking at you all the time.*"

It was exactly what I needed to hear. It was exactly the attitude I needed to take to the pulpit the following Sunday. And it was exactly the gentle rebuke I needed from God regarding my bad attitude about this violation of my precious agenda.

Sometimes God sends us messages when we least expect it. Often he does it through others. Both *what* Kevin said, and the fact that *another person* said it, illustrate the important truth we will focus on in this final chapter.

Transformation is a community project.

Relationships in the Drama of Redemption

As believers, we hunger for both greater Christlikeness (to be less selfish) and for deeper relationships (to feel less isolated). That these two desires work in tandem shouldn't surprise us; God created us for relationships. From the very beginning, God declared that it was not good for man to be alone (Gen. 2:18), and as we saw in this book's opening chapter, one way we bear God's image is by relating to others. Paul Tripp and Tim Lane write:

> God is a community and we as his creation reflect this quality. Moreover, he brings us into community and places the desire for community within us. Ultimately, we can never escape our essential nature, who and what God designed us to be. This relational characteristic is central to who we are . . . you cannot talk about human beings made in God's image without talking about relationships. Yet it is often the first thing we overlook. Only when human beings live in community do we fully reflect the likeness of God.[1]

As God's image-bearers, we are inescapably relational. Our relational nature is reflected in Jesus' summary of God's law in the two great commandments: "You shall love the Lord your God with all your heart and with all your soul and with all your mind and with all your strength," and "You shall love your neighbor as yourself" (Mark 12:30–31). This is the sum of what God requires from us and designs for us. Love God. Love people. It's all about relationships.

The problem, of course, is that relationships aren't easy. Nor are they neutral. They are difficult.

> At one level we want friendships. At another level we don't want them! In creation, we were made to live in community, but because of the fall, we tend to run from the very friendships we need. Quite often, our longing for them is tainted by sin. We pursue them only as long as they satisfy our own desires and needs. We have a love-hate relationship with relationships![2]

Sin hijacks our relationships and exploits them to fortify our rebellion against God. We see this in the first relationships in Scripture. Sin turns Adam and Eve against God, then against one another in history's first marital conflict (Gen. 3). In Cain and Abel we get our initial sour taste of sibling rivalry, which ends tragically in murder (Gen. 4). The rest of human history is filled with reruns of those first bleak episodes.

But in the gospel, God steps in with grace, disarms sin, and by his love recaptures relationships. The dynamic outworking of the gospel

THE MEANS OF PERSONAL CHANGE

is seen in the redemption and restoration of what human beings have lost through sin. The essential first step in the process is a restored relationship with God, who rescues us from the curse and bondage of sin and renews within us hearts to worship him. But this is just the beginning. His ultimate goal is to restore the image of God within us by conforming us to the glorious image of his Son. And the restoration of his image always includes relational transformation, both vertically (with God) and horizontally (with others).

Of course, renewed relationships are not only the *result* of God's transforming grace, they are also a *means* for transformation. God uses relationships as tools for changing our lives. C. S. Lewis remarked that Christ "works on us in all sorts of ways . . . But above all, He works on us through each other."

> Men are mirrors, or "carriers" of Christ to other men . . . That is why the Church, the whole body of Christians showing Him to one another is so important. You might say that when two Christians are following Christ together there is not twice as much Christianity as when they are apart, but sixteen times as much . . . The Church exists for nothing else but to draw men into Christ, to make them little Christs. If they are not doing that, all the cathedrals, clergy, missions, sermons, even the Bible itself, are simply a waste of time. God became Man for no other purpose. It is even doubtful, you know, whether the whole universe was created for any other purpose.[3]

The goal of redemption is to make you a "little Christ." God wants to renew his image within you. But spiritual renewal doesn't happen in isolation from others. It happens in relationships.

Relationships are the stage on which the drama of redemption is enacted. They are an inescapable and necessary aspect of our sanctification. As Shakespeare said, "All the world's a stage"—God's stage.[4] And we are players on this stage, enacting our parts in the drama of redemption, as God calls us to live life together for the glory of his name.

Overcoming Obstacles to Community

We are made for relationships. Sometimes we long for them. And we desperately need them if we're to become more like Jesus. But when we're honest, we have to admit that relationships, both in and outside the church, are hard to build. Community is elusive.

You probably know what it is to hunger for relationship, to long for conversation, only to experience isolation instead. And it's not always because there are no people around you. You can be lonely in a crowd. Sometimes you feel like you are the one piece of a puzzle that doesn't seem to fit with all the others. You might as well be speaking a different language from everyone else. This relational dislocation is both real and painful, and it can leave you feeling hopeless.

At various points in this book we have discussed how, on the individual level, sins such as pride, selfishness, and fear incline us to isolate ourselves from one another spiritually and psychologically. In this closing chapter I want to look at obstacles to community on the cultural level.

Every culture and every age has its unique challenges to community. Let's briefly consider four of the most common phenomena in modern Western society that work against biblical community. These are individualism, compartmentalization, busyness, and misleading expectations.

1. Individualism

When my brothers and I were kids we sometimes played the "I" game. The object was for the players to talk with one another without using the personal pronoun "I." This produced all kinds of amusing grammatical contortions.

"*Me* thinks you are going to lose this game."

"*The person talking* disagrees. *He* knows you will lose."

While silly, the game was surprisingly difficult. Short of keeping silent, I could never avoid saying "I" for more than a few minutes.

Most of us spend our lives talking and thinking about ourselves. Apart from grace, we are hopelessly narcissistic and self-focused. We admire self-made people and covet the independence we think we see in them. We build our lives with the brick and mortar of self-interest and erect monuments to our own delusional self-esteem. Such attitudes are both foreign to Scripture and deadly for relationships. They produce only estranged siblings, broken vows, shattered marriages, alienated children, sour friendships, split churches, and warring nations. We can practice that same blind individualism in our pursuit of personal change. Even though something within us longs for the intimacy of relationships, we try to project an impenetrable image of independence and self-sufficiency. We can't have it both ways. If you and I genuinely desire to grow in grace, we must live in the reality that spiritual formation and our relational commitments are not separate pursuits, but inseparable aspects of the same goal.

2. Compartmentalization

Individualism fools us into seeing relationships in general, and the church in particular, as peripheral to our self-oriented lives. As a result, different aspects of our lives, including church, get sealed off in neat little compartments that we open or close at will. Our closest relationships may be in one box, work in another box, sports and leisure in a third box, church in a fourth box, etc., and we often don't think of them as related to one another. "All too often real-life connections simply run on a different track from 'church' and remain unredeemed and unredemptive."[5] This approach—life as a series of unconnected boxes—makes the growth of authentic, comprehensive Christian relationships impossible.

In their recent book, *Total Church: A Radical Reshaping around Gospel and Community,* Tim Chester and Steve Timmis use a different metaphor to describe the same self-oriented mentality, and offer a helpful alternative.

> The prevailing view of life today is that of an individual standing on his or her own, heroically juggling various responsibilities—family, friendships, career, leisure, chores, decisions, and money. We could also add social responsibilities like political activities, campaigning organizations, community groups, and school associations.
>
> From time to time the pressures overwhelm us, and we drop one or more of the balls. All too often church becomes one of the balls. We juggle our responsibilities for church (measured predominantly by

attendance at meetings) just as we juggle our responsibilities for work and leisure.

An alternative model is to view our various activities and responsibilities as spokes of a wheel. At the center or hub of life is not me as an individual but us as members of the Christian community. Church is not another ball for me to juggle but that which defines who I am and gives Christlike shape to my life.[6]

Do you relate to church as one of many balls you are trying to juggle? One of many compartmentalized, unrelated boxes? Or do you view the body of Christ as a network of gospel-centered relationships at the very hub of life in the Spirit?

Living with community as the hub requires a radical reorientation of our lives. Among other things, it will mean planning our schedules to maximize time with people, so that relationships with other believers are actually treated as a priority. The failure to do this probably accounts for the low levels of satisfaction so many people feel with the church. Our relationships with other believers will not be satisfying if we refuse to invest in them, keeping them walled off from the rest of life. We need a paradigm shift, a change of perspective about the role of community in our lives.

3. Busyness

A third hindrance to community is busyness. As John Ortberg writes, "We try to create first-century community on a twenty-first-century timetable—and it doesn't work. Maybe the biggest single barrier to deep connectedness for most of us is simply the pace of our lives."[7] Similarly, Calvin Miller says, "Hurried Christians beget hurried disciples. Hurried disciples become a hurried church—a hassled fellowship of disciples who serve the clock and call it God."[8]

In this area, the big problem for most of us is that we live under the tyranny of the urgent, letting urgent things push aside more important things. Then, when we get so burned out attending to urgent things— many of them relatively unimportant—we flee for rest and recreation to what is neither urgent nor important. As the pattern repeats we can easily go months or years neglecting the most important relationships in our lives. And when those relationships, which are really important, finally become urgent, they are often filled with tragic and regrettable heartbreak.

We also let many *non*-urgent activities crowd community out of our lives. TV. Sports. Extra-curricular activities for the kids. Maintaining a certain standard of living by working too many hours or too many jobs. Even church activities—which sometimes have little to do with building Christ-centered relationships—can hinder healthy community.

Did you ever see the episode of the *Three Stooges* in which Moe, Curly, and Larry are all trying to sleep in the same double bed? At first, Moe and Curly are in the bed. When Larry gets in on the right side, he pushes the others over and Moe falls off on the left side. Moe runs over to the right side, hops in, and Curly falls off on the left. And so it goes.

Our lives can be like that. We try to do more than is even possible. Most of us keep cramming things in, only to have something else fall out. We are not going to get more time. The bed doesn't get larger. One of the stooges simply can't get in.

> The requirement for true intimacy is chunks of unhurried time. If you think you can fit deep community into the cracks of an overloaded schedule—think again. Wise people do not try to microwave friendship, parenting, or marriage. You can't do community in a hurry.[9]

If you want authentic community, you will have to do less of something else.

4. Misleading Expectations

Have you ever imagined what the ideal church would look like? We would all love to take the best people and the best moments of our Christian experience (isolated, of course, from all the *other* moments and all those *other* people) and bring them together in one warm and loving place . . . where seldom is heard a discouraging word and the skies are not cloudy all day.

Of course, that's nothing but fantasy. The ideal church doesn't exist. How could it? We don't live in an ideal world, and there are no ideal people. We live in the real world, where real people are sinners and relationships are inherently messy and difficult.

The reason relationships are so difficult is because none of us are yet fully conformed to the image of Jesus. Sin remains within us. The process of change has only begun. Though we are saved by grace, the church on this side of glory is still a society of sinners. The failure to realize this sets us up for huge disappointments. If you are easily disillusioned with the church, perhaps you have lost sight of this. But that reality check, even if we have to go through it again and again, is vital to both our own spiritual maturity and the growth of others. If God is going to use us in one another's lives, we must be part of the church that truly exists, not the church we wish would exist. Dietrich Bonhoeffer said:

> The serious Christian, set down for the first time in a Christian community, is likely to bring with him a very definite idea of what Christian life together should be and to try to realize it. But God's grace speedily shatters such dreams . . . Every human wish dream that is injected into the Christian community is a hindrance to genuine community and must be banished if genuine community is to survive. He who loves his dream of a community more than the Christian community itself becomes a destroyer of the latter, even though his personal intentions may be ever so honest and earnest and sacrificial.[10]

So, no one in your church is perfect. But they *are* "instruments in the Redeemer's hands—people in need of change helping people in need of change."[11] They can help you, and you can help them. After all, spiritual transformation is inescapably a community project, a shared task. We need each other. God planned it that way.

A Biblical Portrait of the Church

We experience relationships in a variety of contexts—including the home (spouses, children, parents), the world (friends, neighbors, colleagues), and the church. The gospel informs all of these relationships and we are wise to consider how God specifically employs each in our progressive sanctification.[12]

But we're going to devote the final pages of this book to learning how to better cooperate with God in this task of building biblical community—of building the church. To begin, we need to clear our heads about what the church actually is.

Diverse Metaphors of the Church

For many people, "the church" is primarily a building or an organization. This perception is understandable, but Scripture pictures the church not as a building, but a *people*; not as an organization, but an *organism*. The wealth of metaphors Scripture uses to describe the church is stunning.

- The church is the *bride* of Christ, the object of his special affection and sacrificial love (Rev. 19:7; 21:2, 9; 22:17; cf. Eph. 5:25–33).

- More frequently, the church is called the *body* of Christ—many individual, interdependent members living under the lordship of Christ, the head of the church (Rom. 12:4–5; 1 Cor. 10:17; 12:12–27; Eph. 1:23; 2:16; 3:6; 4:4, 11–16; 5:23, 30; Col. 1:18; 3:15).

- The church is the *temple* of God, made up of living stones and indwelt by the Spirit (1 Cor. 3:16–17; Eph. 2:19–22; 1 Peter 2:4–8).

- Scripture refers to the church as a *flock,* shepherded by faithful leaders who serve under Christ, the Chief Shepherd (Luke 12:32; John 10:16; Acts 20:28–29; 1 Peter 5:1–4).

- The church is the *household*, or family, of God (Eph. 2:19; 1 Tim. 3:15; 1 Peter 4:17).

- Paul describes the church as the *pillar* and *buttress* of the truth; a pillar because the church displays the truth, a buttress because the church protects the truth (1 Tim. 3:15).

- In his letter to believers in the Roman colony of Philippi, Paul likened the church to a *colony* of heaven (Phil. 3:20; cf. 1:27).

- Paul and Peter refer to the church as a *special people* who are possessed by God (Titus 2:14; 1 Peter 2:9), with Peter also using the Old Testament language of *chosen race, royal priesthood,* and *holy nation,* and Paul referring to the church as the *new man* or *new humanity* (Eph. 2:15).

Together these metaphors show us the *value* God places on the church, the intimate *relationship* he shares with it, and the organic *unity* which characterizes its members.

Unifying Marks of the Church

If the church can be likened to many *different* things, what are the most essential characteristics that all churches should have *in common*? While much has been written on this subject, we can benefit by focusing on a single passage that provides us with what John Stott called, "a beautiful little cameo of the Spirit-filled church."[13]

> And they devoted themselves to the apostles' teaching and fellowship, to the breaking of bread and the prayers. And awe came upon every soul, and many wonders and signs were being done through the apostles. And all who believed were together and had all things in common. And they were selling their possessions and belongings and distributing the proceeds to all, as any had need. And day by day, attending the temple together and breaking bread in their homes, they received their food with glad and generous hearts, praising God and having favor with all the people. And the Lord added to their number day by day those who were being saved.
>
> —Acts 2:42–47

This passage describes the church in her infancy as she is indelibly stamped by the Holy Spirit with five distinct characteristics.

A Gospel Community

The church was created by the Word and Spirit on the Day of Pentecost, following Peter's proclamation of the gospel (Acts 2:1–41). The church is therefore a community "devoted . . . [to] the apostles' teaching." Both faith and discipleship—initial conversion and ongoing transformation—are dependent on this devotion to the apostolic teaching of the gospel. The church is a community both *created* by the gospel and *sustained* by the gospel.

A Worshipful Community

The church is devoted to prayer and takes joy in "praising God." Our experience of grace overflows in joyful worship, and Peter reminds us that God has made us "a chosen race, a royal priesthood, a holy nation, a people for his own possession" *so that* we "may proclaim the excellencies of him who called [us] out of darkness into his marvelous light" (1 Peter 2:9). Worship is the ultimate goal of our spiritual formation, with the apex of worship taking place in the gathered community. *This*—the assembled people of God in worship—is the destiny toward which we are moving (Rev. 5:9–10).

A Sacramental Community

"They devoted themselves to . . . the breaking of bread." Stott notes that "the definite article in both expressions (literally, 'the breaking of the bread and the prayers') suggests a reference to the Lord's Supper on the one hand (although almost certainly at that early stage as part of a larger meal) and prayer services or meetings (rather than private prayer) on the other."[14]

Some believers, in an understandable reaction to Catholicism, dislike the word "sacrament." But what I mean by the term is that Christ discloses his presence in a special, sanctifying (but not regenerating or justifying) way to those who receive the elements with faith.

> Worthy receivers, outwardly partaking of the visible elements, in this sacrament, do then also, inwardly by faith, really and indeed, yet not carnally and corporally but spiritually, receive and feed upon, Christ crucified, and all benefits of His death: the body and blood of Christ being then, not corporally or carnally, in, with, or under the bread and wine; yet, as really, but spiritually, present to the faith of believers in that ordinance, as the elements themselves are to their outward senses.[15]

Yet the privilege and sacrament of the Lord's Supper is often neglected in discussions of spiritual formation. This ought not to be. Notice, for example, in Luke 24, that when Jesus ate with his disciples, "he was known to them in the breaking of the bread" (v. 35).

Richard Lovelace believes that, "a return to a stronger view of the Supper, and the more frequent Communion advocated by the Reformers, would be immensely helpful to the spiritual life of Protestantism. This is true because the Communion service is the most graphic embodiment of the primary elements of spiritual renewal secured in Christ's death and resurrection, especially his justifying work for us and his sanctifying life in us."[16] If our transformation is furthered by a deeper understanding and appropriation of the gospel, then we should value more highly this means of "proclaiming the Lord's death until he comes" (1 Cor. 11:26).

A Relational Community

A fourth characteristic of the church found in Acts 2:42 is devotion to "fellowship." The word here is *koinonia*, from the Greek word *koinos*, which meant "common" and is the root of the word *community*. Devotion to *koinonia* means far more than getting together and eating a lot. It means having a common share in something greater than ourselves: fellowship with God, his Son Jesus Christ, and the Holy Spirit (1 John 1:3; 1 Cor. 1:9; 2 Cor. 13:14). To be devoted to fellowship is to be caught up into the Trinitarian life and fellowship of God!

Such fellowship has a hard, practical edge to it. "And all who believed were together and had all things in common. And they were selling their possessions and belongings and distributing the proceeds to all." Notice, however, that the selling was selective, for some of the disciples still had houses in which to meet. The giving was also voluntary, for the imperfect tense of the verbs "selling" and "distributing" indicates that both the "selling and the giving were occasional, in response to particular needs, not once and for all."[17]

Thus, the true meaning of this passage is far more exciting than any socialist notion of collective ownership imposed by coercive pressure or legal force. Rather, this passage shows us the radical results of gospel transformation, which loosens our grip on material possessions and opens our hearts in generosity to others.

A Missional Community

Finally, we see that the church is missional, for "the Lord added to their number day by day those who were being saved." Notice first that their mission was an overflow of their life together. While there is nothing inherently wrong with formalized evangelism programs, the apostolic church didn't need one. They weren't just involved in a mission, they *were* the mission. An authentic community built around the presence of the living God revealed in Jesus Christ and indwelt by the Holy Spirit is the single most powerful argument for the reality of God. Isn't this what Jesus said? "By this all people will know that you are my disciples, if you have love for one another" (John 13:35).

Notice also that although the church actively cooperated with God, it was the Lord who did both the saving and the adding. What was the church's part? They proclaimed the gospel and prayed for the Spirit's power (Acts 4:29–30) as they walked in the transforming power of the gospel *together*.

Transformation Is a Community Project

Having sketched a biblical portrait of the church, let's now ask: *How does God use relationships within the body of Christ to help us become more like Jesus?* If we are convinced that "grace is conveyed through the body of Christ along horizontal channels as well as through the vertical relationship of each believer to God,"[18] and if we can see *how this happens,* we will be better equipped to cooperate with God in receiving this grace and extending it to others.

In Ephesians 4, Paul spells out the implications of one of the dominant metaphors for the church, that of a body. He tells us that just as a victorious king dispenses the spoils of war to his people, so has the ascended Christ granted gifts to his people. The purpose of these gifts is to build up the body of Christ. And the goal of "body-building" is to help us attain to "mature manhood" and "the measure of the stature of the fullness of Christ." Without the "body-building" ministry, we will remain immature children, as susceptible to false teaching as boats are to storms at sea (Eph. 4:7–14).

Then Paul gives us the key for how we can together grow into Christ's image.

> *Speaking the truth in love,* we are to grow up in every way into him who is the head, into Christ, from whom the whole body, joined and held together by every joint with which it is equipped, when each part is working properly, makes the body grow so that it builds itself up in love.
>
> —Ephesians 4:15–16

Speaking the truth in love! That's it. To understand what Paul is saying here is to grasp the key to mutual spiritual growth within local churches. As it turns out, however, "'Speaking the truth in love' is not the best rendering of his expression, for the Greek verb makes no reference to our speech. Literally, it means 'truthing . . . in love,' and includes the notions of 'maintaining,' 'living,' and 'doing' the truth."[19]

We might say, therefore, that spiritual maturity is the result of a mutual, loving, truth-oriented ministry. This is "perhaps the most important ethical guideline in the New Testament, one that summarizes what Christian living is about: truth, love, and continual growth into Christ in everything."[20]

This balance of truth-plus-love is crucial. As Tim Chester writes, "Love without truth is like doing heart surgery with a wet fish. But truth without love is like doing heart surgery with a hammer."[21] We must embody truth, not just express it. So truth, fused with love, is incarnated in our lives as we live it out with one another. Paul David Tripp concurs: "God transforms people's lives as people bring his Word to others . . . . The combination of powerful truth wrapped in self-sacrificing love is what God uses to transform people."[22]

This is all well and good, and absolutely true. But let's step back from the theory for a moment to make a practical point: *We cannot grow up through "truthing in love" if we are not together.* The body builds itself up in love as its various parts are "joined and held *together*." A dismembered body does not grow.

Paul emphasizes the interdependence of the members in verse 16 by saying that the body is "joined and held together by every joint with which it is equipped when each part *is working properly.*" The body only grows as each part is connected to the whole and communicating with the whole. Only under these circumstances can each individual part fulfill its unique role. Christ, as the head of this spiritual body, endows the church with gifts in order to equip us to serve one another. And he supplies each of us with the strength and grace to work properly, each doing his or her part. *Growth in spiritual maturity is a matter of mutual cooperation.* As John Murray wrote:

In reality the growth of the individual does not take place except in the fellowship of the church as the fellowship of the Spirit. If the individual is indifferent to the sanctification of others, and does not seek to promote their growth in grace, love, faith, knowledge, obedience, and holiness, this interferes with his own sanctification in at least two respects. (1) His lack of concern for others is itself a vice that gnaws at the root of spiritual growth. If we are not concerned with, or vigilant in respect of the fruit of the Spirit in others, then it is because we do not burn with holy zeal for the honour of Christ himself . . . (2) His indifference to the interests of others means the absence of ministry which he should have afforded to others. This absence results in the impoverishment of these others to the extent of his failure, and this impoverishment reacts upon himself, because these others are not able to minister to him to the full extent of the support, encouragement, instruction, edification, and exhortation which they owe him.[23]

So, spiritual maturity is the result of "truthing in love" which happens as believers share life together. But what does loving, truth-oriented ministry to one another actually look like? We get the answer from the many "one another" commands given in the New Testament. These commands, which have been called the "house rules for God's family,"[24] guide us in two ways. They highlight how relationships are central to healthy spiritual growth, and they show us in practical ways how to promote such growth.

I will summarize the "one another" commands in five broad categories that together offer a well-balanced prescription for healthy body life. Remember, these commands are reciprocal—we should all be on both the giving *and* receiving ends of these different ways of truthing one another in love.

1. Get Together

Again, at the most basic level, we must begin by getting together! This is implicit in the commands to greet one another (Rom 16:1–16; 1 Cor. 16:20; 2 Cor. 13:12; 1 Peter 5:14) and show hospitality to one another (1 Peter 4:9). You cannot get to know someone *deeply* if you don't know them *at all*! The process begins with greeting. Saying hello. Having a conversation.

After conversation, the New Testament envisions something more meaningful: inviting other believers into your home and into your life. Of course, showing hospitality often requires self-denial and hard work, which may be one reason Peter says "show hospitality to one another without grumbling" (1 Peter 4:9). Most of us only welcome into our homes and lives people who are like us, those with whom we are naturally most comfortable. While it is fine for Christian hospitality to begin more or less inside our comfort zone, the idea is to push beyond it, welcoming fellow believers who may be very different from us.

We see this in Romans 14–15, where Paul exhorts the believers in Rome to extend the love of Christ to one another in spite of their different perspectives and practices in dietary matters.

> May the God of endurance and encouragement grant you to live in such harmony with one another, in accord with Christ Jesus, that together you may with one voice glorify the God and Father of our Lord Jesus Christ. Therefore welcome one another as Christ has welcomed you, for the glory of God.
>
> —Romans 15:5–7

Here, at the height of his argument for Christian unity, Paul points the Romans to the *power*, the *model*, and the *reason* for welcoming one another into their lives.

- The *power* for welcoming one another and living in harmony comes from God himself, "the God of endurance and encouragement," again acknowledging that hospitality and openness are not always easy.
- The *model* is Christ: "live in harmony with one another, in accord with Christ Jesus, . . . Therefore welcome one another as Christ has welcomed you."
- The *reason* is the glory of God: "live in harmony with one another in accord with Christ Jesus, that together you may with one voice glorify the God and Father of our Lord Jesus Christ" and "Welcome one another . . . for the glory of God."

Greeting one another. Showing hospitality to one another. Welcoming one another. These are the first steps to community. *To build transforming relationships with others, we have to get together.*

2. Show Love

The most often repeated command regarding Christian relationships is simply, "love one another" (John 13:34–35; 15:12, 17; 1 Thess. 4:9; 1 John 3:11, 16, 23; 4:7, 11–12; 2 John 1:5). "A new commandment I give to you, that you love one another: just as I have loved you, you also are to love one another" (John 13:34). Paul teaches that we fulfill the law through loving one another (Rom. 13:8). And Peter says that we are to "love one another earnestly from a pure heart" (1 Peter 1:22).

But, of course, love is not just a sweet, sentimental feeling. Loving one another requires treating one another with the same grace and kindness, forgiveness and forbearance that Christ has extended to us. In other words, loving others is often costly and painful. But it is in the very costliness of loving others that we become more like Jesus. In fact, as the following passages of Scripture indicate, God *intends* our relationships to be the primary contexts for learning to follow Jesus in the path of costly love.

> Let all bitterness and wrath and anger and clamor and slander be put away from you, along with all malice. Be kind to one another, tenderhearted, forgiving one another, as God in Christ forgave you. Therefore be imitators of God, as beloved children. And walk in love, as Christ loved us and gave himself up for us, a fragrant offering and sacrifice to God.
>
> —Ephesians 4:31–5:2

> Put on then, as God's chosen ones, holy and beloved, compassion, kindness, humility, meekness, and patience, bearing with one another and, if one has a complaint against another, forgiving each other; as the Lord has forgiven you, so you also must forgive.
>
> —Colossians 3:12–13

> By this we know love, that he laid down his life for us, and we ought to lay down our lives for the brothers. But if anyone has the world's goods and sees his brother in need, yet closes his heart against him, how does

God's love abide in him? Little children, let us not love in word or talk but in deed and in truth.

—1 John 3:16–18

Have you recognized how impossible it would be to imitate Christ in his love without relationships? There is simply no way to become like Jesus without following him in the path of love. And that requires people *to* love. Without relationships we will not grow in Christlikeness. As John Wesley said, "There is nothing more unchristian than a solitary Christian."[25]

3. Share Truth

While "speaking the truth in love" need not always include the direct quotation *of* Scripture, when rightly practiced it will always orbit tightly *around* Scripture, bringing the truth of God's Word to bear in one another's lives. Indeed, Scripture itself commands us to instruct one another (Rom. 15:14), admonish one another through psalms, hymns, and spiritual songs (Col. 3:16), and edify (or build up) one another (1 Thess. 5:11). The clear implications are (1) that we must begin from Scripture, and (2) that God has so arranged his church that we *need* others to help us better see, understand, and apply the truth of the gospel to our lives.

A similar point was made by C. S. Lewis in his book, *The Four Loves*. In an allusion to his good friends Charles Williams (deceased at the time Lewis wrote this) and J. R. R. Tolkien, Lewis wrote:

In each of my friends there is something that only some other friend can fully bring out. By myself I am not large enough to call the whole man into activity; I want other lights than my own to show all his facets. Now that Charles is dead, I shall never again see Ronald's reaction to a specifically Caroline joke. Far from having more of Ronald, having him "to myself" now that Charles is away, I have less of Ronald. Hence true friendship is the least jealous of loves. Two friends delight to be joined by a third, and three by a fourth . . . we possess each friend not less but more as the number of those with whom we share him increases. In this, Friendship exhibits a glorious "nearness by resemblance" to Heaven . . . for every soul, seeing Him in her own way, communicates that unique vision to all the rest... The more we share the Heavenly Bread between us, the more we shall all have.[26]

The more we share... the more we shall all have. To put it as simply as possible, you and I should pursue relationships with others because our vision of Christ and his glory will be impoverished to whatever degree we are disengaged from relationships with others.

When we are in meaningful relationships with one another, we each bring a unique perspective and experience to our knowledge of Christ's love. One person has been rescued from a menacing addiction. Another has been brought through deep suffering. Still another has been sustained by God's grace in a difficult marriage. The list goes on. When we gather to share our stories, we see a different aspect of the diamond that is the love of Christ.[27]

4. Confront Sin

Not only do I need the help of others to see more of Christ and his glory. I also need their help to see the sinfulness of my own heart more clearly.

Take care, brothers, lest there be in any of you an evil, unbelieving heart, leading you to fall away from the living God. But exhort one another every day, as long as it is called "today," that none of you may be hardened by the deceitfulness of sin. For we have come to share in Christ, if indeed we hold our original confidence firm to the end.

—Hebrews 3:12–14

This is a serious warning that both diagnoses the problem of sin (the hardening of heart in unbelief) and prescribes the cure (exhorting one another every day). The writer warns us that an evil, unbelieving heart can lead us to fall away from the living God. This is the danger for those whose hearts are hardened by the deceitfulness of sin. And the scary thing is that because sin is so insidiously deceitful, we may not even recognize the hardening process at work in our souls. But the passage also prescribes the cure: *community.* "Exhort one another every day

... that none of you may be hardened by the deceitfulness of sin." We can't see ourselves very well by ourselves! As Paul Tripp writes:

> Personal insight is the product of community. I need you in order to really see and know myself. Otherwise, I will listen to my own arguments, believe my own lies, and buy into my own delusions. My self-perception is as accurate as a carnival mirror. If I am going to see myself clearly, I need you to hold the mirror of God's Word in front of me.[28]

The warning from Hebrews might feel unsettling to some. Does it imply that you could lose your salvation? Or, is this passage actually addressed to false professors of faith, to unbelievers? The answer to both questions is No. The author is clearly addressing Christians, because he calls them "brothers" in verse 12 and in verse 14 he confirms that "we share in Christ." So, this is not a warning to unbelievers. But neither is he suggesting that a true believer can lose salvation.[29] The warning is intended not to frighten us into thinking that we are unbelievers or that we can lose our salvation, but rather to keep us walking in faith, to keep us holding onto Christ, to keep us using the means of grace God has provided for us—including community. As John Piper says, *"Eternal security is a community project."*[30]

5. Stir Up

Finally, we help one another become more like Jesus by considering one another in order to stir up love and good works. As the dying embers of a fire need to be stoked and stirred into flame again, so our hearts need to be stirred into action by the encouragement of others.

> And let us consider one another in order to stir up love and good works, not forsaking the assembling of ourselves together, as is the manner of some, but exhorting one another, and so much the more as you see the Day approaching.
> —Hebrews 10:24–25 NKJV

Notice that stirring up love and good works requires that we "*consider* one another."[31] I need people in my life who consider me, who study my soul, who look deeply into the patterns of my thinking, the ways of my heart. I need people who know me so well, that they know how to effectively motivate me into obedient action. So do you.

This passage also shows us that one of the motives for considering and exhorting one another is the approaching Day of the Lord. If we are tempted to give short shrift to the importance of relationships, it's because we have adopted a mentality more characterized by this age than the age to come. This grounds our relationships in an eternal perspective, reminding us that we are all headed for an eternal destiny.

In *The Weight of Glory*, C. S. Lewis clarifies what is at stake:

> It may be possible for each to think too much of his own potential glory hereafter; it is hardly possible for him to think too often or too deeply about that of his neighbour. The load, or weight, or burden of my neighbour's glory should be laid daily on my back, a load so heavy that only humility can carry it, and the backs of the proud will be broken. It is a serious thing to live in a society of possible gods and goddesses, to remember that the dullest and most uninteresting person you talk to may one day be a creature which, if you saw it now, you would be strongly tempted to worship, or else a horror and a corruption such as you now meet, if at all, only in a nightmare. All day long we are, in some degree, helping each other to one or other of these destinations. It is in the light of these overwhelming possibilities, it is with the awe and the circumspection proper to them, that we should conduct all our dealings with one another, all friendships, all loves, all play, all politics. There are no ordinary people. You have never talked to a mere mortal. Nations, cultures, arts, civilization—these are mortal, and their life is to ours as the life of a gnat. But it is immortals whom we joke with, work with, marry, snub, and exploit—immortal horrors or everlasting splendours.[32]

Relationships matter because you and I, to some degree, are helping each other to one or the other of these destinations. We will either help one another move toward increasing Christlikeness and everlasting glory, or we will further the progressive disintegration and corruption of our souls.

The stakes are high! The people in your life will last forever. Keep an eternal perspective and, under God's grace, do everything in your power to use relationships for both your own and your friends' progressive conformity to the character of Christ.

Joining the Dance of Community

As we bring this chapter to a close, let's return to a word introduced earlier in this chapter: *fellowship.* To live in Christian fellowship is to share something in common with others that is much greater than our individual selves.

In his first letter, John reminds a group of believers that the apostles had proclaimed to them "the eternal life, which was with the Father and was made manifest to us . . . so that you too may have fellowship with us" (1 John 1:2–3a). We know from verse 1 that "the eternal life" which they proclaimed was none other than Jesus Christ himself, living and incarnate, the one which the disciples had heard, seen, looked upon, and touched with their own hands. But the apostles proclaimed eternal life *in order that* we might have *fellowship* with them. But then he goes further and says, "and indeed our fellowship is with the Father and with his Son Jesus Christ" (v. 3b). In other words, the goal of the apostolic preaching was to draw people into the eternal fellowship that exists within the Trinitarian life of God!

This takes us back to where we began this book. God's goal in creating human beings in the first place was that they image forth his glory. But he never intended us to do it alone. Being image-bearers of God necessarily involves us in relationships—with him, one another, and the world. The reason community is essential is because it has its foundation in the being of God. As Dallas Willard writes, "God's aim in human history is the creation of an all inclusive community of loving persons, with himself included as its primary sustainer and most glorious inhabitant."[33]

We get a taste of this in John 17, when Jesus prays for believers "that they may all be one, just as you, Father, are in me, and I in you, that they also may be in us, so that the world may believe that you have sent me" (v. 21). We will spend eternity exploring the impenetrable depths contained in those few words! The Father is in the Son. The Son is in the Father. And Jesus prays that *we* may be in *them*—the Father and the Son. But then Jesus takes it further, as he prays not only for this mysterious union of relationships, but also explains that the purpose for this is "so that the world may know that you sent me and loved them even as you loved me" (vv. 22–23). In other words, God's mission of being known in the world is accomplished precisely through this—the union of believers with one another and their union with God in Christ.

C. S. Lewis helpfully compared the Trinitarian fellowship of God to a dance. He wrote:

> In Christianity God is not a static thing—not even a person—but a dynamic, pulsating activity, a life, almost a kind of drama. Almost, if you will not think me irreverent, a kind of dance.[34]

This dance, or drama, stands at the very center of ultimate reality. For God is not a solitary personality, but a community of three persons who eternally coexist in mutual, indwelling, self-giving relationships of love with one another. This is what the early church fathers called *perichoresis,* which comes from two Greek words: *peri* (around) and *chorea* (dance). Lewis then describes how you and I must be drawn into the *choreography* of this eternal dance.

> The whole dance, or drama, or pattern of this three-Personal life is to be played out in each one of us: or (putting it the other way round) each one of us has got to enter that pattern, take his place in that dance. There is no other way to the happiness for which we were made.[35]

The problem, of course, is that we sometimes refuse to dance. Let me illustrate. A few years ago my youngest brother got married. It was a beautiful ceremony and I felt honored to be the Best Man—until that moment in the reception when the DJ yelled into his microphone for everyone in the wedding party to make their way to the dance floor and do the Hokey-Pokey. That's when the panic kicked in. Joyful heart to sweaty palms in about ten seconds. You see, I was raised a no-dancing Baptist. Add to that my general lack of coordination, combined with a natural introversion, and the fact that I had literally never danced in my life.

Yes, this was my brother's wedding. Yes, I had agreed to dedicate the day, not to indulging my insecurities, but to playing a key role in joyfully celebrating his marriage. This was supposed to be about Andy and Alissa, his bride—not me and my pride. Yet somehow, as the rest of the wedding party rose and moved toward the dance floor, I managed to slip off in the opposite direction. Who am I kidding? I exited the main hall and lurked in less visible parts of the building until the dancing was over!

We all have a similar tendency to shrink away from personal relationships, especially when they stretch us beyond our comfort zones. But in doing so, we miss the opportunity to grow closer to the people God has put in our lives. This in itself would be sad enough. But consider the *Imago Dei*. Consider everything we have learned in this book about the extraordinary measures God has taken to rescue us from our sins, reconcile us to himself through the gospel, renew us in his image, and make us part of the new community he is redeeming for his glory. You see, the saddest thing about neglecting community with other believers is that it sets us at cross purposes with the very reason for which we were redeemed. We are, in fact, setting ourselves against the heart of reality itself. For God, who is ultimate reality, is a community. And to experience the joy of his love, you cannot remain outside of the party. You have to join the dance.

Lewis went on to say:

> Good things as well as bad, you know, are caught by a kind of infection. If you want to get warm you must stand near the fire: if you want to get wet you must get into the water. If you want joy, power, peace, eternal life, you must get close to, or even into, the thing that has them. They are not a sort of prize which God could if He chose, just hand out to anyone. They are a great fountain of energy and beauty spurting up at the very centre of reality. If you are close to it, the spray will wet you: if you are not, you will remain dry.[36]

Victoria Falls is the largest waterfall in the world. During a mission trip to Africa several years ago, I got to visit this incredible spectacle of wonder, power, and beauty. Prior to our arrival, we stopped several miles away and enjoyed a panoramic view of the entire area. A great swell of mist rose from the falls in the distance. When we arrived, the roar of the water was thunderous and the mist was everywhere. It was like walking through a tropical rain forest, and by the end of the tour, I was soaked to the skin!

The Triune God, much like Victoria Falls, is an inexhaustible wonder of power, majesty, grace, and beauty. The Father has loved us with an everlasting love. He gave his Son to live as our perfect representative, to die as our spotless substitute. And now, the Father, together with his risen and exalted Son, has sent his Spirit to dwell within his people with transforming grace and power. You can hear the thunderous roar of his power from afar, but to be drenched with his grace you have to draw near to him. You can't get close if you shrink away—from either God or his people. But through grace alone, you can press in. As we read in the final chapter of Scripture, *"The Spirit and the Bride say, 'Come.'"*

It's time to join the dance.

Notes

Introduction

1. Dietrich Bonhoeffer, *The Cost of Discipleship* (New York, NY: Collier Books, Macmillan Publishing Company, 1963 Revised Edition) 47.

2. Timothy Keller, "The Centrality of the Gospel," Redeemer Presbyterian Church of New York City. Available online at: http://download.redeemer.com/pdf/learn/resources/Centrality_of_the_Gospel-Keller.pdf. Accessed February 16, 2010.

3. Ibid.

4. John Owen, *A Discourse Concerning the Holy Spirit*, in William H. Gould, ed., *The Works of John Owen*, vol. 3 (Carlisle, PA: The Banner of Truth Trust, 1967 reprint of 1850–53 edition) 370–371.

Chapter 1—Restoring God's Broken Image: The Goal

1. *Westminster Shorter Catechism*, Question 1: "What is the chief end of man?"

2. Sinclair B. Ferguson, *The Holy Spirit* (Downers Grove, IL: InterVarsity Press, 1996) 139–140

3. *The Heidelberg Catechism*, Question 6: "Did God then create man so wicked and perverse?"

4. Irenaeus, *Against Heresies*, Book IV, Chapter 20, Number 7. Quoted in Ben Patterson, *Deepening Your Conversation with God: Learning to Love to Pray* (Minneapolis, MN: Bethany House Publishers, 2001) 87.

5. Herman Bavinck uses the same metaphor, saying: "The entire world is a revelation of God, a mirror of his attributes and perfections. Every creature in its own way and degree is the embodiment of a divine thought. But among creatures, only man is the image of God, God's highest and richest self-revelation and consequently the head and crown of the whole creation . . . While all creatures display vestiges of God, only a human being is the image of God. And he is such totally, in soul and body, in all his faculties and powers, in all conditions and relations. Man is the image of God because and insofar as he is truly human, and he is

truly and essentially human because, and to the extent that, he is the image of God." Herman Bavinck, John Bolt, gen. ed., John Vriend, trans., *Reformed Dogmatics: Volume 2: God and Creation* (Grand Rapids, MI: Baker Academic, 2004) 530–531, 555. By saying that man is the image of God totally, "in soul and body," Bavinck does not infer that God has physical attributes. "God, after all, is 'spirit' (*pneuma*, John 4:24) and has no body. The human body is a part of the image of God in its organization as instrument of the soul, in its formal perfection, not in its material substance as flesh (*sarx*)" (559–560). While beyond the scope of this chapter, Bavinck's fuller unpacking of the meaning of "image of God" is very helpful. He explores how God's image is "demonstrable in the human soul" (555); that "belonging to the image of God . . . are the human faculties" (556); that "the image of God manifests itself in the virtues of knowledge, righteousness, and holiness with which humanity was created from the start" (557); "how the human body belongs integrally to the image of God" (559); and that "also belonging to this image is man's habitation in paradise" (561). Bavinck also traces the interpretive history of the *imago Dei* in Christian theology and carefully distinguishes the Reformed view from both the Roman Catholic and Lutheran positions.

6. Anthony A. Hoekema, *Created in God's Image* (Grand Rapids, MI: Wm B. Eerdmans Publishing Co., 1986) 52.

7. John Ortberg, *Everybody's Normal Till You Get to Know Them* (Grand Rapids, MI: Zondervan, 2003) 34, 35, 39.

8. Hoekema, 75.

9. See references in ibid., 83.

10. J. I. Packer, *Rediscovering Holiness* (Ann Arbor, MI: Vine Books, 1992) 50.

11. John Calvin, John T. McNeil, ed., Ford L. Battles, trans., *Institutes of the Christian Religion*, Book I, Chap. XV, 4 (Philadelphia, PA: The Westminster Press, 1960) 189.

12. Alistair Begg, *What Angels Wish They Knew: The Basics of True Christianity* (Chicago, IL: Moody Press, 1998) 37.

13. Though his original name was Abram, I am using the name God later gave him in Genesis 17:5.

14. For a fascinating study on the themes of seed (descendants) and land in the Old Testament, see Stephen G. Dempster, *Dominion and Dynasty: A Biblical Theology of the Hebrew Bible* (Downers Grove, IL: InterVarsity Press, 2004).

15. "Who did [Jesus] think he was? What did he think he was to do? The answers came from his Bible, the Hebrew scriptures in which he found a rich tapestry of figures, historical persons, prophetic pictures and symbols of worship. And in this tapestry, where others saw only a fragmented collection of various figures and hopes, Jesus saw his own face." Christopher J. H. Wright, *Knowing Jesus Through the Old Testament* (Downers Grove, IL: InterVarsity Press, 1992) 108.

16. Herman Bavinck, John Bolt, gen. ed., John Vriend, trans., *Reformed Dogmatics: Volume 1: Prolegomena* (Grand Rapids, MI: Baker Academic, 2003) 112.

17. Herman Ridderbos, *Paul: An Outline of His Theology* (Grand Rapids, MI: Wm B. Eerdmans Publishing Co., 1975) 70.

18. Ibid., 70–71.

19. "In Christ we see not only the radiance of God's glory, but also the true image of humanity." David Peterson, *Possessed by God: A New Testament Theology of Sanctification and Holiness* (Downers Grove, IL: InterVarsity Press, 1995) 124.

20. Hoekema, 73, 22.

21. Colin Kruse explains Paul's reference to the veil: "Ex. 34:33–35 tells how Moses veiled his face after communicating God's law to the Israelites, so that they would not have to look upon its brightness. Paul interprets this as an attempt to conceal from the Israelites the fading nature of the splendour which accompanied the old covenant, and he contrasts Moses' lack

of boldness with the boldness he himself has as a minister of the new covenant (vv. 12–13). He also sees in the veiling of Moses' face something analogous to the *veil* which lay over the minds of many of his Jewish contemporaries, who could not properly understand the law of Moses when it was read in their synagogues (vv. 14–15). Believers, those who have turned to the Lord, have the veil removed from their minds (16), and so *with unveiled faces* they reflect (or perhaps contemplate) the glory of the Lord, and in so doing are *being transformed into his likeness* (18). Paul's primary purpose in highlighting the superior splendour of the ministry of the new covenant was to explain why he was very bold and did not lose heart (v. 12; *cf.* 4:1). He may also have wanted to use this argument to counteract the teaching of his opponents at Corinth, who placed great stress on their Jewish ancestry (*cf.* 11:21b–22)." Colin Kruse, "2 Corinthians 3:12–18" in D. A. Carson, R. T. France, J. A. Motyer, G. J. Wenham, editors, *New Bible Commentary: 21st Century Edition*. 4th ed. (Downers Grove, IL: Inter-Varsity Press, 1994) 1195–1196.

22. John Newton, "Amazing Grace," 1779.

23. Jonathan Edwards saw this as the critical difference between false and true Christianity. "And this is indeed the very main difference between the joy of the hypocrite, and the joy of the true saint. The former rejoices in himself; self is the first foundation of his joy: the latter rejoices in God. The hypocrite has his mind pleased and delighted, in the first place, with his own privilege, and the happiness which he supposes he has attained, or shall attain. True saints have their minds, in the first place, inexpressibly pleased and delighted with the sweet ideas of the glorious and amiable nature of the things of God." Jonathan Edwards, *Religious Affections*, John E. Smith, ed., *The Works of Jonathan Edwards*, vol. 2 (New Haven, CT: Yale University Press, 1959) 249–250.

24. "Observe that the purpose of the Gospel is the restoration in us of the image of God which had been cancelled by sin, and that this restoration is progressive and goes on during our whole life, because God makes His glory to shine in us little by little." John Calvin, D. W. Torrance and T. F. Torrance, eds., T. A. Smail, trans., *The Second Epistle of Paul the Apostle to the Corinthians and the Epistles to Timothy, Titus, and Philemon* (Grand Rapids, MI: Wm. B. Eerdmans Publishing Co. , 1976) 50.

25. "Workmanship" is the Greek word *poiema*, from which we get our English word "poem." The word was "used in classical times for the work of a craftsman, such as the making of a crown" (in Herodotus). It occurs twenty-eight times in the Septuagint, the Greek translation of the Old Testament. It is used of God's works (Ps. 64:9; 92:4; 143:5; Eccl. 3:11; 8:9) and of a person's deeds, both good (1 Sam. 19:4; Eccl. 2:4, 11, 17; 3:22; 8:14) and evil (Eccl. 4:3; 8:14). It is also used of a person's skillful work or art (Eccl. 4:4; Isa. 29:16). It is used only one other time in the New Testament, in Romans 1:20, to describe the natural created world. See Harold W. Hoehner, *Ephesians: An Exegetical Commentary* (Grand Rapids, MI: Baker Academic, 2002) 346–347.

26. Calvin's comment on this passage well fits the theme of this chapter: "Adam was at first created in the image of God, so that he might reflect, as in a mirror, the righteousness of God. But that image, having been wiped out by sin, must now be restored in Christ. The regeneration of the godly is indeed, as is said in 2 Cor. 3.18, nothing else than the reformation of the image of God in them . . . our highest perfection consists in our conformity and resemblance to God. Adam lost the image which he had originally received, therefore it is necessary that it shall be restored to us by Christ." John Calvin, D. W. Torrance and T. F. Torrance, eds., T. H. L. Parker, trans., *The Epistles of Paul the Apostle to the Galatians, Ephesians, Philippians and Colossians*, (Grand Rapids, MI: Wm. B. Eerdmans Publishing Co. , 1976) 191.

27. The Puritan, Walter Marshall wrote: "God first created you to live a holy life. This is what he wanted when he first made humans in his image. Now, God is re-creating this kind of holiness in your life through the new birth and through sanctification in Jesus Christ.

God's image is now being restored to you and it will be finally, perfectly complete when you are glorified with God in heaven." Walter Marshall, *The Gospel Mystery of Sanctification: Growing in Holiness by Living in Union with Christ. A New Version Put Into Modern English by Bruce H. McRae* (Eugene, OR: Wipf & Stock Publishers, 2005) 16.

28. "In a word, for the New Testament, sanctification or holiness, is Christlikeness or, as various theologians throughout the history of the church have described it, 'Christiformity.' Set within the context of justification is the growth of the seed of regeneration and the outworking of union with Jesus Christ. Man was made as the image of God and bore his likeness (Gn. 1:26–27). He was called to express it in every aspect of his being. But he fell from that high estate. Salvation, and its outworking in sanctification, consequently have in view the restoration of man as the image of God." Ferguson, 139.

29. Charles Wesley, "O for a Heart to Praise my God," 1742. The final verse says, "Thy nature, gracious Lord, impart / Come quickly from above / Write Thy new name upon my heart / Thy new, best name of Love."

30. Kenneth Boa, *Conformed to His Image: Biblical and Practical Approaches to Spiritual Formation* (Grand Rapids, MI: Zondervan, 2001) 515. Dallas Willard similarly defines spiritual formation as "the Spirit-driven process of forming the inner world of the human self in such a way that it becomes like the inner being of Christ himself." Dallas Willard, *Renovation of the Heart: Putting on the Character of Christ* (Colorado Springs, CO: NavPress, 2002) 22. I'm using the term synonymously with transformation.

31. C. S. Lewis, *The Lion, the Witch and the Wardrobe* (New York, NY: Collier Books, 1970) 16.

32. Ibid., 165.

Chapter 2—The Key to Transformation: The Gospel

1. The Greek word is *katoptrizomai*. It can mean either to gaze or to reflect. Translations differ in how they render the word; but both meanings are implied, because when a person looks in a mirror, he is both gazing and reflecting.

2. Timothy Keller, "The Centrality of the Gospel," Redeemer Presbyterian Church of New York City. Available online at: http://download.redeemer.com/pdf/learn/resources/Centrality_of_the_Gospel-Keller.pdf. Accessed February 16, 2010.

3. For an excellent overview of this passage and a careful articulation of the meaning of the gospel, see D. A. Carson, "The Gospel of Jesus Christ (1 Corinthians 15:1–19)" at http://www.thegospelcoalition.org/articles.php?a=81. Accessed June 12, 2008.

4. J. Oswald Sanders, *The Incomparable Christ* (Chicago, IL: Moody Press, 1971) 150.

5. Philip P. Bliss, "Hallelujah! What a Savior," 1875.

6. John R. W. Stott, *The Cross of Christ* (Downers Grove, IL: InterVarsity Press, 1986) 89, 159.

7. As Jonathan Edwards said, in one of his characteristically Christ-centered sermons, "Christ by His obedience, by that obedience which he undertook for our sakes, has honored God abundantly more than the sins of any of us have dishonored him, how many soever, how great soever . . . God hates our sins, but not more than he delights in Christ's obedience which he performed on our account. This is a sweet savour to him, a savour of rest. God is abundantly compensated, he desires no more; Christ's righteousness is of infinite worthiness and merit." Jonathan Edwards, *The Works of Jonathan Edwards*, vol. 2 (Carlisle, PA: The Banner of Truth Trust, 1974 reprint) 930.

8. Richard B. Gaffin Jr., *By Faith, Not by Sight: Paul and the Order of Salvation* (Waynesboro, GA: Paternoster Press, 2006) 27.

9. Ibid.

10. Ibid., 59.

11. Ibid., 60–61.

12. C. S. Lewis, *Miracles* (New York, NY: HarperCollins, 1947) 236–237.

13. J. R. R. Tolkien, *The Tolkien Reader* (New York, NY: Del Rey Books, 1966) 86.

14. J. R. R. Tolkien, *The Return of the King* (New York, NY: Del Rey Books, 1966) 246.

15. Tolkien, *The Tolkien Reader*, 88–89.

16. See Acts 2:22–24, 31–32; 3:13–15, 26; 4:2, 10–12, 33; 5:30; 10:36–41; 13:23–37; 17:3, 18, 31; 18:5; 26:23.

17. Harold W. Hoehner, *Ephesians: An Exegetical Commentary* (Grand Rapids, MI: Baker Academic, 2002) 283–284.

18. D. Martyn Lloyd-Jones, *God's Ultimate Purpose: An Exposition of Ephesians 1:1 to 23* (Grand Rapids, MI: Baker Book House, 1978) 441.

19. Irenaeus, *Against Heresies*, Book III, Chapter 18, Number 7, in Alexander Roberts & James Donaldson, ed., *The Writings of the Fathers Down to A.D. 325, Ante-Nicene Fathers, Volume 1: The Apostolic Fathers, Justin Martyr, Irenaeus* (Peabody, MA: Hendrickson Publishers, 2004) 448.

20. C. S. Lewis, "The Grand Miracle," in *God in the Dock: Essays on Theology and Ethics* (Grand Rapids, MI: Wm. B. Eerdmans Publishing Co. , 1970) 82.

21. Calvin commented: "Christ alone, therefore, is the mirror in which we can contemplate that which the weakness of the cross hinders from being clearly seen in ourselves. When our minds rise to a confident anticipation of righteousness, salvation, and glory, let us learn to turn them to Christ. We still lie under the power of death; but he, raised from the dead by heavenly power, has the dominion of life. We labor under the bondage of sin, and, surrounded by endless vexations, are engaged in a hard warfare, but he, sitting at the right hand of the Father, exercises the highest government in heaven and earth, and triumphs gloriously over the enemies whom he has subdued and vanquished. We lie here mean and despised; but to him has been 'given a name' which angels and men regard with reverence, and devils and wicked men with dread. We are pressed down here by the scantiness of all our comforts: but he has been appointed by the Father to be the sole dispenser of all blessings. For these reasons, we shall find our advantage in directing our views to Christ, that in him, as in a mirror, we may see the glorious treasures of Divine grace, and the unmeasurable greatness of that power, which has not yet been manifested in ourselves." John Calvin, D. W. Torrance and T. F. Torrance, eds., T. H. L. Parker, trans., *The Epistles of Paul the Apostle to the Galatians, Ephesians, Philippians and Colossians* (Grand Rapids, MI: Wm. B. Eerdmans Publishing Co. , 1976) 136.

22. Sinclair B. Ferguson, *The Holy Spirit* (Downers Grove, IL: InterVarsity Press, 1996) 33.

23. As Ferguson explains, the last phrase of 2 Cor. 3:18, "'from the Lord, who is the Spirit' translates three Greek words: *apo* (from), *kyrio* (Lord, genitive case following the preposition *apo*) and *pneumatos* (Spirit, also in the genitive case). The statement is amendable to more than one interpretation: (1) 'from the Spirit of the Lord.' (2) 'from the Lord who is the Spirit'; (3) 'from the Lord of the Spirit.' The third option may, at first glance, seem to be the least likely, but it is the most natural rendering and one that is highly illuminating theologically. Paul is then saying that the Lord Jesus Christ is the Lord of the Spirit. There is no ontological confusion here, but an economic equivalence; nor is there an ontological subordinationism, but rather a complete intimacy of relationship between Jesus and the Spirit. In effect, Paul is teaching that through his life and ministry Jesus came into such complete possession of the Spirit, receiving and experiencing him 'without limit' (John 3:34), that he is now 'Lord' of the Spirit (2 Cor. 3:18). With respect to his economic ministry to us, the Spirit has been 'imprinted' with the character of Jesus." Ibid., 55.

24. Ibid., 37.

25. John Calvin, *Instruction in Faith (1537)*, Paul T. Fuhrmann, trans., (Louisville, KY: Westminster John Knox Press, 1977) 52.

26. Ferguson, 91–92.

27. Martin Luther, "The Ninety-Five Theses" in John Dillenberger, ed., *Martin Luther: Selections from His Writings* (New York, NY: Anchor Books, 1962) 490.

28. Westminster Confession of Faith, Chapter XIV.

29. Richard Lovelace, *Dynamics of Spiritual Life: An Evangelical Theology of Renewal* (Downers Grove, IL: Inter-Varsity Press, 1979) 102.

30. Isaac Watts, "No More My God," n.d.

Chapter 3—The Curse is Canceled: Justification

1. As quoted in Roland H. Bainton, *Here I Stand: A Life of Martin Luther* (New York, NY: Meridian Press, 1995) 30.

2. Ibid., 34.

3. Ibid., 44.

4. Ibid., 49–50.

5. Ibid., 64.

6. Or, as Richard Lovelace writes, "The law is like a 'tracer chemical' which makes the invisible course of a disease evident or a medicine which aggravates a hidden illness until it breaks out in surface symptoms. . . [but] without concurrent light on the provisions of grace, the law will not cure sin but only aggravate it." Richard Lovelace, *Dynamics of Spiritual Life: An Evangelical Theology of Renewal* (Downers Grove, IL: InterVarsity Press, 1979) 110–111, 113.

7. "Justifying is the judge's act," says J. I. Packer. "From the litigant's standpoint, therefore, 'be justified' means 'get the verdict.'" J. I. Packer, "Justification," in J. D. Douglas, D. R. W. Wood, I. H. Marshall, J. I. Packer, A. R. Millard, D. J. Wiseman, eds., *New Bible Dictionary: Third Edition* (Downers Grove, IL: InterVarsity Press, 1996) 636.

8. This is Packer's point when he says, "Lexical support is wanting for the view of Chrysostom, Augustine, and the Council of Trent that when Paul and James speak of present justification they refer to God's work of *making* righteous by inner renewal, as well as of *counting* righteous through remission of sins. James seems to mean neither, Paul only the latter. His synonyms for 'justify' are 'reckon righteousness,' 'remit sins,' 'not reckon sin' (see Rom. 4:5–8, RV)—phrases expressing the idea, not of inner transformation, but of conferring a legal status and canceling a legal liability. Justification, to Paul, is a judgment passed on man, not a work wrought within man." Packer, 637.

9. If this question seems irrelevant to us, it is only because we have failed to grasp the gravity of our sinful condition. As theologian John Murray wrote, "If we are to appreciate that which is central to the gospel . . . our thinking must be revolutionized by the realism of the wrath of God, of the reality and gravity of our guilt, and of the divine condemnation. It is then and only then that our thinking and feeling will be rehabilitated to an understanding of God's grace in the justification of the ungodly. The question is really not so much: how can man be just with God; but how can sinful man *become* just with God? The question in this form points up the necessity of a complete reversal in our relation to God. Justification is the answer and justification is the act of God's free grace. 'It is God who justifies: who is he that condemns?' (Rom. 8:33)." John Murray, *Redemption: Accomplished and Applied* (Grand Rapids, MI: Wm. B. Eerdmans Publishing Co., 1955) 118.

10. I am echoing Tim Keller who writes, "The Christian gospel is that I am so flawed that Jesus had to die for me, yet I am so valued that Jesus was glad to die for me." Timothy Keller, *The Reason for God: Belief in an Age of Skepticism* (New York, NY: Dutton, 2008) 181.

11. Most versions read, "vindicated in [or by] the Spirit" (so NIV, ESV, NASB) with "justified" as a marginal reading. But the Greek word *dikaioo* means "to render or declare as righteous or just" and is usually translated "justify." I take this phrase to refer to the resurrection of Christ by the power of the Spirit (cf. Rom. 1:4) viewed as the public declaration of his righteous and exalted status as representative of the new creation in his capacity as Second Adam. In his helpful exegesis of this passage, Richard Gaffin says that as long as Jesus "remained in a state of death, the righteous character of his work, the efficacy of his obedience unto death remained in question, in fact, was implicitly denied. Consequently, the eradication of death in his resurrection is nothing less than the removal of the verdict of condemnation and the effective affirmation of this (adamic) righteousness. His resurrected state is the reward and seal which testifies perpetually to his perfect obedience." Richard B. Gaffin, Jr., *Resurrection and Redemption: A Study in Paul's Soteriology* (Phillipsburg, NJ: P & R Publishing, 1987) 121–122.

12. Herman Bavinck, with the Greek words omitted, in Herman Bavinck, John Bolt, gen. ed., John Vriend, trans., *Reformed Dogmatics: Volume 4: Holy Spirit, Church, and New Creation* (Grand Rapids, MI: Baker Academic, 2008) 211.

13. Lovelace, 101.

14. Martin Luther, *A Commentary on St. Paul's Epistle to the Galatians* (London: James Clarke & Co., 1953) 101.

15. John Owen, *Of the Mortification of Sin in Believers* in William H. Gould, ed., *The Works of John Owen*, vol. 6, (Carlisle, PA: The Banner of Truth Trust, 1967 reprint of 1850–53 edition) 33.

16. Augustus Toplady, "From Whence This Fear and Unbelief," 1772.

17. John R. W. Stott, *The Message of Galatians* (Downers Grove, IL: InterVarsity Press, 1984) 109.

18. By keeping the term "sons" (as opposed to the more gender-neutral "children" or "sons and daughters") I do not mean to infer any inferiority in a female's status with God. The terminology, rather, reflects the cultural norms of the first-century, when the New Testament was written, when sons had unique rights as heirs.

19. William Cowper, "Love Constraining to Obedience" in *The Complete Poetical Works of William Cowper*, ed., H. S. Milford, MA, (London: Henry Frowde, 1905) 468.

20. William Gadsby, "Mercy Speaks by Jesus' Blood," *A Selection of Hymns for Public Worship*, 1814.

Chapter 4—The Cure Has Begun: The Heart

1. Oscar Wilde, *The Picture of Dorian Gray* (New York, NY: Barnes & Noble Classics, 2003 reprint, originally published in 1891) 28.

2. C. S. Lewis, *Surprised by Joy* (New York, NY: Harcourt Brace & Company, 1955) 226.

3. This is not to say that every person is as evil as they could be. In fact, no one is. God's common grace often restrains human wickedness—keeping us from descending as deeply into evil as we otherwise would. The "total" in total depravity does not mean that we are *utterly* evil—as sinful as we could be, but that we are *pervasively* evil—tainted with sin in every part: mind, heart, will, and body—and *potentially* evil—the seeds of all forms of wickedness lying dormant in the soil of our souls. While no human being will ever commit every sin he or she is capable of, wickedness is so deeply ingrained within us that every human being is capable of committing the worst sins imaginable.

4. Jonathan Edwards, *Charity and Its Fruits* (Carlisle, PA: The Banner of Truth Trust, 1998 reprint) 157–158.

5. Derek Webb, "Crooked Deep Down," © 2002 Derek Webb Music (admin. by Music Services) All Rights Reserved. Used By Permission.

6. "True holiness is a matter of the heart. True holiness means that you have holy thoughts, motives, and feelings. This holiness consists chiefly in love, from which all other good works flow. Every good thing you do must flow from this kind of inner life, or else it is not acceptable to God. God commands you to love him with your whole heart, soul, mind, and strength." Walter Marshall, *The Gospel Mystery of Sanctification: Growing in Holiness by Living in Union with Christ. A New Version Put Into Modern English by Bruce H. McRae* (Eugene, OR: Wipf & Stock Publishers, 2005) 15.

7. Bavinck writes, "The heart, according to Scripture, is the *organ* of man's life. It is, first, the center of physical life but then also, in a metaphorical sense, the seat and fountain of man's entire psychic life, of emotions and passions, of desire and will, even of thinking and knowing. From the heart flow "the springs of life" (Prov. 4:23). This life, which originates in the heart, then splits into two streams. On the one hand, we must distinguish the life that embraces all impressions, awarenesses, perceptions, observations, thoughts, knowledge, and wisdom. Especially in its higher forms, the central organ of this life is the *mind (nous)*. This life further embodies itself in words and language. On the other hand, the heart is the seat of all the emotions, passions, urges, inclinations, attachments, desires, and decisions of the will, which have to be led by the mind *(nous)* and express themselves in action." Herman Bavinck, John Bolt, gen. ed., John Vriend, trans., *Reformed Dogmatics: Volume 2: God and Creation* (Grand Rapids, MI: Baker Academic, 2004) 556–557.

8. Johannes Behm, καρδια, in Gerhard Kittel, ed., Geoffrey W. Bromiley, trans., *Theological Dictionary of the New Testament, Volume III:* (Grand Rapids, MI: Wm. B. Eerdmans Publishing Co. , 1965) 611. Behm further says that "a. In the heart dwell feelings and emotions, desires and passions; b. The heart is the seat of understanding, the source of thought and reflection; c. The heart is the seat of the will, the source of resolves; d. Thus the heart is supremely the one centre in man to which God turns, in which the religious life is rooted, which determines moral conduct" (612). Numerous references to Scripture are provided with each definition.

9. David Powlison, *Seeing With New Eyes: Counseling and the Human Condition Through the Lens of Scripture* (Phillipsburg, NJ: P & R Publishing, 2003) 162.

10. See the many excellent books and articles by David Powlison, Paul David Tripp, Timothy Lane, and Edward T. Welch.

11. John Piper, *Desiring God: The Meditations of a Christian Hedonist* (Sisters, OR: Multnomah, Third Edition, 2006) 87–88.

12. David Powlison, "Idols of the Heart and Vanity Fair," *The Journal of Biblical Counseling*, Vol. 13, No. 2, 1995, 36.

13. John Calvin, John T. McNeil, ed., Ford L. Battles, trans., *Institutes of the Christian Religion*, Book I, Chap. XI, 8 (Philadelphia, PA: The Westminster Press, 1960) 108.

14. For a thoughtful treatment of idolatry in contemporary culture, see Timothy Keller, *Counterfeit Gods: The Empty Promises of Money, Sex, and Power, and the Only Hope that Matters* (New York, NY: Dutton, 2009).

15. Paul David Tripp, *Instruments in the Redeemer's Hands: People in Need of Change Helping People in Need of Change* (Phillipsburg, NJ: P & R Publishing, 2002) 63.

16. Powlison, "Idols of the Heart and Vanity Fair," 36. Similarly, Tripp says: "You and I are always desiring. Desires precede, determine and characterize everything you do. Desires get you up in the morning and put you to bed at night. Desire makes you work with discipline to get one thing done, and run as hard as you can to avoid another. Desires sculpt every relationship in your life. They are the lenses through which you examine every situation. At the foundation of all worship, whether true or false, is a heart full of desire" (Tripp, 78).

17. Tim Chester, *You Can Change* (Nottingham, England: Inter-Varsity Press, 2008) 116. Much of my thinking in this section was influenced by Chester's helpful chapter, "What desires do you need to turn from?".

18. C. H. Spurgeon, "The Great Reservoir," in *The New Park Street Pulpit*, vol. 4 (Grand Rapids, MI: Baker Book House, 1994) 113–120.

19. I view "heart," "soul," and "spirit" as virtually synonymous terms. I agree with Hoekema who says: "The Bible does not use exact scientific language. It uses terms like *soul, spirit,* and *heart* more or less interchangeably." Anthony A. Hoekema, *Created in God's Image* (Grand Rapids, MI: Wm. B. Eerdmans Publishing Co., 1986) 203. Hoekema gives three reasons for rejecting a belief in trichotomy ("the view that, according to the Bible, man consists of body, soul, and spirit," 205), but also rejects dichotomy ("the view that man consists of body and soul," 209). Instead, he contends that "the Bible describes the human person as a totality, a whole, a unitary being . . . the Bible's primary concern is not the psychological or anthropological constitution of man but his inescapable relatedness to God" (210).

20. See Jonathan Edwards' penetrating analysis of the nature and importance of the affections to genuine spirituality in Jonathan Edwards, *Religious Affections*, John E. Smith, ed., *The Works of Jonathan Edwards*, vol. 2 (New Haven, CT: Yale University Press, 1959). The summary of Scriptural teaching on the necessity of various affections included in this chapter is largely dependent on Edwards.

21. Quoted by John Piper in *The Legacy of Sovereign Joy: God's Triumphant Grace in the Lives of Augustine, Luther, and Calvin* (Wheaton, IL: Crossway Books, 2000) 62–63. Similarly, one of the early Puritans, Richard Sibbes, wrote: "There is nothing that characterizeth and sets a stamp upon a Christian as much as desires. All other things may be counterfeit. Words and actions may be counterfeit, but the desires and affections cannot, because they are the immediate issues and productions of the soul . . . A man may ask his desires what he is? According to the pulse of the desires, so is the temper of the man. Desires are better than actions a great deal; for a man may do a good action, that he doth not love, and he may abstain from an ill action, that he hates not. But God is a Spirit, and looks to the spirit especially. It is a good character of a Christian, that his desire, for the most part, is to good." Richard Sibbes, *The Works of Richard Sibbes*, vol. 2 (Carlisle, PA: The Banner of Truth Trust, 1983 reprint) 219.

22. Ridderbos points out that in the "renewal of the inward man . . . the significance of the heart and of the understanding (the *nous*) comes to the forefront" and that the conceptual material with which the New Testament describes heart renewal is both rich and diverse. For example, Ridderbos points out how Christ "dwells" in the hearts of believers through faith (Eph. 3:17); God "sends" the Spirit of his Son into our hearts (Gal. 4:6) as the earnest and seal of complete redemption (Eph. 1:13–14; 4:30; 2 Cor. 1:22); He "pours" his love into our hearts through the Holy Spirit (Rom. 5:5) and "writes" his will on our hearts by the Spirit (2 Cor. 3:3), "illumines" our hearts with the knowledge of Christ (2 Cor. 4:6), and "enlightens the eyes of [our] hearts" through the Spirit of wisdom and revelation (Eph. 1:18). Furthermore, the peace of Christ rules (Col. 3:15), guards (Phil. 4:7) and directs (2 Thess. 3:5) our hearts. And the Spirit works within our hearts, even in prayer and intercession (Rom. 8:15, 26–27). Herman Ridderbos, *Paul: An Outline of His Theology* (Grand Rapids, MI: Wm. B. Eerdmans Publishing Co., 1975) 227.

23. David Peterson's comments on the relationship between sanctification and regeneration are helpful: "Regeneration involves a new birth to faith, hope and love, made possible by the Holy Spirit. Sanctification has to do with the new status and orientation of those who belong to God and to one another as his people. Sanctification means having a new identity, with the obligation to live according to that identity. Regeneration, which is a definitive, life-transforming work of the Spirit at the beginning of the Christian life, has its continuation

in the process of renewal (*cf.* Eph. 4:22–24; Col. 3:9–11; Tit. 3:5–6). Sanctification has its continuation or extension in the life of holiness which the Spirit makes possible through faith in Christ." David Peterson, *Possessed by God: A New Testament Theology of Sanctification and Holiness* (Downers Grove, IL: InterVarsity Press, 1995) 63–64.

24. Richard F. Lovelace, *Dynamics of Spiritual Life: An Evangelical Theology of Renewal* (Downers Grove, IL: Inter-Varsity Press, 1979) 104.

25. I'm echoing Wayne Grudem who defines regeneration as the "secret act of God by which he imparts new life to us." Wayne Grudem, *Systematic Theology: An Introduction to Biblical Doctrine* (Grand Rapids, Mich.: Zondervan Publishing House, 1994) 699.

26. John Piper, *Finally Alive: What Happens When We Are Born Again* (Ross-shire, Scotland: Christian Focus Publications, 2009) 22.

27. Lovelace, 108.

28. Charles Wesley, "And Can it Be," 1738.

29. Saint Augustine, R. S. Pine-Coffin, trans., *Confessions*, (New York, NY: Penguin Books, 1961) 236 (X, 31).

30. C. S. Lewis, *The Voyage of the "Dawn Treader"* (New York, NY: Collier Books, 1952) 1.

31. Ibid., 75.

32. Ibid., 67–93.

33. Ibid., 93.

Chapter 5—Closing the Gap: Sanctification

1. Sanctification "is an integral part of the redemptive work of Jesus Christ. It is regularly portrayed as a once-for-all, definitive act and primarily has to do with the holy status or position of those who are 'in Christ.'" David Peterson, *Possessed by God: A New Testament Theology of Sanctification and Holiness* (Downers Grove, IL: InterVarsity Press, 1995) 24. Peterson warns that "when the terminology of sanctification is simply used to describe everything that happens to us after conversion, the definitive emphasis of the New Testament is soon obscured. The call to 'be holy' can so easily degenerate into a moralistic and perfectionistic programme for believers to pursue" (137).

2. "Christians are called to live out the practical consequences of knowing God in Jesus Christ and of being consecrated by his saving work. Everything that is said about moral change and personal transformation in the New Testament is to be related to God's sanctifying initiative in Christ." Ibid., 24–25.

3. "Practical holiness means working out in everyday life and relationships the moral consequences of our union with Christ." Ibid., 114.

4. Quoted in Douglas Moo, *The Epistle to the Romans* (Grand Rapids, MI: Wm. B. Eerdmans Publishing Co., 1996) 356.

5. Ibid., 358.

6. When Paul says that Christ died to sin, it is helpful to note that he is speaking of sin as a "ruling power." In Moo's words: "Just as death once had 'authority' over Christ because of his full identification with sinful people in the 'old age,' so that other ruling power of the old age, sin, could be said to have 'authority' over Christ. As a 'man of the old age,' he was subject to the power of sin—with the critical difference that he never succumbed to its power and actually sinned" (Ibid., 379). Moo points out that the advantage of this interpretation is that it allows "died to sin" to have the same meaning in verse 10 as it has in verse 2. "When these salvation-historical perspectives are given their due place, we are able to give 'die to sin' the same meaning here as it had in verse 2: a separation or freedom from the rule of sin."

7. John Calvin, John T. McNeil, ed., Ford L. Battles, trans., *Institutes of the Christian Religion*, Book III, Chap. I, 1 (Philadelphia, PA: The Westminster Press, 1960) 537.

8. Charles Wesley, "O For a Thousand Tongues To Sing," 1739.

9. "Paul's reference to baptism is to the Roman Christian's water baptism as their outward initiation into Christian experience . . . By the date of Romans, 'baptize' had almost become a technical expression for the rite of Christian initiation by water, and this is surely the meaning the Roman Christians would have given the word" (Moo, 359).

10. Walter Marshall, *The Gospel Mystery of Sanctification: Growing in Holiness by Living in Union with Christ. A New Version Put Into Modern English by Bruce H. McRae* (Eugene, OR: Wipf & Stock Publishers, 2005). At the heart of Marshall's book is the doctrine of our union with Christ and the necessary implications of union with Christ for sanctification. "This is the key error Christians fall into in their lives: they think that even though they have been justified by a righteousness produced totally by Christ, they must be sanctified by a holiness produced totally by themselves" (39–40).

11. "Sanctification, like justification, is grounded in union with Christ. The power of sin to rule their lives has been *destroyed* in the cross of Christ; we have died with Christ, and have been raised up together with him in newness of life. Therefore we are not to set the estimates of our power to conquer sin according to past experiences of our will power, but are to fix our attention on Christ and the power of his risen life in which we participate: for we have died, and our life is hidden with Christ in God." Richard F. Lovelace, *Dynamics of Spiritual Life: An Evangelical Theology of Renewal* (Downers Grove, IL: Inter-Varsity Press, 1979) 115.

12. Sinclair B. Ferguson, *The Holy Spirit* (Downers Grove, IL: InterVarsity Press, 1996) 143–144.

13. I am echoing the words of Tim Chester and Steve Timmis in their helpful book, *Total Church: A Radical Reshaping around Gospel and Community* (Wheaton, IL: Crossway Books, 2008) 143. Richard Lovelace makes the same emphasis: "The Triple Way of classical mysticism, which moves from the stage of cleansing one's life through illumination toward union with God, seems to reverse the biblical order, which starts from union with Christ claimed by faith, leading to the illumination of the Holy Spirit and consequent cleansing through the process of sanctification" (Lovelace, 19).

14. John Murray comments: "We are not commanded to become dead to sin and alive to God; these are presupposed. And it is not by reckoning these to be facts that they become facts. The force of the imperative is that we are to reckon with and appreciate the facts which already obtain by virtue of our union with Christ." John Murray, *The Epistle to the Romans*, vol. 1 (Grand Rapids, MI: Wm. B. Eerdmans Publishing Co. , 1968) 225–226. Similarly, Moo writes, "In union with Christ we *have been made* dead to sin and alive to God; it remains for us to appropriate (v. 11) and apply (vv. 12–13) what God has done for us" (Moo, 380).

15. "The assumption that "old man" and "new man" refer to parts, or natures, of a person is incorrect. Rather, they designate the person as a whole, considered in relation to the corporate structure to which he or she belongs . . . They do not, at least in the first place, speak of a change in nature, but of a change in relationship. "Our old man" is not our Adamic, or sin "nature" that is judged and dethroned on the cross, but to which is added in the believer another "nature," "the new man." Rather, the "old man" is what we were "in Adam"—the "man" of the old age, who lives under the tyranny of sin and death. As J. R. W. Stott puts it, "what was crucified with Christ was not a part of me called my old nature, but the whole of me as I was before I was converted" (Moo, 374).

16. Quoted in Josiah Bull, *"But Now I See:" The Life of John Newton* (Carlisle, PA: The Banner of Truth Trust, 1998 reprint, 1868 orig.) 333–334. The fuller context is worth reading: "The tradition is still preserved that on one of these occasions, at the house of Mr. Ring, Mr. Newton, speaking on 1 Cor. xv. 10, 'By the grace of God I am what I am.' uttered himself—in brief—to the following effect: '1. I am not what I ought to be. Ah, how imperfect and deficient! 2. Not what I might be, considering my privileges and opportunities. 3. Not what I

wish to be. God, who knows my heart, knows I wish to be like Him. 4. I am not what I hope to be,—ere long to drop this clay tabernacle, to be like Him, and see Him as He is (1 John 3:2). 5. Not what I once was—a child of sin and slave of the devil. Though not all these—not what I ought to be, not what I might be, not what I wish or hope to be, and not what I once was—I think I can truly say with the apostle, "By the grace of God I am what I am." Thanks to Mack Tomlinson for supplying me with this reference.

17. As Stott writes: "The major secret of holy living is in the mind. It is in knowing (6) that our former self was crucified with Christ, in knowing (3) that baptism into Christ is baptism into his death and resurrection, and in considering (11, RSV) that through Christ we are dead to sin and alive to God. We are to recall, to ponder, to grasp, to register these truths until they are so integral to our mindset that a return to the old life is unthinkable. Regenerate Christians should no more contemplate a return to unregenerate living than adults to their childhood, married people to their singleness or discharged prisoners to their prison cell. For our union with Jesus Christ has severed us from the old life and committed us to the new." John R. W. Stott, *Romans: God's Good News for the World* (Downers Grove, IL: InterVarsity Press, 1994) 180.

18. "'Body' (*soma*) may be the physical body; but it is probably, as in 6:6, the whole person, viewed in terms of the person's interaction with the world. As Nygren puts it, 'the arena of the battle is in the world.' The battle is a spiritual one, but it is fought, and won or lost, in the daily decisions the believer makes about how to use his body." (Moo, 383).

19. I agree with Peterson's position on Romans 7, that "the struggle that Romans 7 portrays cannot be divorced from the picture of conflict in the Christian life set forth in 6:12–23 . . . The Christian does not any longer live a life fundamentally determined and controlled by the flesh. Nevertheless, 'flesh' continues to be a powerful force in our experience. The conflict with sin does not diminish with conversion but actually intensifies, because we begin to experience the possibilities of a Spirit-directed life (*cf.* Gal. 5:16–26)" (Peterson, 108). However, not all scholars view Romans 7:14–25 as descriptive of the regenerate. Douglas Moo, for example, believes Paul is describing the unregenerate (see Moo, 442–467). Martyn Lloyd-Jones suggests that Paul is describing the experience of someone "neither unregenerate nor regenerate"— someone experiencing "conviction but not conversion." D. Martyn Lloyd-Jones, *The Law: Its Function and Limits (Romans 7:1–8:4)* (Grand Rapids, MI: Zondervan, 1973) 256, 262. On the other hand, in his summary description of the person speaking in this passage, John Stott says that "such a person, deploring evil in his fallen nature, delighting himself in God's law, and longing for the promised full and final salvation, seems to provide ample evidence of being regenerate and even mature" (Stott, 206). With Peterson and Stott, I believe Paul is describing his experience as a believer struggling with indwelling sin. Yet, it is important to note that Paul's primary focus in this passage is the inadequacy of the law to deliver from sin. As Moo says, "What Paul says about the Mosaic law comes much to the same thing, whatever we decide about the identity and spiritual condition of the person whose situation is depicted in these verses" (Moo, 442).

20. Regarding the believer's two natures, Andy Naselli writes, "Keswick's error is not in speaking of two natures in the believer but in how it speaks of those natures, namely, its view of the sinful nature or flesh . . . the Keswick view incorrectly understands the flesh to be an equally powerful nature alongside the believer's new nature: both natures are unchanging entities within the believer, and only one is in total control at any given moment. Thus, the flesh either controls the believer or is counteracted by the Spirit. According to Keswick theology, a believer in 'category 1' lives in the flesh. It is all or nothing. A believer is either in the flesh or in the Spirit. His two natures are two opposing principles that vie for supremacy, like two fierce dogs: if the believer feeds the white dog and starves the black dog, then the white dog wins. Believers in 'category 1' feed their flesh, which dominates their life resulting

in a fleshly lifestyle. For believers in 'category 2', the Spirit counteracts their sinful nature with the result that their new nature prevails over all known sin." Andrew D. Naselli, "Keswick Theology: A Historical and Theological Survey and Analysis of the Doctrine of Sanctification in the Early Keswick Movement, 1875–1920" (Ph.D. diss., Bob Jones University, 2003) 223. This dissertation is a thorough analysis and charitable critique of the teaching of the Early Keswick Movement, popularized in the writings of Andrew Murray, F. B. Meyer, Evan Hopkins and others.

21. This view also misunderstands the nature of sin, viewing it in terms of intentional actions, while neglecting to address sin on the motivational level. The victory over sin promised (and sometimes claimed) produces superficial triumphalism, at best. Worse, it may lead to naïve self-righteousness that is lacking in the self-awareness Paul demonstrated by calling himself the foremost of sinners (1 Tim. 1:15).

22. Related to this is the problem of dividing Christians into two categories—those who struggle with sin ("carnal") and those who live in victory ("spiritual"). The "victorious life" is often described with biblical language –such as abiding in Christ or being filled with the Spirit. But the assumption is that some who are genuinely saved need still need something in addition to the gospel to lift them out of the "self life" into the "Christ life." The net effect of this unfortunate division is to create a "haves" and "have nots" mentality among Christians. This mentality can lead to superiority and self-righteousness in the "haves" and disillusionment and discouragement for the "have nots." But a careful examination of Scripture shows that *all* believers abide in Christ and are filled with his Spirit *to some degree*. We all have been blessed with every spiritual blessing in Christ (Eph. 1:3). God's divine power has granted us all things that pertain to life and godliness (2 Peter 1:3). All believers—not just a few elite super saints—are being transformed by God's grace. While believers can behave in carnal ways (1 Cor. 3:1–3), "carnal Christian" is not a permanent category in which a believer can remain. For a very helpful overview of the exegetical arguments in favor of viewing abiding in Christ and being filled with the Spirit as something true of all believers to some degree, see Naselli, 194–218, 271–277. See also D. A. Carson's comments on abiding in the vine in John 15 in D. A. Carson, *The Gospel According to John: An Introduction and Commentary* (Grand Rapids, MI: Wm. B. Eerdmans Publishing Co., 1991) 510–519. For further critique on the holiness teaching of the early Keswick movement see J. I. Packer, *Keep in Step with the Spirit* (Grand Rapids, MI: Fleming H. Revell, 1984)132–164. For an extensive scholarly overview and critique see B. B. Warfield's writings in *The Works of Benjamin B. Warfield*, vols. 7 and 8 (Grand Rapids, MI: Baker Book House, 2000 reprint).

23. Naselli's comments were particularly helpful to me: "The Spirit transforms the whole believer—not just one part of him. Rather than merely counteracting sin, the Spirit gradually transforms the believer by restoring the image of God in him and gradually mortifying sin . . . . Even Christians will never be entirely free from sin's effects until glorification. God does not help the believer to be holy by counteracting sin as a hot air balloon counteracts gravity. Rather, God progressively makes the whole believer holy, that is, conformed into the image of Jesus Christ. Through the Spirit's power, the believer progressively mortifies sins while simultaneously cultivating and nourishing holiness (Rom. 8:13; 2 Thess. 2:13)." (224–226).

24. "If 'body' has the general meaning we have suggested, these 'passions' would include not only the physical lusts and appetites but also those desires that reside in the mind and will: the desire to have our own way, the desire to possess what other people have (cf. 7:7–8), the desire to have dominance over others." (Moo, 383).

25. Moo comments, "If 'body' in v. 12 means 'person in contact with the world' instead of 'physical body,' then 'members' also will mean 'natural capacities' rather than limbs, or parts, of the body" (Moo, 384). Though, I think it's likely that *both* bodily members and natural capacities could be in view.

26. I have adapted this imagery from John Piper's helpful sermon entitled, "Do Not Let Sin Reign in Your Mortal Body, Part 1" (Minneapolis, MN: Bethlehem Baptist Church, 5 November 2000), available online at: http://www.desiringgod.org/ResourceLibrary/Sermons/ByScripture/10/34_Do_Not_Let_Sin_Reign_in_Your_Mortal_Body_Part_1/. Accessed September 16, 2008.

27. In the interest of simplicity, I have not included discussion on verse 14, which gives an additional promise and assurance to ground the commands of verses 11–13: "For sin will have no dominion over you, since you are not under law but under grace." As Moo helpfully comments, "That the law is so suddenly brought onto the scene at the end of this paragraph reveals the extent to which Paul's presentation of his gospel in this letter never moves too far from the salvation-historical question of Old Covenant and New, Jew and Gentile. This allusion is one of a series of interjections about the negative effects of the law in salvation history (cf. 3:19–20, 21, 27–28; 4:13–15; 5:13–14, 20) that culminate in chap. 7. These texts—especially 5:20 and 7:1–6—furnish the context in which the enigmatic and much-debated phrase 'not under the law' must be interpreted. As in all these references, *nomos* here must be the Mosaic law, the torah. And while most of the (Gentile-) Christians in Rome have never lived 'under the law,' the situation of the Jews under the Mosaic law, as we will see in 7:4, is used by Paul as representative of the situation and need of all people. . . . Paul is thinking of 'law' and 'grace' as contrasting salvation-historical powers. . . . 'Under law,' then, is another way of characterizing 'the old realm.' This explains why Paul can make release from the law a reason for the Christian's freedom from the power of sin: as he has repeatedly stated, the Mosaic law has had a definite sin-producing and sin-intensifying function: it has brought 'knowledge of sin' (3:20), 'wrath' (4:15), 'transgression' (5:13–14), and an increase in the severity of sin (5:20). The law, as Paul puts it in 1 Cor. 15:56, is 'the power of sin.' . . . To be 'under law' is to be subject to the constraining and sin-strengthening regime of the old age; to be 'under grace' is to be subject to the new age in which freedom from the power of sin is available." (Moo, 387–389). For arguments in favor of this interpretation, see Moo's commentary.

28. For more on these themes, see Timothy Keller, *Counterfeit Gods: The Empty Promises of Money, Sex, and Power, and the Only Hope that Matters* (New York, NY: Dutton, 2009).

29. C. S. Lewis, *Surprised by Joy* (New York, NY: Harcourt Brace & Company, 1955) 229.

30. John Donne, "Holy Sonnet XIV" in *Selected Poems* (New York, NY: Penguin Classics, 2006) 183–184.

31. Peterson, 101.

32. John F. MacArthur, *Our Sufficiency in Christ* (Wheaton, IL: Crossway Books, 1998 reprint) 37–39, 169, 241–242.

33. Book II, Chap. XVI. 19 in Calvin, 527–528.

Introduction to Part Two
1. Martin Luther, "An Argument in Defense of All the Articles of Dr. Martin Luther Wrongly Condemned in the Roman Bull." Available online at: http://www.godrules.net/library/luther/NEW1luther_c4.htm. Accessed 12 March 2008.

Chapter 6—Captivated by Beauty: Holiness
1. C. S. Lewis, *Letters to an American Lady* (Grand Rapids, MI: Wm. B. Eerdmans Publishing Co., 1971) 19.

2. Thanks to several regular readers of my blog whose comments suggested many of the words, images, and associations, that opened this chapter. See http://www.brianghedges.com/2008/08/holiness.html. Accessed August 20, 2008.

3. Jonathan Edwards, *The Miscellanies: a—500*, Thomas A. Schafer, ed., *The Works of Jonathan Edwards*, vol. 13 (New Haven, CT: Yale University Press, 1994) 163.

4. Rudolf Otto, quoted in R. C. Sproul, *The Holiness of God* (Carol Stream, IL: Tyndale House Publishers, 1998) 42.

5. Flannery O'Connor, "The Fiction Writer and His Country," in *Flannery O'Connor: Collected Works* (New York, NY: Library of America, 1988) 806.

6. The Hebrew word is *qadash*.

7. For the implications of this passage and the broader biblical teaching on Sabbath for believers today, see D. A. Carson, ed., *From Sabbath to Lord's Day: A Biblical, Historical, and Theological Investigation* (Grand Rapids, MI: Zondervan Publishing House, 1982).

8. The Hebrew word is *qodesh*.

9. Arthur W. Pink, *The Attributes of God* (Pensacola, FL: Mt. Zion Publications, 1993) 45.

10. Stephen Charnock, *The Existence and Attributes of God*, vol. 2 (Grand Rapids, MI: Baker Books, 1996 reprint) 113–114.

11. I am borrowing this phrase from William Blake's poem, "The Tyger" (1794).

12. A. W. Tozer, *The Knowledge of the Holy* (New York, NY: HarperCollins, 1992) 163.

13. John Calvin, John T. McNeil, ed., Ford L. Battles, trans., *Institutes of the Christian Religion*, Book I, Chap. 1, 3 (Philadelphia, PA: The Westminster Press, 1960) 39.

14. Sproul, 45.

15. Sinclair B. Ferguson, *The Holy Spirit* (Downers Grove, IL: InterVarsity Press, 1996) 52.

16. Saint Augustine, R. S. Pine-Coffin, trans., *Confessions* (New York, NY: Penguin Books, 1961) 260 (XI.9).

17. J. C. Ryle, *Holiness: It's Nature, Hindrances, Difficulties, and Roots* (Darlington, England: Evangelical Press, 1997 reprint) xx.

18. Ferguson, 140–142.

19. John Owen, *A Discourse Concerning the Holy Spirit*, in William H. Gould, ed., *The Works of John Owen*, vol. 3 (Carlisle, PA: The Banner of Truth Trust, 1967 reprint of 1850–53 edition) 370–371.

20. "Something much deeper is contemplated here than replacing bad habits with good habits through sheer willpower. We are to detach ourselves from the compulsive organism of sin rooted in unregenerate human nature and to put ourselves in gear with the living power of Christ's resurrection which will then express his character through our lives. But choice and will enter in along with faith and understanding, and neither is spiritually alive without the other." Richard Lovelace, *Dynamics of Spiritual Life: An Evangelical Theology of Renewal* (Downers Grove, IL: InterVarsity Press, 1979) 117.

21. "The tenses in these three verses are important. The laying aside the old being (v. 22) and the putting on the new (v. 24) are both described by aorist infinitives. This tense is used for *undefined* action; it is merely mentioned without further specification. The most important issue is the contrast these words provide. The present tense, which shows ongoing action, describes the continual corruption of the old being (v. 22) and the continual renewing of the mind (v. 23). Both items are important. The old being is in a state of ever-deepening corruption, and the Christian life is an ever-increasing renewal of the mind (see 2 Cor. 3:18; 4:16)." Klyne Snodgrass, *The NIV Application Commentary: Ephesians* (Grand Rapids, MI: Zondervan, 1996) 234–235.

22. "To 'learn Christ' is to grasp the new creation which he has made possible, and the entirely new life which results from it. It is nothing less than putting off our old humanity like a rotten garment and putting on like clean clothing the new humanity recreated in God's image." John R. W. Stott, *The Message of Ephesians: God's New Society* (Downers Grove, IL: InterVarsity Press, 1979) 189.

23. "God's purpose is to conform us to the image of his Son; to reproduce the family likeness in us. He does that by employing the pattern he used when his Son sanctified himself for our sake. It was necessary for him to die and rise again, that he might enter into his

glory. It is no less necessary for that pattern to be worked out analogously in our lives, that we too, ultimately, may be conformed to the glory-image of God when we finally experience the adoption, the redemption of our bodies and face-to-face knowledge and reflection of the glory of Christ." Ferguson, 172.

24. David Brainerd, *The Life and Diary of the Rev. David Brainerd*, in Jonathan Edwards, *The Works of Jonathan Edwards*, vol. 2 (Carlisle, PA: The Banner of Truth Trust, 1974 reprint) 329.

Chapter 7—Killing Sin: Mortification

1. Adapted from Patricia Yollin, "Horrified zoogoer recalls tiger attack," *The San Francisco Chronicle*, Monday, January 1, 2007. Available online at: http://www.sfgate.com/cgi-bin/article. cgi?f=/c/a/2007/01/01/MNG3CNB93Q1.DTL&feed=rss.news. Accessed August 17, 2008.

2. John Owen, *The Mortification of Sin: Abridged and made easy to read by Richard Rushing* (Carlisle, PA: The Banner of Truth Trust, 2004) 5. For the original, see John Owen, *Of the Mortification of Sin in Believers* in William H. Gould, ed., *The Works of John Owen*, vol. 6 (Carlisle, PA: The Banner of Truth Trust, 1967 reprint of 1850–53 edition) 9. Most of my quotations from Owen's book on mortification in this chapter are from the abridged version. But I have also included references to the original in the notes. For a contemporary synthesis of Owen's thought, see "The Spirituality of John Owen" in J. I. Packer, *A Quest for Godliness: The Puritan Vision of the Christian Life* (Wheaton, IL: Crossway Books, 1990) 191–218, and Sinclair B. Ferguson, *John Owen on the Christian Life* (Carlisle, PA: The Banner of Truth Trust, 1995). More accessible is Kris Lundgaard's excellent popular level treatment of mortification, *The Enemy Within: Straight Talk about the Power and Defeat of Sin* (Phillipsburg, NJ: P&R Publishing, 1998).

3. Gerald Bray, "Asceticism and Monasticism," in Sinclair B. Ferguson, David F. Wright, J. I. Packer, ed., *New Dictionary of Theology* (Downers Grove, IL: InterVarsity Press, 1988) 47.

4. "Someone may change an obvious sin for a hidden one. Mortification is not just the substitution of one sin for another. He may simply have changed from one road to hell to a safer path than he was on before. He may even have a different heart than he had, which is more cunning; not a new heart, which is more holy!" Owen, 27; original: vol. 6, 25.

5. David F. Wells, *Losing Our Virtue: Why the Church Must Recover Its Moral Vision* (Grand Rapids, MI: Wm. B. Eerdmans Publishing Co. , 1998) 203–204.

6. John Calvin, John T. McNeil, ed., *Institutes of the Christian Religion* in *The Library of Christian Classics Volume XX*, Book III, Chap. VII, 10 (Philadelphia, PA: The Westminster Press, 1960) 700.

7. Owen, 5; original: vol. 6, 9.

8. Ibid., 7; original: vol. 6, 11.

9. John Brown, a theologian from another century put it well: "Crucifixion . . . produced death not suddenly but gradually . . . True Christians . . . do not succeed in completely destroying it (that is, the flesh) while here below; but they have fixed it to the cross, and they are determined to keep it there till it expire." Quoted in John R. W. Stott, *The Message of Galatians* (Downers Grove, IL: InterVarsity Press, 1984) 151.

10. John Owen, *A Discourse Concerning the Holy Spirit,* in William H. Gould, ed., *The Works of John Owen*, vol. 3 (Carlisle, PA: The Banner of Truth Trust, 1967 reprint of 1850–53 edition) 548.

11. Stott, 151–152. Owen writes, "When a man is nailed to a cross, he at first struggles, strives, and cries out with great strength and might; but as his blood and spirits waste, his strivings are faint and seldom, his cries low and hoarse, and scarce to be heard. So when a man first determines to conquer a lust or sin, and to deal with it in earnest, it struggles with great violence to break loose; it cries with earnestness and impatience to be satisfied and

relieved. By mortification, the blood and spirits of it are let out, it moves seldom and faintly, cries sparingly, and is scarce to be heard in the heart; it may sometimes have a dying pang that makes the appearance of great vigour and strength, but it is quickly over, especially if it is kept from considerable success." Owen, *Mortification*, 35; original: vol. 6, 30.

12. Owen, *Mortification*, 85 (author's emphasis); original: vol. 6, 62.

13. Ibid., 8: original: vol. 6, 12.

14. William L. Lane, *The Gospel of Mark* (Grand Rapids, MI: Wm. B. Eerdmans Publishing Co. , 1974) 348.

15. Owen, vol. 3, 552. Emphasis added.

16. John Bunyan, *The Holy War* (Ross-shire, Scotland: Christian Focus Publications, 1993) chapter nine.

17. Joshua Harris, *Not Even a Hint: Guarding Your Heart Against Lust* (Sisters, OR: Multnomah Publishers, 2003) 131.

18. Owen, *Mortification*, 41; original: vol. 6, 33.

19. Ibid., 116–117; original: vol. 6, 79.

20. John Owen, *Indwelling Sin in Believers: Abridged and Made Easy to Read* (Carlisle, PA: The Banner of Truth Trust, 2010) 99–100 ; original: vol. 6, 250–251.

21. Owen, *Mortification*, 3; original: vol. 6, 7.

22. Owen, vol. 6, 34.

23. See Owen, *Mortification*, 129; original: vol. 6, 85–86.

24. C. S. Lewis, *The Great Divorce* (New York, NY: HarperOne, 1946, 1973) chapter eleven. Perhaps I should add that the point of Lewis's story (and my use of it) is not that post-mortem salvation is possible, but that love for sin is what bars us from the enjoyment of heavenly pleasures.

Chapter 8—Growing in Grace: Vivification

1. J. M. Barrie, *Peter Pan* (New York, NY: Viking Penguin, 1991) 1. I owe the idea for this illustration to J. I. Packer, *Rediscovering Holiness* (Ann Arbor, MI: Vine Books, 1992) 197–198.

2. John Murray, *Collected Writings of John Murray, Volume Two: Select Lectures in Systematic Theology* (Carlisle, PA: The Banner of Truth Trust, 1977) 298.

3. J. C. Ryle, *Holiness: Its Nature, Hindrances, Difficulties, and Roots* (Darlington, England: Evangelical Press, 1997 reprint) 83.

4. Klyne Snodgrass, *The NIV Application Commentary: Ephesians* (Grand Rapids, MI.: Zondervan, 1996) 96. "Walk" also has significance in the Old Testament. Both Enoch and Noah were commended because they walked with God (Gen. 5:22–24; 6:9). When Abraham was ninety-nine years old, God appeared to him, saying, "I am God Almighty; walk before me, and be blameless" (Gen. 17:1).

5. Dallas Willard, *The Great Omission: Reclaiming Jesus' Essential Teachings on Discipleship* (San Francisco, CA: HarperSanFrancisco, 2006) 76.

6. Packer, 165.

7. God's mercies include: righteousness (3:21–26), redemption (3:24), grace (3:24), peace (5:1), grace (5:2), justification (5:1), hope (5:4–5), the love of God poured out in our hearts (5:5), union with Christ (6:1–11); freedom from sin (6:1–23); eternal life (6:22), freedom from the law (7:1–25); no condemnation (8:1), the Spirit (8:9), sonship (8:14–16); the hope of the future redemption of our bodies (8:23); the Spirit interceding (8:26–27); all things working together for our good (8:28), conformity to Jesus Christ (8:29), calling (8:30), glorification (8:30), and so on.

8. This is what A. W. Tozer called "The Sacrament of Living," describing the person for whom "every act of his life is or can be as truly sacred as prayer or baptism or the Lord's

Supper. To say this is not to bring all acts down to one dead level; it is rather to lift every act up into a living kingdom and turn the whole life into a sacrament." A. W. Tozer, *The Pursuit of God* (Camp Hill, PA: Christian Publications, 1993 reprint) 115.

9. C. S. Lewis, *Mere Christianity* (New York, NY: HarperOne, 1952, 1980) 196–197.

10. David Peterson helpfully connects the dots between the biblical concepts of sanctification and renewal. "Sanctification is specifically associated with covenant theology and the notion of belonging to God because of the redemptive work of his Son. In its broadest sense, renewal is a more comprehensive term, covering what is meant by sanctification and glorification, but setting these themes in a creation-recreation framework." David Peterson, *Possessed by God: A New Testament Theology of Sanctification and Holiness* (Downers Grove, IL: InterVarsity Press, 1995) 133.

11. J. I. Packer, *A Quest for Godliness: The Puritan Vision of the Christian Life* (Wheaton, IL: Crossway Books, 1990) 195. Similarly, the Puritan, Thomas Manton said, "The influences of heaven (i.e. sunlight) pass through the air, but they produce their effects in the earth; they do not make the air fruitful, but the earth; so do the influences of grace pass through the understanding, but they produce their fruit in the will, and show forth their strength in the affections; and therefore, when we would have our affections for God, the way is to enlarge the understanding." Thomas Manton, *Psalm 119*, vol. 1 (Carlisle, PA: The Banner of Truth Trust, 1990) 303.

12. Richard F. Lovelace, *Dynamics of Spiritual Life: An Evangelical Theology of Renewal* (Downers Grove, IL: InterVarsity Press, 1979) 19–20.

13. Ibid., 79.

14. "The principle work of the Spirit in applying redemption lies in making us holy, and being filled with the Spirit simply means having all our faculties under his control rather than under the control of sin." Ibid., 125.

15. John F. MacArthur, *Our Sufficiency in Christ* (Wheaton, IL: Crossway Books, 1998 reprint) 207–208.

16. J. I. Packer, *Rediscovering Holiness*, 103.

17. G. C. Berkouwer, *Faith and Sanctification* (Grand Rapids, MI: Wm. B. Eerdmans Publishing Co., 1952) 122.

18. J. I. Packer observes that "holiness teaching that skips over disciplined persistence in the well-doing that forms holy habits is thus weak; habit forming is the Spirit's ordinary way of leading us on in holiness. The fruit of the Spirit itself is, from one standpoint, a series of habits of action and reaction." J. I. Packer, *Keep in Step with the Spirit* (Grand Rapids, MI: Fleming H. Revell, 1984) 109. In a later chapter, Packer says that passivity "is altogether wrong, for the Holy Spirit's way of working in us is through the working of our minds and wills. He moves us to act by causing us to see reasons for moving ourselves to act. Thus our conscious, rational selfhood, so far from being annihilated, is strengthened, and in reverent, resolute obedience we work out our salvation, knowing that God is at work in us to make us '. . . both . . . will and . . . work for his good pleasure' (Philippians 2:13). This is holiness, and in the process of perfecting it there is, properly speaking, no passivity at all." Packer, 156. Another helpful book that thoughtfully explores the dynamic interplay between the believer's will and God's will in the process of transformation is Jerry Bridges, *The Discipline of Grace: God's Role and Our Role in the Pursuit of Holiness* (Colorado Springs, CO: NavPress, 2006).

19. Jonathan Edwards, *The Works of Jonathan Edwards*, vol. 2 (Carlisle, PA: Banner of Truth Trust, 1974 reprint) 557.

20. It would be difficult to overstate the significance Scripture gives to the Spirit and his role in our lives. Meditate for a moment on the Spirit's work.

 Christ bore our curse and died in our place so we could receive the promised
Spirit through faith (Gal. 3:2–3, 5, 14).

Jesus teaches that we must be born of the Spirit in order to see and enter the kingdom of God (John 3:1–8).

The Spirit gives us understanding of the gospel and makes it effective in our lives (1 Cor. 2:4, 12; 1 Thess. 1:4–5).

The ministry of the new covenant is a ministry of the life-giving Spirit who brings freedom and transformation (2 Cor. 3:5–18).

The Spirit is the agent of our sanctification, spiritual cleansing, and renewal (2 Thess. 2:13; 1 Cor. 6:11; Titus 3:5).

The kingdom of God consists of life and joy in the Spirit (Rom. 14:17), and the Spirit causes us to abound in hope (Rom. 15:13).

Our access to God is in the Spirit (Eph. 2:18); in the Spirit we worship God (Phil. 3:3) and pray (Eph. 6:18; Jude 20).

We are joined to the body of Christ by the Spirit (1 Cor. 12:13) and God inhabits us as his new temple through the Spirit's indwelling of the church (1 Cor. 3:16; Eph. 2:22).

We know that we abide in God and God in us, because he has given us his Spirit (1 John 3:24; 4:13).

The Spirit secures our salvation by sealing us for the future day of redemption (Eph. 1:13; 4:30; 2 Cor. 1:22).

God gives his Spirit as the down-payment and guarantee of our inheritance in Christ. The Spirit assures us that all of God's promises will be fulfilled (Eph. 1:13–14; 2 Cor. 1:19–22; 2 Cor. 5:5).

God pours his love into our hearts through his Spirit (Rom. 5:5), and gives us assurance of our sonship by causing us to cry, "Abba, Father" (Rom. 8:15–16; Gal. 4:6).

The law of the Spirit of life in Christ Jesus has set us free from the law of sin and death (Rom. 8:2).

We now serve God not under the old written code of the law, but in the new life of the Spirit (Rom. 7:6).

We walk in the Spirit and set our minds on the things of the Spirit (Rom. 8:4–6).

God's glorious Spirit rests on us when we suffer for Christ (1 Peter 4:14).

The Spirit opens the eyes of our hearts to know God better (Eph. 1:16–19), strengthens us in our inner being (Eph. 3:14–16), and fills us with the fullness of God (Eph. 3:17–21; 5:18).

The same Spirit who raised Jesus from the dead dwells in our hearts and enables us to put sin to death, promising to give life to our mortal bodies (Rom. 8:9–14).

21. My understanding and explanation of this passage was shaped by a helpful sermon by Tim Keller on Galatians 5:16–18, 23–25 called "How to Change." This sermon is available for download at http://download.redeemer.com/rpcsermons/storesamplesermons/How_to_Change.mp3. Accessed 3 September 2008.

22. Peterson, 135.

23. James Montgomery Boice, "Galatians" in Frank E. Gaebelein, ed., *The Expositor's Bible Commentary*, Volume 10 (Grand Rapids, MI: Zondervan, 1976) 498.

24. Ibid.

25. Jonathan Edwards, *Religious Affections*, John E. Smith, ed., *The Works of Jonathan Edwards*, vol. 2 (New Haven, CT: Yale University Press, 1959) 365.

26. Keller, "How to Change."

27. Packer, *Keep In Step with the Spirit*, 109.

28. Sinclair B. Ferguson, *The Holy Spirit* (Downers Grove, IL: InterVarsity Press, 1996) 52.

29. Ferguson writes, "With respect to his economic ministry to us, the Spirit has been 'imprinted' with the character of Jesus." Ibid., 55.

30. Lovelace, 131.

31. Berkouwer, 66.

32. Lewis, 93.

33. John Newton, "Prayer Answered by Crosses," 1779.

Chapter 9—The Quest for Joy: Motivation

1. Thomas Brooks, *The Crown and Glory of Christianity, or Holiness the Only Way to Happiness,* in Alexander B. Grosart, ed., *The Works of Thomas Brooks,* vol. 4 (Carlisle, PA: The Banner of Truth Trust, 2002 reprint of 1861–67 edition) 37.

2. C. S. Lewis, *Mere Christianity* (San Francisco, CA: HarperSanFrancisco, 1952) 50.

3. Quoted in John Piper *Desiring God: The Meditations of a Christian Hedonist* (Sisters, Oregon: Multnomah Books, Third Edition, 2003) 12.

4. Jonathan Evans, "Jesus Is All I Wish or Want" n. d.

5. John Newton, "How Tedious and Tasteless the Hours," 1779.

6. Piper, 28.

7. Piper, 10.

8. This is not to infer that we should never act from duty, or that duty itself is a bad thing. But as C. S. Lewis said, "A *perfect* man [would] never act from a sense of duty; he'd always *want* the right thing more than the wrong one. Duty is only a substitute for love (of God and of other people) like a crutch which is a substitute for a leg. Most of us need the crutch at times; but of course it is idiotic to use the crutch when our own legs (our own loves, tastes, habits etc.) can do the journey on their own." C. S. Lewis, ed. Walter Hooper, *The Collected Letters of C. S. Lewis: Volume III: Narnia, Cambridge, and Joy* (New York, NY: HarperCollins, 2007) 872.

9. Piper, 25.

10. Ibid., 53.

11. Thomas Brooks, *An Ark for All God's Noahs* in Alexander B. Grosart, ed., *The Works of Thomas Brooks,* vol. 2 (Carlisle, PA: The Banner of Truth Trust, 2002 reprint of 1861–67 edition) v.

12. Ibid, 32–33

13. Dietrich Bonhoeffer, *The Cost of Discipleship* (New York, NY: Collier Books, MacMillan Publishing Company, 1963 Revised Edition) 99.

14. Bonhoeffer, 103.

15. Saint Augustine, R. S. Pine-Coffin, trans., *Confessions* (New York, NY: Penguin Books, 1961) 21 (I, 1).

16. Elisabeth Elliot, *Shadow of the Almighty: The Life & Testament of Jim Elliot* (San Francisco, CA: HarperSanFrancisco, 1958) 19.

17. C. S. Lewis, *The Weight of Glory and Other Addresses* (New York, NY: HarperOne, 1949, 1976 revised) 25–26.

18. John Calvin, whose first point in laying down directions for the Christian life was the practice of self denial, also understood this dynamic. Calvin viewed "meditation on the future life" as "our sole comfort" which, if taken away, would leave us "captivated by the empty solace of this world." Calvin said that believers would "have been desperately unhappy unless, with mind intent upon heaven, they had surmounted whatever is in this world, and passed beyond the present aspect of affairs . . . [but if they are troubled by wicked men] they will without difficulty bear up under such evils also. For before their eyes will be the day when the Lord will receive his faithful people into the peace of his Kingdom, "will wipe away every

tear from their eyes" [Rev. 7:17; cf. Isa. 25:8], will clothe them with "a robe of glory . . . and rejoicing" [Ecclus. 6:31, EV], "will feed them with the unspeakable sweetness of his delights, will elevate them to his sublime fellowship—in fine, will deign to make them sharers in his happiness." John Calvin, John T. McNeil, ed., Ford L. Battles, trans., *Institutes of the Christian Religion* Book III, Chap. IX.6 (Philadelphia, PA: The Westminster Press, 1960) 718–719. C. S. Lewis similarly covers the scope of God's promises when he writes, "The promises of Scripture may very roughly be reduced to five heads. It is promised (1) that we shall be with Christ; (2) that we shall be like Him; (3) with an enormous wealth of imagery, that we shall have glory; (4) that we shall, in some sense, be fed or feasted or entertained; and (5) that we shall have some official position in the universe—ruling cities, judging angels, being pillars of God's temple." Lewis, 34.

19. John Newton, "Glorious Things of Thee are Spoken," 1779.

20. John Piper, *The Purifying Power of Living by Faith in FUTURE GRACE* (Sisters, OR: Multnomah Books, 1995) 335.

21. Thomas Chalmers, "The Expulsive Power of a New Affection," in Andrew Watterson Blackwood, comp., *The Protestant Pulpit: An Anthology of Master Sermons from the Reformation to Our Own Day* (New York, NY: Abingdon, 1947) 50, 56.

22. Milton Vincent, *A Gospel Primer for Christians: Learning to See the Glories of God's Love* (Bemidji, MN: Focus Publishing, 2008) 45–46.

23. John Piper's *Future Grace* contains nearly 450 pages of extensive meditation and application on how God's promises sever the promises of sin. Most of what I have written in this chapter I first learned from Piper. The theological debt I owe to him is incalculable. I hope my readers will savor the rich feast of both *Desiring God* and *Future Grace* for themselves. For more on how to fight specific sins with the promises of God, see also Piper's *Battling Unbelief: Defeating Sin with Superior Pleasure* (Sisters, OR: Multnomah Books, 2007), an abridgement of *Future Grace* which teaches how to battle the unbelief of anxiety, pride, misplaced shame, impatience, covetousness, bitterness, despondency, and lust.

24. For a short biographical sketch see: http://en.wikipedia.org/wiki/Guy_de_Maupassant. Accessed March 25, 2008.

25. John Calvin, D. W. Torrance and T. F. Torrance, eds., *The Epistles of Paul The Apostle to the Galatians, Ephesians, Philippians and Colossians* (Grand Rapids, MI: Wm. B. Eerdmans Publishing Co. , 1976) 289.

26. Augustine, *Confessions*, 178 (VIII, 12).

27. Ibid., 181 (IX, 1).

28. For a fascinating biographical sketch of Augustine that focuses on the power of pleasure in Augustine's conversion and transformation, see John Piper, *The Legacy of Sovereign Joy: God's Triumphant Grace in the Lives of Augustine, Luther, and Calvin* (Wheaton, IL: Crossway Books, 2000).

29. Piper, *Future Grace*, 9–10. Emphasis added.

30. Sam Storms, *One Thing: Developing a Passion for the Beauty of God* (Ross-shire, Scotland: Christian Focus Publications Ltd., 2004) 124–127.

31. Ibid., 129.

Chapter 10—Training in the Spirit: Disciplines

1. John Ortberg, *The Life You've Always Wanted: Spiritual Disciplines for Ordinary People* (Grand Rapids, MI: Zondervan, 2002) 43. All of my thinking on training vs. trying, including the marathon illustration, is dependent on Ortberg. His book is a helpful and accessible introduction to spiritual disciplines.

2. Ibid., 44.

3. Donald S. Whitney, *Spiritual Disciplines for the Christian Life* (Colorado Springs, CO: NavPress, 1991) 15.

4. Sinclair Ferguson, *Grow in Grace* (Carlisle, PA: The Banner of Truth Trust, 1989) 20.

5. Richard Foster, *Celebration of Discipline: The Path to Spiritual Growth* (San Francisco, CA: HarperSanFrancisco, 1998) 20.

6. Charles Bridges, *An Exposition of Psalm 119* (Carlisle, PA: The Banner of Truth Trust, 1974 reprint) 32.

7. Whitney, 44.

8. Ibid., 95.

9. Quoted in Whitney, 69.

10. Thomas Watson, *The Saints Spiritual Delight and A Christian on the Mount* (London, England: London Tract Society, 1830) 76. Available for free download from http://books.google.com/books?id=D9MCAAAAQAAJ. Accessed September 5, 2008.

11. Watson, 93.

12. Here is the fuller quotation: "Endeavor to Promote spiritual appetites by Laying yourself in the way of allurement. [W]e are to avoid being the way of temptation with Respect to our Carnal appetites. Job made a Covenant with his Eyes. But we ought to take all opportunities to Lay our selves in the way of Enticement with Respect to our Gracious Inclinations . . . [Thus] you should be often with G[od] in Prayer and then you will be in the way of having your heart drawn forth to him . . . [We ought] to be . . . frequent in Reading & Constant in hearing the word. [A]nd particularly to this End we ought . . . Carefully & with the utmost seriousness & Consideration about the sacrament of the Lord's supper. [T]his was appointed for this End to draw forth the . . . Longings of our souls towards J[esus Christ]." Punctuation is original, bracketed words supply the full words for Edwards' abbreviations. Jonathan Edwards, "117. Sermon on Cant. 5:1," in *Works of Jonathan Edwards Online, Volume 44, Sermons, Series II, 1729* (Jonathan Edwards Center, Yale University, 2008) L. 10r.

13. Ben Patterson, *Deepening Your Conversation with God: Learning to Love to Pray* (Minneapolis, MN: Bethany House Publishers, 2001) 27–28.

14. Quoted in George Smith, *Life of William Carey* (New York, NY: Hard Press, 2006) 77.

15. Paul Miller, *A Praying Life: Connecting with God in a Distracting World* (Colorado Springs, CO: NavPress, 2009) 32.

16. As Lovelace writes, "Deficiency in prayer both reflects and reinforces inattention toward God." Richard Lovelace, *Dynamics of Spiritual Life: An Evangelical Theology of Renewal* (Downers Grove, IL: Inter-Varsity Press, 1979) 153.

17. To further explore the importance of praying in Jesus' name see Bryan Chapell, *Praying Backwards: Transform Your Prayer Life by Beginning in Jesus' Name* (Grand Rapids, MI: Baker Books, 2005).

18. Horatius Bonar, "Not What My Hands Have Done," 1861.

19. Miller, 30–31.

20. Ibid.

21. Ibid., 32

22. Ibid.

23. F. F. Bruce, *The Epistles to the Colossians, to Philemon, and to the Ephesians* (NICNT), (Grand Rapids, MI.: Wm. B. Eerdmans Publishing Co., 1984) 330.

24. Thanks to my friend, Rodney Tolleson, for providing me with this illustration.

25. John Newton, "Come, My Soul, Thy Suit Prepare," 1779.

26. I'm borrowing these categories from Richard Foster who lists a total of twelve disciplines: the inward disciplines of meditation, prayer, fasting, and study; the outward disciplines of simplicity, solitude, submission, and service; and the corporate disciplines of confession, worship, guidance, and celebration. See Richard Foster, *Celebration of Discipline: The Path*

to Spiritual Growth (San Francisco, CA: HarperSanFrancisco, 1998). Dallas Willard divides the disciplines into two categories: disciplines of abstinence (solitude, silence, fasting, frugality, chastity, secrecy, sacrifice) and engagement (study, worship, celebration, service, prayer, fellowship, confession, submission). See Dallas Willard, *The Spirit of the Disciplines: Understanding How God Changes Lives* (San Francisco, CA: HarperSanFrancisco, 1988) 156–192. John Ortberg considers eight disciplines—celebration, slowing, prayer, servanthood, confession, receiving guidance from the Holy Spirit, secrecy, and reflection on Scripture. See John Ortberg, *The Life You've Always Wanted: Spiritual Disciplines for Ordinary People* (Grand Rapids, MI: Zondervan, 2002). And, in the two most helpful and Scripture-centered books on spiritual disciplines I've read, Don Whitney writes about various spiritual disciplines for both individuals and the church. In *Spiritual Disciplines for the Christian Life*, Whitney gives biblical and practical instruction on the disciplines of Bible intake (including hearing, reading, studying, memorizing, meditating, and applying the Word), prayer, worship, evangelism, serving, stewardship, fasting, silence and solitude (dealt with together), journaling and learning. *Spiritual Disciplines Within the Church*, on the other hand, discusses baptism, church membership, listening to preaching, worship, witness, serving, giving, observing the Lord's Table, fellowship, prayer, and learning. See Donald S. Whitney, *Spiritual Disciplines for the Christian Life* (Colorado Springs, CO: NavPress, 1991) and *Spiritual Disciplines Within the Church: Participating Fully in the Body of Christ* (Chicago, IL: Moody Publishers, 1996).

27. Del Fehsenfeld III, "Spiritual Formation," unpublished paper.

28. Quoted in *Spirit of Revival* (Buchanan, MI: Life Action Ministries, Vol. 39, No. 1, Spring 2008) 22.

29. If you haven't read anything on the disciplines and desire to learn more, I suggest starting with either Ortberg's *The Life You've Always Wanted* or Whitney's *Spiritual Disciplines for the Christian Life.*

30. Bryan Chapell, *Holiness by Grace: Delighting in the Joy that is Our Strength* (Wheaton, IL: Crossway Books, 2001) 57.

31. Andrew Bonar, *Memoir & Remains of Robert Murray M'Cheyne* (Carlisle, PA: The Banner of Truth Trust, 2004 reprint of 1892 edition) 54.

32. John Owen, *Meditations and Discourses Concerning the Glory of Christ; Applied unto Unconverted Sinners and Saints under Spiritual Decays* in William H. Gould, ed., *The Works of John Owen*, vol. 1 (Carlisle, PA: The Banner of Truth Trust, 1967 reprint of 1850–53 edition) 460–461.

33. G. C. Berkouwer, *Faith and Sanctification* (Grand Rapids, MI: Wm. B. Eerdmans Publishing Co., 1952) 160.

34. Eugene H. Peterson, *Eat this Book: A Conversation in the Art of Spiritual Reading* (Grand Rapids, MI: Wm. B. Eerdmans Publishing Co., 2006) 18.

35. Similarly, Tim Chester and Steve Timmis write, "Biblical spirituality does not take place in silence; it takes place bearing a cross. It is not a spirituality of withdrawal but a spirituality of engagement. You do not practice it on retreat in a secluded house; you practice it on the streets in the midst of broken lives." Tim Chester and Steve Timmis, *Total Church: A Radical Reshaping around Gospel and Community* (Wheaton, IL: Crossway Books, 2008) 146.

Chapter 11—The Refiner's Fire: Suffering

1. William Cowper, "Light Shining Out of Darkness," 1779.

2. Bob Dylan, "Everything is Broken," Copyright ©1989 Special Rider Music.

3. D. A. Carson, *How Long, O Lord? Reflections on Suffering and Evil* (Grand Rapids, MI: Baker Academic, 2nd Edition, 2006) 159.

4. Edward Shillito, "Jesus of the Scars," quoted in Carson, 170.

NOTES

5. Three excellent books that treat the topic of suffering more thoroughly are D. A. Carson's, *How Long, O Lord?* (referenced above), Joni Eareckson Tada and Steve Estes, *When God Weeps: Why Our Sufferings Matter to the Almighty* (Grand Rapids, MI: Zondervan Publishing House, 1997), and Jerry Bridges, *Trusting God: Even When Life Hurts* (Colorado Springs, CO: NavPress, 1994).

6. C. S. Lewis, *The Problem of Pain* (New York, NY: HarperCollins, 1940, 1996, 2001) 110–111.

7. David Peterson, *Possessed by God: A New Testament Theology of Sanctification and Holiness* (Downers Grove, IL: InterVarsity Press, 1995) 117.

8. *The Heidelberg Catechism*, Question 27. The following passages from Scripture are listed in support of this definition: Acts 17:25–28; Jer. 23:23–24; Isa. 29:15–16; Ezek. 8:12; Heb. 1:3; Jer. 5:24; Acts 14:17; John 9:3; Prov. 22:2; Matt. 10:20; and Prov. 16:33.

9. Ibid., Question 28, with the following Scripture references: Rom. 5:3; Jas. 1:3; Ps. 39:9; Job 1:21–22; Deut. 8:10; 1 Thess. 5:18; Ps. 55:22; Rom. 5:4; Rom. 8:38–39; Job 1:12; Job 2:6; Acts 17:28; Acts 17:25; and Prov. 21:1.

10. Jerry Bridges notes two errors we often make when we talk about the Providence of God. First, "we almost always use the expression 'the providence of God' in connection with apparently 'good' events . . . But you almost never hear anyone say something such as, 'In the providence of God I had an accident and was paralyzed from my waist down'. . . The second problem with our popular use of the expression 'the providence of God' is that we either unconsciously or deliberately imply that God intervenes at specific points in our lives but is largely only an uninterested spectator most of the time." Jerry Bridges, *Trusting God: Even When Life Hurts* (Colorado Springs, CO: NavPress, 1994) 24–25.

11. Gene Edwards, *The Inward Journey: A Story of God's Transforming Love* (Wheaton, IL: Tyndale House Publishers, Inc., 1993) 61–62.

12. Though I have been unable to locate the original source, these words are often attributed to Charles Spurgeon.

13. Milton Vincent, *A Gospel Primer for Christians: Learning to See the Glories of God's Love* (Bemidji, MN: Focus Publishing, 2008) 31–32.

14. Richard Baxter, *The Saints Everlasting Rest* (Welwyn, UK: Evangelical Press 1978 reprint) 246.

15. Thomas Watson, *All Things for Good* (Carlisle, PA: The Banner of Truth Trust, 1998 reprint) 27.

16. Quoted in John Piper, *A Godward Life: Book Two* (Sisters, OR: Multnomah, 1999) 305.

17. Tim Chester, *You Can Change* (Nottingham, England: InterVarsity Press, 2008) 160.

18. Quoted in John Piper, *The Hidden Smile of God: The Fruit of Affliction in the Lives of John Bunyan, William Cowper, and David Brainerd* (Wheaton, IL: Crossway Books, 2001) 139

19. Piper, *A Godward Life*, 307.

20. Watson, 28.

21. William Cowper, "Welcome Cross."

22. The Greek word is used in the Septuagint, a Greek translation of the Old Testament.

23. Douglas J. Moo, *The Letter of James* (Grand Rapids, MI: Wm. B. Eerdmans Publishing Co., 2000) 54.

24. To anneal is to toughen glass or metal through a process of heating and slow cooling.

25. C. H. Spurgeon, "The Sorrowful Man's Question," in *The Metropolitan Tabernacle Pulpit* (Pasadena, TX: Pilgrim Publications, 1977 reprint) 121–132. Available online at: http://www.spurgeon.org/sermons/2666.htm. Accessed August 23, 2008.

26. Moo, 55.

27. John Flavel, *The Mystery of Providence* (Carlisle, PA: The Banner of Truth Trust, reprint) 202.

28. A. W. Tozer, *The Root of the Righteous* (Harrisburg, PA: Christian Publications, 1955) 137.

29. C. S. Lewis, *The Great Divorce* (New York, NY: HarperOne, 1946, 1973) 69.

30. C. S. Lewis, *Mere Christianity* (New York, NY: HarperOne, 1952, 1980) 205.

31. John Flavel, *The Fountain of Life* (Grand Rapids, MI: Baker, 1977 reprint) 322–323.

Chapter 12—Life Together: Community

1. Tim Lane and Paul Tripp, *Relationships: A Mess Worth Making* (Greensboro, NC: New Growth Press, 2006) 25–26.

2. Timothy S. Lane and Paul David Tripp, *How People Change* (Greensboro, NC: New Growth Press, 2006) 75.

3. C. S. Lewis, *Mere Christianity* (New York, NY: HarperOne, 1952, 1980) 190, 199.

4. William Shakespeare, *As You Like It*, Act 2, Scene 7.

5. Dallas Willard, quoted in Randy Frazee, *The Connecting Church: Beyond Small Groups to Authentic Community* (Grand Rapids, MI.: Zondervan, 2001) 17.

6. Tim Chester and Steve Timmis, *Total Church: A Radical Reshaping around Gospel and Community* (Wheaton, IL: Crossway Books, 2008) 44–45. Frazee agrees: "The writings of Scripture lead one to conclude that God intends the church, not to be one more bolt on the wheel of activity in our lives, but the very hub at the center of one's life and community" (Frazee, 37).

7. John Ortberg, *Everybody's Normal Till You Get to Know Them* (Grand Rapids, MI: Zondervan, 2003) 46.

8. Calvin Miller, *Into the Depths of God* (Minneapolis, MN.: Bethany House Publishers, 2000) 48.

9. Ortberg, 46.

10. Dietrich Bonhoeffer, *Life Together: The Classic Exploration of Faith in Community* (San Francisco, CA.: HarperSanFrancisco, 1954) 26–27. Similarly, Jean Vanier wrote, "There is no ideal community. Community is made up of people with all their richness, but also with their weakness and poverty, of people who accept and forgive each other, who are vulnerable with each other. Humility and trust are more at the foundation of community than perfection" (Quoted in Ortberg, 48).

11. See bibliographical information above.

12. To further explore how God uses marriage and parenting in our sanctification, I recommend the following books. On marriage: Dave Harvey, *When Sinners Say "I Do": Discovering the Power of the Gospel for Marriage* (Wapwallopen, PA: Shepherd Press, 2007) and Gary Thomas, *Sacred Marriage* (Grand Rapids, MI: Zondervan, 2000). On parenting: Tedd Tripp, *Shepherding a Child's Heart* (Wapwallopen, PA: Shepherd Press, 1995) and Gary Thomas, *Sacred Parenting: How Raising Children Shapes Our Souls* (Grand Rapids, MI: Zondervan, 2005).

13. John R. W. Stott, *The Spirit, the Church, and the World: The Message of Acts* (Downers Grove, IL: InterVarsity Press, 1990) 81.

14. Stott, 84–85.

15. *The Westminster Confession of Faith*, 29.7. Interestingly enough, the only significant difference between this and the *Baptist Confession of 1689* is the substitution of the word "ordinance" for "sacrament," while the explanation for how the Lord's Supper works is almost identical. Though he doesn't use the term "sacrament," I am in essential agreement with Don Whitney's explanation of the Lord's Table: "Participation in the Lord's Supper allows us an experience with Christ that cannot be enjoyed in any other manner. Neither prayer,

the preaching of God's Word, public or private worship, nor any other means of encounter with the Lord can bring us into the presence of Jesus Christ in exactly the same way. God has given to His children several means of communion with His Son, but one is unique to the Lord's Supper. Further, this communion is spiritual—that is, it does not occur merely by eating the bread and drinking from the cup, but by faith. And even though the bread and the cup do not contain the physical body and blood of Jesus, nor are they changed into them, they really do minister Christ to those who believe." Donald S. Whitney, *Spiritual Disciplines Within the Church: Participating Fully in the Body of Christ* (Chicago, IL: Moody Publishers, 1996) 141.

16. Richard Lovelace, *Dynamics of Spiritual Life: An Evangelical Theology of Renewal* (Downers Grove, IL: Inter-Varsity Press, 1979)170.

17. Stott, *The Message of Acts*, 84.

18. Lovelace, 168.

19. John R. W. Stott, *The Message of Ephesians: God's New Society* (Downers Grove, IL.: InterVarsity Press, 1979) 172.

20. Klyne Snodgrass, *The NIV Application Commentary: Ephesians* (Grand Rapids, MI: Zondervan, 1996) 206.

21. Tim Chester, *You Can Change* (Nottingham, England: InterVarsity Press, 2008) 158.

22. Tripp, *Instruments in the Redeemer's Hands*, 21.

23. John Murray, *Collected Writings of John Murray, Volume Two: Select Lectures in Systematic Theology* (Carlisle, PA: The Banner of Truth Trust, 1977) 299–300.

24. John Loftness in C. J. Mahaney, ed., *Why Small Groups? Together Toward Maturity* (Gaithersburg, MD: Sovereign Grace Ministries, 1996) 26. A good book-length study of the "one another" commands is Wayne Jacobsen and Clay Jacobsen, *Authentic Relationships: Discover the Lost Art of "One Anothering"* (Grand Rapids, MI: Baker Books, 2001).

25. Quoted in Whitney, 159.

26. C. S. Lewis, *The Four Loves* (New York, NY: Harcourt, Inc., 1960, 1988) 61–62.

27. Tripp and Lane, *How People Change*, 85

28. Paul David Tripp, *Instruments in the Redeemer's Hands: People in Need of Change Helping People in Need of Change* (Phillipsburg, NJ: P & R Publishing, 2002) 54.

29. If this is neither a warning for unbelievers or implying that Christians can lose their salvation, you might still be wondering what the "if" is there for. "For we share in Christ, *if* indeed we hold our original confidence firm to the end." In a sermon on a related passage, entitled "Final Perseverance," Charles Spurgeon helpfully explained the role of these kinds of "if" statements. Spurgeon said:

What is the use of putting this "if" in, like a bugbear to frighten children, or like a ghost that can have no existence? My learned friend, "Who art thou that repliest against God?" If God has put it in, he has put it in for wise reasons and for excellent purposes. Let me show you why. First, O Christian, it is put in to keep thee from falling away. God preserves his children from falling away; but he keeps them by the use of means; and one of these is, the terrors of the law, showing them what would happen if they were to fall away. There is a deep precipice: what is the best way to keep any one from going down there? Why, to tell him that if he did he would inevitably be dashed to pieces. In some old castle there is a deep cellar, where there is a vast amount of fixed air and gas, which would kill anybody who went down. What does the guide say? "If you go down you will never come up alive." Who thinks of going down? The very fact of the guide telling us what the consequences would be, keeps us from it. Our friend puts away from us a cup of arsenic; he does not want us to drink it, but he says, "If you drink it, it will kill you." Does he suppose for a moment that we should drink it. No; he tells us the consequences, and he is sure we will not do it. So God says, "My child, if you fall over this precipice you will be dashed to pieces." What does the child do? He says, "Father, keep me; hold thou me up, and I shall be safe." It leads the believer to greater dependence on God, to a holy fear and caution, because he knows that if he were to fall away he could not be renewed, and he stands far away from that great gulf, because he knows that if he were to fall into it there would be no salvation for him." Charles H. Spurgeon, "Final Perseverance," in *The New Park Street Pulpit*, vol. 2 (Grand Rapids, MI: Baker Book House, 1856, 1994 reprint) 169.

I discovered this passage from Spurgeon in Thomas R. Schreiner & Ardel B. Caneday, *The Race Set Before Us: A Biblical Theology of Perseverance and Assurance* (Downers Grove, IL: InterVarsity Press, 2001), a thoughtful, yet accessible, exploration of the doctrines of perseverance and assurance and the role of the warning passages in Scripture.

30. John Piper, "Eternal Security is a Community Project," (Minneapolis, MN: Bethlehem Baptist Church, August 18, 1996), available online at: http://www.desiringgod.org/ResourceLibrary/Sermons/ByDate/1996/964_Eternal_Security_Is_a_Community_Project/. Accessed March 15, 2010.

31. I'm using the NKJV because it rightly shows that "one another" is the direct object of "consider."

32. C. S. Lewis, *The Weight of Glory and Other Addresses* (New York, NY: HarperOne, 1949, 1976 revised) 45–46.

33. Quoted in Ortberg, 34.

34. Lewis, *Mere Christianity*, 175.

35. Ibid., 176.

36. Ibid., 176.

General Index

Scripture Index